Sr Robert Atkyns

J. Kip Delin. et Sculp.

Elinor Fettiplace's Receipt Book

To make serop of tobaccho. 5 [illegible]

Take a quart of water & three ounces of tobaccho, put the tobaccho in the water, & let it lie a night & a day close couered, then boile it from a quart to a pinte, then straine it, & put to euerie pinte a pound of sugar, then put in the whites of three or fowre eggs finelie beaten, then set it on the fire, & when it boiles scum it, then couer it close, & let it boile, till it bee serop.

A water for a sore throte; by m^tis Higgs.

Take a quart of claret wine, & put therunto a pound of brown sugar candie bruised, of large mace half an ounce, on handfull of rosemarie, boile them well together till part of the wine bee wasted, then straine it & keep it, in the boyling put to it a little allome, & so wash the throte with it.

A pouder for a Canker.

Take a quantitie of burnt allome, & the like of white coperas burned, grind them small, then shake into them so much bole armonak as may collor it, & with the finger lay it to the sore once a day, & within three or fowre dayes it will flatlie heale the Canker.

For the Goute.

Take a quarter of a pound of barrowes grease, a quarter of a pound of wax, a quarter of a pound of rosin, then lay three paire of tongs in the fire, when they bee hot, take on paire of them, & melt the rosin with them in the pot, & so doo with the other two paire, & melt it all in one pot, then dip clothes in it, & make searclothes therof, & lay it to the sore place.

For the scurfe in ones throte.

Take Smithes water that hee cooles his iron in, & as much honie as will make it sweet, & the whites of two or three eggs, & put them in, then set it on the fire & let it boile, then scum it, let it boile after till it bee inough, then straine it, & when it is cold, wash your throte with it.

A page from Elinor Fettiplace's original manuscript.

Elinor Fettiplace's Receipt Book

Elizabethan Country House Cooking

Hilary Spurling

Elisabeth Sifton Books
VIKING

First published in 1986 by
The Salamander Press, 18 Anley Road, London W14 9BY, England
in association with
Penguin Books Ltd, Harmondsworth, Middlesex, England
Elisabeth Sifton Books · Viking Penguin Inc., 40 West 23rd Street, New York,
New York 10010, U.S.A.
Penguin Books Australia Ltd, Ringwood, Victoria, Australia
Penguin Books Canada Limited, 2801 John Street, Markham, Ontario, Canada L3R 1B4
Penguin Books (N.Z.) Ltd, 182–190 Wairau Road, Auckland 10, New Zealand

Library of Congress Cataloging in Publication Data available

ISBN 0-670-81592-6

Acknowledgement

Some of these recipes were first published
in articles by the author in the *London Evening Standard*
and the *New Statesman*

Designed by Humphrey Stone

Set in Monophoto Garamond
Printed and bound in Great Britain
by Richard Clay Ltd, Bungay, Suffolk

For Amy, Nat and Gilbert,
testers and tasters

Contents

'When I reflect upon the Number of Books already in print upon this Subject, and with what Contempt they are read, I cannot but be apprehensive that this may meet with the same Fate ...'

ELIZABETH RAFFALD
The Experienced English Housekeeper
1769

'I must frankly own, that if I had known, beforehand, that this book would have cost me the labour which it has, I should never have been courageous enough to commence it ...'

ISABELLA BEETON
The Book of Household Management
1861

Foreword

I have been cooking for ten years now from a small, stout, handwritten book, bound in leather and stamped in gold, with endpapers made from odd scraps of mediaeval Latin manuscript, and an inscription at the front: 'Lady Elinor Fetiplace. 1604.'

It came from the last of my husband's great-aunts, the unmarried youngest daughter of a large Victorian family, whose semi-detached London house had become by the end of her life a sort of family repository for mementoes, old diaries, photographs, water-colours, dusty collections of coins, medals, games, mother-of-pearl counters and curios. When she died, the book itself had lain untouched for perhaps fifty years, unused for practical purposes for at least a hundred, possibly two hundred or more years before that. The last of the Fettiplaces died at the end of the eighteenth century when the manuscript passed, by inheritance and marriage, eventually into my husband's family. It undoubtedly started as a working cookery book but, although it contains additions at the back in various late seventeenth-, possibly even eighteenth-century hands, there is no way of telling who was the last person to cook from it.

Elinor herself was the wife of Sir Richard Fettiplace, heir to the heavily mortgaged estates of an old but impoverished Berkshire family. Her own family were the Pooles of Sapperton in Gloucestershire. Her grandmother was Elizabeth Whittington who inherited Pauntley, the village Dick Whittington set out from (with or without his cat) to become three times mayor of London in the fourteenth century. One of her uncles by marriage was Sir John Thynne who built Longleat. Another was Carew Raleigh whose younger brother, Sir Walter, contributed a couple of recipes to her book. Besides food and drink, she collected a great many remedies, including cures for bubonic plague—'A medicine of King Henry the eighth for the plague or pestilence'—and a prescription for nosebleeds supplied by a surgeon named Hall, who was almost certainly Shakespeare's son-in-law. There is also a herbal poultice from Dr Thomas Muffet, the scientist and leading authority on insects, whose only daughter, Patience, was the Little Miss Muffet terrorised by a spider in the nursery rhyme.

But ten years ago, when I came across this book, I knew nothing about its fairytale and nursery rhyme associations, let alone its actual origins. Nor did I know anything at all about the food of the period, beyond a vague idea that it must have been hearty, heavily spiced, probably rather monotonous with nothing to speak of in the way of fresh vegetables and far too many rich dishes. The first thing I cooked, for curiosity's sake, was The Lord of Devonshire his Pudding, because it sounded surprisingly like a de luxe version of ordinary, nursery, bread-and-butter pudding. Next I tried a barley cream, roast mutton with orange juice and claret wine in the gravy, chicken with spinach sauce, and something called 'bisket bread', which turned out to be a sort of fine langue-de-chat biscuit.

The more I experimented, the clearer it became that this food was proving pretty well the opposite of what I had expected. Lady Fettiplace's cooking is on the whole simple but subtle, and by no means unsophisticated. It belongs to the European tradition that subsequently produced both French *haute cuisine* and the French bourgeois cooking that underlies so much of the current revival of interest in food in this country. In Lady Fettiplace's day, English cooking was well abreast, if not ahead of the most advanced practice in France: why the French went on to cherish and develop a repertoire that was almost entirely (if only temporarily) submerged or spoilt in England is a mystery for historians to solve. In the meantime, anyone inquisitive about food might find it worth sampling some of these Renaissance dishes whose ancestral influence is still, nearly four hundred years later, faintly discernible, if anywhere, in humble, homely, familiar, British nursery food.

Admittedly, Lady Fettiplace incorporates a great many unfamiliar and what might have been thought of as un-English touches: seasonings of sugar and spice in a spinach tart, rosewater in both sweet and savoury dishes, sauces for meat thickened (in the best approved manner of the *nouvelle cuisine* today) with egg yolks and vegetables instead of flour. But the great advantage of this early English cooking is that, unlike the exotic cuisines of, say, China, India, even the Mediterranean, it was evolved specifically to suit the climate and produce of this country. It is at once alien and conveniently local, adventurous and entirely practical, now that electric mixers, blenders and liquidisers have eliminated so much of the manual drudgery of a seventeenth-century kitchen. A great many luxury imported goods—sugar from the New World, lemons, Seville oranges and sweet potatoes from Spain, sherry and canary wines, claret and malmsey, spices from the East—were taken for granted then as now. Others—tea, coffee, potatoes, tomatoes, bananas, sweet oranges—had not yet reached England in 1604. But the only staple ingredients I have found at all hard to come by are rosewater, rennet (for setting milk to make junkets, sweet creams and cream cheeses), mace and beef marrow. Other more expensive rarities—musk, ambergris, frankincense and myrrh, sheet gold and seed pearls—I have treated as optional extras, which they must often have been at the time.

Lady Fettiplace left her book in 1647 to her niece and god-daughter, Ann Poole, who had married Sir George Horner of Mells (great-grandson of Sir John Horner—the Little Jack Horner of the nursery rhyme—who made a good thing out of picking up confiscated church lands under Henry VIII). The Horner daughters or their descendants must have handed it back at some point to their Fettiplace cousins, perhaps keeping copies themselves, since this sort of household manual was normally passed down from mother to daughter (in this case, god-daughter, for Lady Fettiplace had no surviving daughter of her own), or from one wife to the next, descending—unlike virtually any other form of inheritance—as a rule in the female line.

Manuscripts like this one were, so far as I know, the only form of historical record produced exclusively by and for women which is why, though I am neither a professional cook nor an historian, I think that, as the latest wife in this chain, I may lay a peculiar claim to Lady Fettiplace's book. I have followed her round the calendar from Oringe Marmalad, made with pippins and the first Seville oranges in January or February, through Baked Rabbatt, Boyled Troute, Preserved Apricocks, Pickled Cowcumbers and Creamapple Pie to Christmas pudding and mince pies, mixed with mutton and moistened with rosewater, in December. I began simply for the pleasure of cooking from a book written in such fine, clear, cranky Shakespearean English. But I went on because these recipes, standing in much the same relation to modern cooking as Shakespeare's language to what we speak now, are not only entertaining to read but easy to follow, straightforward to make and, in my experience, nearly always excellent eating.

FOREWORD

I learned to cook, like a great many others of my second world war generation growing up in the age of austerity, from reading Elizabeth David, who not only explained how to do it but somehow turned cooking from boring, repetitive housework into one of the potential pleasures of life, worth taking as much trouble about as music or travel or books. Elinor Fettiplace's manuscript, when it first turned up, struck me as an oddity, but one apparently in working order which might possibly interest Mrs David. Now that I know a little more about it, I understand better why she suggested it ought to be published; and, although the format of this book and the mistakes in it are mine, the writing of it owes more than I can say to her inexhaustible patience, generosity and scholarship.

I should particularly like to thank Brian Frith, F.S.G., who combed Gloucestershire archives for me, and Mr and Mrs Michael Wallis of Scotts Nurseries (Merriott) in Somerset, who hospitably allowed me time and again to strip their damask rose bushes for experiments with rose syrup and conserves. Among published sources, Karen Hess's comprehensive, practical and learned edition of *Martha Washington's Booke of Cookery* proved invaluable in an area not much patronised so far by professional historians. I am also grateful for information, advice and more bags full of rose petals to Caroline Barron, Sybille Bedford, Rev R. A. Bowden of Coates, John Broad, Jane Fowles of Longleat, David Gibson, Mark Girouard, J. A. S. Green, M.A., Berkshire County Archivist, Trevor and Valerie Grove, Dr John Hayes, Director of the National Portrait Gallery, Brian Halliwell of the Royal Botanic Gardens, Kew, Sophie Hughes of Kingstone Cottage Plants, Caryl and John Hubbard of Chilcombe, Mary Jenner of Whitbread and Co., Moll Lampard, Rev Raymond Martin of Redmarley d'Abitot with Pauntley, Helen Rogers, Prof A. L. Rowse, Ian Roy, D. J. H. Smith, B.A., Gloucestershire County Archivist, Andrew Spurling, W. J. Tighe, S. W. Taylor, B.A., A.G.R.A., and C. Anne Wilson. Lastly, my thanks go to James and Tom Fenton whose idea it was in the first place.

HILARY SPURLING
HOLLOWAY, FEBRUARY 1986

* = contributors of recipes

Sir Thomas Fettiplace = Beatrice, Lady Talbot

William

John

Ann Fettiplace = Hugh Unton
(sole heir) of Wadley

Richard of E. Shefford
and Besselsleigh d.1511

John d.1524 = Dorothy Danvers

Edward d.1540

Sir Edward

Sir John = 1. Elizabeth Hungerford
1527–1580 2. Jane Covert

Thomas
of Fernham

Bessels = Elinor Covert

Thomas

5 daughters 5 sons

RICHARD POLE of Sapperton d.1517 = 1. Alice Stradling
2. Eliz. Nottingham
3. ? DANVERS

Sir Giles Brydges

Sir Anthony Cooke
of Gidea Hall
1504–1576

John, 1st Baron Chandos

KATHARINE = LEONARD POOLE d.1539

Mary = R. Arnold
of Highnam

Edward,
2nd Baron Chandos

1. ELIZ. = SIR GILES d.1589 = 2. Elinor = 1. Sir William Wroughton
WHITTINGTON Lewknor of Broad Hinton

William

Eliz. = Henry Tracy
of Toddington

Sir Thomas
d.1597

Dorothy = 1. Sir John Thynne = Christian Gresham
of Longleat (1st wife)
2. Carew, brother to
Sir Walter Raleigh*

SIR HENRY d.1616 = ANN

Gresham Thynne*

Dorothy = Sir Thomas Lucy
of Stratford-
on-Avon

Giles,
3rd Baron

William,
4th Baron

Dorothy = Sir Henry Unton

Devereux

Giles

Frances =
Sir Nevill Poole

Dorothy =
Sir John Savage

Ann =
Sir Theo.
Georges

ELINOR c.1570–c.1647 = SIR RICHARD FETTIPLACE
1564–1615

Sir William Cooke = Joyce (sole heir)
of Highnam

Henry

2 daughters d.s.p.

JOHN c.1590–1619 = Margaret d.1638

Grey Bridges, 5th Baron Chandos

Beata = Sir Henry Poole 1593–1645

? Elizabeth d.1630 = Thos. Addis

Sir John Tracy = Anne Shirley,
of Toddington, the Lady Tracy*
1st Viscount Rathcoole

EDMUND b.1601

3 daughters

2 sons

Robert, 2nd Viscount

EDMUND d.1711

Meriel Tracy = Sir William 1620–1651

Ann = Sir George Horner 1604–1677

ELIZ. = John Blandy

Sir Henry d.s.p.

Mildred = Wm. Cecil,
Lord Burghley

Ann = Sir Nicholas Bacon

Eliz., Lady Russell = 1. Sir Thos. Hoby
2. John, Lord Russell

William Shaw = ELIZ. d.1758

Fettiplace
d.s.p. 1719

Robert Cecil,
Earl of Salisbury

Sir Francis Bacon

Sir Thos. = Margaret,
Lady Hoby (diarist)

Edward Hoby = Cecily, sister to
Sir Henry Unton

FETTIPLACE SHAW = Rev. Francis Merewether
d.1796

Introduction
A Family and its Fortunes

I

Lady Fettiplace lived at Appleton Manor in Berkshire (now in Oxfordshire), a few miles south west of Oxford: the long, low, grey Cotswold stone house—twelfth-century with Tudor additions—still stands, and so does the church over the garden wall where her husband, Sir Richard, and her eldest son John both lie buried. The Fettiplaces were an ancient family, said to have supplied a gentleman usher to William the Conqueror, first heard of for certain in the person of Adam Fettiplace, who was imprisoned in 1232 for beating up clerks of the Oxford schools, going on to become mayor of Oxford and lord of the manor of North Denchworth, ten miles south of Appleton, in Berkshire.[1] His son was knight of the shire, his grandson fought at Crécy and the siege of Calais in 1347. Fettiplaces crop up over the next three centuries and more in various capacities at court—securing a loan or serving as ambassador for Henry VI, employed as Esquire of the Body by Henry VII, attending Henry VIII at the Field of the Cloth of Gold, fighting fairly regularly on the battlefields of France, Scotland, Ireland and eventually England (when more than one Berkshire and Oxfordshire Fettiplace, mostly supporting the Royalist cause in the civil war, fought or was forced into hiding and ruined[2]). Like other families on the make after the Conquest, the Fettiplaces in their heyday put out many branches, spreading up through the midlands, along the Thames valley, down into the West country, making advantageous marriages, picking up land, doing so well that at one point they were rumoured to hold thirteen counties:

The Tracys, the Laceys and the Fettiplaces
Own all the manors, the parks and the chases.

'The Lady Tracy' supplied Lady Fettiplace in 1604 with the recipe for crystallised fruit on p. 163, a Dyett Drinke and a prescription for calamine eye drops. She was the wife of Sir John Tracy of Toddington in Gloucestershire, an old friend and neighbour of Elinor's family, the 'deer and loving cousin' who inherited a short sword in 1616 from Elinor's father, Sir Henry Poole.[3] There had been Tracys at Toddington for longer even than there had been Fettiplaces in Berkshire. Both families still regularly supplied high sheriffs, members of parliament and J.P.s in their respective counties, but by the middle of the sixteenth century they were being rapidly overhauled by a post-Reformation breed of ambitious, energetic, acquisitive new men who prospered exceedingly under the Tudors.

Elinor Fettiplace's father was one of them. Sir Henry Poole of Sapperton in Gloucestershire had inherited a comfortable estate, built up from scratch over three generations, which he set himself to consolidate and extend by shrewd purchase, exchange, investment and by his own and his children's marriages. By the time of his death his estates, solidly based on rich sheep-farming land in the Cotswolds round Cirencester, stretched south down through Wiltshire, eastwards into Berkshire and north as far as Pauntley near the Herefordshire border.[4] It was what Sir Henry's contemporaries called a solid bottom. He lived latterly in his newly built great house at Sapperton, but seems to have been based during Elinor's childhood in the manor house at Pauntley which had belonged to his mother, Elizabeth Whittington (she died in 1543, when Henry was two), the eldest of six Whittington heiresses who were the last of that famous name in the village that had been Dick Whittington's birthplace.

Sir Richard Whittington, London's best known lord mayor, died worth a fortune in 1423, and Whittington money helped fill the Poole sails at a critical juncture just over a century later. Henry's father, Giles Poole, was one of Henry VIII's handpicked group of gentlemen pensioners, serving with the army in France in 1544 and again three years later on a triumphant march into Scotland, where he was knighted after the battle of Pinkie by the great Duke of Somerset. He had his court pension increased under Edward VI, was returned as a good Catholic knight of the shire to Queen Mary's parliament, and became provost martial for Ireland under Queen Elizabeth.[5] There were family links with Elizabeth's two favourites, the Earl of Leicester and his stepson Robert Devereux, second Earl of Essex. Henry Poole, a soldier like his father, chose the name Devereux for his eldest son, born at Pauntley in 1572. A year later Sir Giles, mustering men for what turned out to be a disastrous expedition into Ireland under Walter Devereux, first Earl of Essex, reported from Sapperton that he had rounded up twelve reluctant recruits and meant to meet his master at Chartley, 'yf I be able to light uppon my horse'.[6]

Elinor Poole was born probably within a year or two of her brother Devereux. Their mother was Anne Wroughton, daughter of Sir William Wroughton of Broad Hinton in Wiltshire, another prosperous West country squire knighted, like Poole, by Protector Somerset on the field of battle in 1547. Landing a bride with a sizeable portion, or marrying a well-to-do widow, was a crucial part of contemporary strategy for building up an estate: when Wroughton died in 1559, Sir Giles brought off a double coup by taking the widow, Elinor Wroughton, as his second wife as well as marrying his son Henry to her daughter Anne (who chose her mother's name of Elinor for her own eldest daughter).

Another of Protector Somerset's loyal band of followers, knighted with Poole and Wroughton on the Scottish campaign in 1547, was Sir John Thynne whose fortune was founded on his pickings as Somerset's steward augmented, as he said himself, by judicious marriages. His first wife was Christian Gresham, daughter and sister to two of the wealthiest financiers in England; and it was partly on the strength of this marriage that he built Longleat in the 1560s and 70s, followed probably a decade or two later by the Pooles, who incorporated several features first seen at Longleat into their own palatial Renaissance mansion at Sapperton. As a young man, Giles Poole is thought to have found a footing in Thynne's household[7] and, when Lady Thynne died, Sir John prudently followed Sir Giles' example by marrying as his second wife Dorothy Wroughton, respectively daughter and sister to the two Poole ladies at Sapperton. Her daughter, Gresham Thynne, was first cousin and contemporary to Elinor Poole, whose recipe book contains a remedy for heart trouble, a Red Cockle Syrup and a Dyet Drinke all marked in the margin, in the owner's handwriting, 'By Mrs Gresham Thinne'.

If Elinor's grandfather had begun his career as a retainer of Thynne's so, thirty or more years later, did Carew Raleigh, whose younger brother Walter got off to a rather more spectacular start at court. Sir Carew, according to John Aubrey, 'was Gentleman of the horse to Sir John Thynne of Longleate, and after his death maryed his lady, by whom he had children ...'[8] These children, nieces and nephews to Sir Walter Raleigh, were also Elinor Fettiplace's first cousins; and two of her recipes, both for cordials based on tobacco, are endorsed at the side in her hand 'By Sr W. R.' and 'By S^{r} W rallygh'.

Her grandfather seems to have retired to the country under a cloud after Somerset's fall in 1552, though both he and his son always retained friends at court. Sir Henry later kept considerable state at Sapperton, entertaining courtiers like Lord Sidney and Queen Elizabeth's Secretary of State, Robert Cecil (son of the most powerful of all the Duke of Somerset's old servants, William Cecil), carrying out government business, sitting on committees, supervising levies, and generally taking a prominent part in local politics. He was a close friend of Cecil's cousin, Sir William Cooke of Highnam in Gloucestershire, the 'beloved cousin' who came in for a gold ring and a gilt falchion, or broadsword, under the terms of Sir Henry's will.* He was Sheriff of the county in 1588, and captain of three hundred footmen in the Gloucestershire trained bands sent up to London to resist the Armada. His son Devereux went up to Oxford that autumn, by which time negotiations must have been already in hand for the marriage between Elinor, eldest of his four daughters, and Richard Fettiplace, that took place early in 1589.

Sir Giles died that February, bequeathing Elinor £400 already earmarked for her marriage portion,[9] and leaving Sapperton perhaps still unfinished, since Sir Henry's youngest child—another Henry—was born at Pauntley in October, 1590 (a middle son, Giles, had died young). Elinor's own son, John Fettiplace, was born probably a little before this new brother. Her nearest brother, Devereux, was killed a year later, fighting alongside his father in France under Robert Devereux, Earl of Essex, who commanded the English expeditionary force shipped over to support Henri of Navarre against the Catholic league. Sir Henry was a captain in Essex's personal cornet of horse at the unsuccessful siege of Rouen in the autumn of 1591,[10] when Devereux died a few months before his twentieth birthday: 'Sir Devereux Poole, being but of tender age, was for his worthyness and valoure knighted in France by Henry

*Cooke made his fortune by marrying a relation of the Pooles, Joyce Lucy, only child and heiress of Sir Thomas Lucy of Charlcote, Stratford-on-Avon (his father was the Sir Thomas Lucy said to have modelled for Shakespeare's Justice Shallow): a match enthusiastically promoted by another of Cecil's hard-up cousins, Francis Bacon, who recommended the bridegroom beforehand as poor but honest, and afterwards regularly relied on touching 'my cos. Cooke' for a loan (J. Spedding, *Letters and Life of Francis Bacon*, 1862, vol. ii, p. 369; vol. iv, p. 40). Joyce Cooke's grandmother was Mary Arnold of Highnam, née Bridges, daughter of Sir John Bridges, first Baron Chandos, who was Giles Poole's maternal aunt.

the 4, the French King, after his owne order and there ended his dayse ...' runs the inscription in Sapperton church.* Devereux may still be seen, sculpted in stone and kneeling in full armour beside his father's tomb, with Elinor and her three younger sisters kneeling at the front.

Elinor's marriage had brought her a great name and prestige, even if the Fettiplace fortunes were founded by now on what seems to have been an increasingly shaky bottom. She was marrying into the senior branch of a family that still owned vast tracts of land in and around the Vale of the White Horse—an area bounded today by the M4 and A40 roads, between Newbury and Swindon to the south, Oxford and Burford to the north—in the century between the Reformation and the civil war. Her father-in-law, Bessells Fettiplace, and his father Sir John, had both been sheriffs of Berkshire as their forbears had been at least since the time of a fifteenth-century Sir Thomas Fettiplace who married into the Portuguese royal family (his wife was the widow of Gilbert, Lord Talbot, killed on another French battlefield fighting for Henry V). Sir Thomas was buried in 1442 at East Shefford, still part of the ancestral estates right down to Lady Fettiplace's day, though the family had long since migrated a few miles north to the adjacent manors of Appleton (a comparatively recent acquisition in 1564) and Besselsleigh.[11]

Elinor's new in-laws seem to have paid dearly for her dowry of £400. Signs of crisis that year suggest that the terms of her settlement involved substantial selling up to clear the debts and mortgages of a heavily encumbered estate. Bessells Fettiplace had already sold Ockholt-in-Bray—known as 'Fettiplace manor'—and in 1589 he conveyed Compton Beauchamp to Elinor's father. In January he and his son Richard sold Radecott for '£1700 in hand paid' to their neighbour and kinsman, Sir Henry Unton, who also bought from them and their wives three months later the manor and hundred of Shrivenham with its 40 houses and gardens, 30

*The tablet at Sapperton, put up presumably twenty-five years after the event, when Sir Henry died, gives the date of Devereux's death as 1590; but it is 1591 in the *Victoria County History*, in W. A. Shaw, *Knights of England*, 1906, and in W. C. Metcalf, *Book of Knights*, 1885, where he is listed as one of four English knights dubbed by Henri IV (who was desperate by this stage to rally troops already badly demoralised by lack of pay or reinforcements, military failure, sickness and even starvation). A letter dated December 5, 1591, from Lord Burghley to Devereux Poole's kinsman Sir Henry Unton, the English ambassador at Rouen, urges him to prevent the French King knighting any more of the Queen's subjects on pain of her extreme displeasure (*Correspondence of Sir Henry Unton*, Rev Joseph Stevenson, ed., 1847, pp. 192–3).

orchards, 40 barns, 4 dovehouses and nearly 2,000 acres of mixed pasture, meadow, and woodland. The great moated grange at East Shefford—where the ancient arms of Fettiplace (two silver chevrons on a red ground, with a griffin's head crest) and the five blue shields of the royal house of Portugal were emblazoned on the corbels and windows of the high, oak-beamed hall—went for a princely £3,000 the same year.[12] So did the outlying manor of Septvans in Kent, and from then on, every three years or so, Bessells and his son sold more land. Provision had to be made for five younger sons: one of them, Michael Fettiplace, was apprenticed in 1590 to Richard Covert, a London merchant taylor who married Michael's sister Cecily the year after.[13] Bessells would also have had to find portions for his five daughters, two married, and one still to come when he secured for his eldest son a bride whose £400 must have represented a considerable prize. The great Lady Russell, a neighbour of the Fettiplaces at Donnington castle in Berkshire, marrying off her own daughter to the Earl of Worcester's eldest son a few years later, reckoned a hundred pounds, coupled with expectations to come, 'will be a sufficient portion for an Earl of so small revenue and so many children as the Earl of Worcester'.[14]

The Queen herself danced at this Russell wedding—the bride's cousin, Robert Cecil, was her Secretary of State, the bride one of her Maids of Honour—at Blackfriars on June 15, 1600; and so did Richard Fettiplace. It was a sumptuous affair and singularly auspicious for anyone seeking preferment, especially through Cecil, whose papers at Hatfield House include several letters from Richard's father-in-law, Sir Henry Poole, accompanying parcels and presents, issuing invitations, requesting jobs or perks for local candidates (including 'my near kinsman', Sir Edmund Fettiplace of Swinbrook in Oxfordshire, another captain in Essex's army, for whom Elinor's father successfully sought a reward on August 24, 1605).[15] Sir Henry's three younger daughters all married men who were eventually knighted; his only surviving son would in due course marry a daughter of the fourth Baron Chandos (Cecil's elder brother, Lord Burghley, married another of Chandos' daughters in 1609); two of his Poole granddaughters married earls. Perhaps he thought it was high time his eldest child was honoured, and perhaps Cecil owed him a favour.

The Queen, always sparing of knighthoods, must have been even more reluctant than usual to confer one at this particular juncture, when she was seriously considering degrading all the knights made against her express orders the previous summer in Ireland by Essex (who had been imprisoned since Christmas on this and other charges, and was publicly disgraced in the Star Chamber the day before the Russell wedding). But something or somebody changed her mind: 'I doubt not but you have heard of the great marriage at the Lady Russell, where the Queen was present ...' wrote John Chamberlain to his friend Dudley Carleton on June 24,[16] 'and of the knighting of Sir Fetipher with many goode wordes more than God knowes he was worthy of.' This letter must have crossed with an equally supercilious packet of country gossip and news, dated 22 June, from young Carleton,[17] in attendance on Sir Edward Norris at Englefield in Oxfordshire: 'Lady Unton holds her court at Faringdon, but in discontent with her husband for seeking to contract his household. Mrs Fettiplace, whose husband has been knighted now just a week, comes from her father's where she now is, to be our neighbour, on our return from Englefield, I mean to see how she becomes her Ladyship.'*

The unmistakeably patronising tone of this exchange between two bachelor wits—Chamberlain was a dedicated, lifelong London gossip; Carleton, afterwards ambassador at the Hague, acquired a name as one of the shrewdest observers in Europe—suggests that, at any rate to their more sophisticated contemporaries, 'Sir Fetipher'† and his ambitious wife had somewhat the air of country cousins. But there can be no doubt that this day's work gave great satisfaction at Appleton. The Lady Unton holding court at Faringdon was another of the new Lady Fettiplace's cousins, Dorothy Wroughton, eldest daughter of Elinor's uncle, Sir Thomas Wroughton of Broad Hinton. She had married Queen Elizabeth's ambassador, Sir Henry Unton of Wadley near Faringdon, nearly ten years before Elinor married a kinsman of his, and moved to a nearby household in Berkshire.

A painted panel (now in the National Portrait Gallery), commissioned by Dorothy to illustrate scenes from her husband's life,

*This triumphal visit to Sapperton can hardly have gone unnoticed at Longleat whose current chatelaine, plain Mrs Thynne, remained sharply critical of her own husband's failure to secure a knighthood from the Queen: 'It is reported here my brother Townshend shall be knighted; if it be true I can but be sorry that your standing and credit at Court can not procure you as much grace as he were [in]. Mr Thynne as you are I would not have been without it if I had given well for it. If all your courtly friends can not procure you that title I think they will do very little for you; if men can not procure it, yet methinks some of your great Ladies might do so much for you.' Joan Thynne to John Thynne, June 18, 1601. J. and M. Thynne, *Two Elizabethan Women*, pp. 19–20.

†Posterity may have settled for 'Fettiplace' but Elinor (alternatively Elynor, and Elianor) and her contemporaries spelt it as the whim took them 'Fettyplace', 'Feteplace', 'Phetiplace', etc. (I have found both ffeteplace and Ffetiplact.)

shows her presiding over a dinner party at Wadley: bearded gentlemen in black doublet and hose and high-crowned black hats, each with a napkin politely draped over his left shoulder, talk and drink with elaborately coiffed and jewelled ladies, some in black, some in pink and silver, their long, pale, slender fingers set off by huge puffed and embroidered sleeves, their faces framed in stiff gauzy collars edged with pearls. Behind the diners are three attendants proffering books (presumably to show the bookish taste of Sir Henry, who amassed a substantial library of two hundred and twenty volumes), while in front six musicians play for a masque in progress. Lady Unton left inventories[18] listing everything from cellar to wheatloft at Wadley which, together with her strip-cartoon illustrations, give a pretty fair notion of the sort of entertaining that went with the food Lady Fettiplace (herself perhaps one of the guests in pink or silver at her cousin's party) describes in her book.

Sir Henry Unton, weakened financially and physically by the French wars which killed Devereux Poole, had died prematurely in 1596, leaving staggering debts of £23,000 and a clutch of litigious heirs, none of which prevented his determined young widow from hanging on to his manor of Wadley. She kept his illustrious name too, even though she was married again two years later to the husband, George Shirley, whose notions of thrift and economy were clearly cramping her style as a housekeeper by 1600. She had mourned her first husband energetically (Dorothy Unton is the full-sized lady in marble kneeling beside the tomb she erected for him in Faringdon church) before remarrying on terms impressive even by modern feminist standards.

Any sort of independent life for a woman, single or widowed, was virtually impossible in Elizabethan England, where the possession of an income or property simply made a woman all the more desirable, legitimate prey to marauding males; but the contract Lady Unton negotiated for herself as a widow gives a pretty fair inkling of what it felt like, for heiresses like herself and her cousin Elinor, to be bought and sold like cows by their fathers and husbands. The conditions Dorothy Unton laid down for George Shirley amount to a real-life version—equally hard-headed, if financially and sexually a good deal more explicit—of Millamant's marriage settlement, worked out just over a century later, at the end of Congreve's *The Way of the World*: 'first, she requires to reserve her own living entire to herself, and to bestow it without any control,' Carleton reported to Chamberlain on March 6, 1598, 'second, she demands a jointure [widow's pension] of £1000 a year;

thirdly, £500 in land to be tied on her son, if there be one [Lady Unton had no children, then or afterwards]; fourthly, if it should happen that she and her husband fall out, she requires £500 a year out of his living, and to live apart from him, with that added to her living of Faringdon; and fifth, if she chance to find fault with her husband's unsufficiency to choose another bedfellow.'[19]

Even allowing for exaggeration or ribaldry on Carleton's part, Lady Unton plainly had the upper hand, and the masculine world was aghast: 'for mine owne part as poore a man as I am,' replied Chamberlain, 'I wold not buy such another of the price'.[20] If Dorothy Unton had no choice but to sell herself, at least she drove a hard bargain. Her sister Mary seems to have been one of the very few women who ended up unsold (Lady Unton left her household goods in 1634 to 'my sister Mary Wroughton', deducting among other bequests 'one little silver cawdle-cupp' for 'my Lady Frances Poole', who was Elinor Fettiplace's younger sister);[21] and perhaps her fate is not entirely surprising in the light of Carleton's account of her, on October 13, 1600, as a headstrong girl gallivanting about on horseback in the deer park at Windsor, or careering from house to house—'and to some places where they were little known'—all over Berkshire at the head of 'a company of mad wenches ... attended with a concert of musicians, as if they had undertaken the like adventure as Kemp did from London to Norwich'[22] (Will Kemp, for whom Shakespeare wrote the part of Dogberry in *Much Ado About Nothing*, had made an immensely successful publicity stunt out of morris-dancing to Norwich the year before Mary's escapade).

Clearly both Mary and Dorothy laid claim to some of the same freedoms as their male contemporaries; and what little is known of Elinor Fettiplace suggests a character quite as forceful as her Wroughton cousins with the same firm view of her own importance. Like Dorothy Unton, she remained her Ladyship long after she, too, had been remarried to a commoner and widowed for a second time. Titles, never easily come by under Elizabeth, were not to be lightly given up in that inordinately class-conscious age pullulating, as Philip Stubbes complained (in his *Anatomie of Abuses*, 1583), with social climbers, 'every man crying out with open mouth I am a gentleman, I am worshipful, I am Honorable, I am noble, and I cannot tell what ...' Virtually the only decoration in Lady Fettiplace's elegant but austere manuscript is the series of exuberant twiddles and curlicues executed round her name and rank at the foot of the front inside cover: 'Right Wor: the Ladie Elynor Fetiplace, her Book'.

A nicely brought-up girl in the sixteenth century would normally have been taught to dance, sing, play the lute, to sew and embroider, as well as to master all the housewifely activities—ranging from cookery, confectionery and the distilling of spirits to medicinal prescribing and dispensing, laundry work and the routine manufacture of household items like ink and insecticide—covered in Lady Fettiplace's book. But owning a book in the first place (not to mention knowing how to read and write in it) may have been more unusual at a time when, not so very much earlier, the great Earl of Pembroke saw nothing to be ashamed of, according to Aubrey, in being unable to sign his own name. Literacy, let alone Latin, was far from universal among well-bred Tudor women, and perhaps it is no coincidence that Elinor Fettiplace was connected on her father's side to the Cookes of Gidea Hall in Essex, a family well known for advanced views on the education of girls.

Her father's 'beloved cousin' and neighbour, Sir William Cooke of Highnam, was nephew to the five Cooke sisters, generally agreed to be (after the Queen) the most learned women in England: one became Lady Russell, another Lady Burghley—Robert Cecil's mother—a third the mother of Francis Bacon. Lady Fettiplace's book is one of very few household manuscripts known to have survived from so early a date. It was apparently made, or at any rate copied out, in her father's newly finished and thoroughly modern establishment at Sapperton, and its contents reflect clearly and coherently, if on an exclusively domestic front, the inquiring, empirical, sceptical, in short Baconian bent of the age. Its owner must have been, like the formidable Cooke sisters, at the very least an efficient and practical manager. Apart from organising her household, she would have been expected to take over management of the estate in her husband's absence, supervising farm work and maintenance, making up accounts, receiving and paying out rents ('money walks away a pace here, for Woodlands hath had sixty pounds of me since you went,' wrote Elinor's slightly younger contemporary, Maria Thynne, in a business letter from Longleat to her husband in London[23]). There was a clear obligation on a knight and his lady to keep up a certain state which meant, for someone like Elinor Fettiplace, who came from a background of lavish entertaining at Pauntley and Sapperton, applying the same hospitable principles to running her own smaller but still sizeable household in Berkshire.

Not that she would have been in charge right away. It was customary after an early marriage for an eldest son to settle in his father's house where his wife might finish her education under the eye of her mother-in-law. Richard's mother, also called Elinor or Helen, was one of the Coverts, wealthy ironfounders and squires of Slaugham in Sussex with whom the Fettiplaces prudently intermarried over three generations at this critical stage in their fortunes. Marrying for money, though standard practice, did not always make for smooth relations between the parties. Elinor Fettiplace's own aunt, Lady Thynne, had had considerable trouble at Longleat when her eldest stepson married the eighteen-year-old Joan Hayward, a rich merchant's daughter who threatened to run away nine months after the marriage on the grounds that her new in-laws treated her like a servant.* Twenty years later when her own son and heir married, Joan Thynne herself proved an even more implacable mother-in-law to his bride. Part of her grievance was that the young couple had married in secret (this match in 1595 between Thomas Thynne and Maria Audley, both aged sixteen, which intensified the longrunning feud between their two families, is said to have given Shakespeare ideas for *Romeo and Juliet*[24]), which meant that there was no parental contract, and so no dowry to build up the Longleat estates and, more specifically, provide portions for the younger, unmarried Thynne girls.

Elinor Fettiplace's own handsome dowry perhaps helped finance the marriage two years later of her sister-in-law, Cecily Fettiplace, to another of the Coverts. She herself cannot have been much more than seventeen or so when her husband installed her at Appleton alongside his younger brothers and sisters, the last of whom—Elizabeth or Parnell—was born five years after Elinor's own son John. The family seem to have used Appleton as a base with the adjacent manor of Besselsleigh (owned by the family since a previous Richard Fettiplace of East Shefford had married Elizabeth Bessells in the fifteenth century) serving as an annexe or overflow: one of Bessells' brothers, who was living there in the 1590s, was succeeded

*Joan Thynne, who married John Thynne the younger in 1576, complained of being 'vilely abused' by Elinor's Aunt Dorothy, forcibly restrained, denied food and drink, nicknamed to her face, mocked and scorned behind her back, but, though Joan's parents were sympathetic, she was obliged to return to Longleat where Lady Thynne (staunchly supported by her own indignant friends) was equally obliged to put up with her. Roles were reversed with the death of old Sir John Thynne in 1580, when Joan was triumphantly installed at Longleat while the widowed Lady Dorothy retired to her dower house just as, when Joan's own husband died in 1604, she in turn was forced to hand over to a daughter-in-law she detested (see J. and M. Thynne, *Two Elizabethan Women*, pp. xxix, 4, 55–6).

by Richard's brother Thomas, and possibly at one point by Richard himself. Nothing now remains of the Besselsleigh house except for a single stone gate pier in the field next to the tiny church. Cromwell is said to have slept there, and the place was gutted in the civil war (like the Wroughtons' family home at Broad Hinton) by Royalists anxious to prevent its ever again housing a parliamentary garrison.

Elinor's children may have been baptised or buried there, since none are recorded in the Appleton register. Besides her son and heir John, she had another son Henry, baptised after the Twelfth Night celebrations at Pauntley in January 1602, of whom nothing further is known. The deaths of two baby daughters are recorded on their great-grandfather's tomb erected in 1593 in Appleton church, and there may possibly have been a third, the young bride mourned by her husband at Pauntley in 1630:

She was by birth a fettiplace
Elizabeth by name
her parentes joy, my swete solace
free from deceit or blame
who being of a milde conceyt
and modest still of minde
on vertue ever her thoughts did wayt
*she was so well inclinde . . .**

All that is known for certain is that, in 1604, the date on her book, Elinor Fettiplace had one two-year-old son and another who, at fifteen, was already nearing marriageable age. John Fettiplace was married at Appleton in 1606 to a cousin—Margaret Fettiplace of Fernham—who bore him a son the year after, making four generations of Fettiplaces under one roof. Bessells' death in 1609 made Sir Richard head of a household that included his son's wife and child (his widowed mother would have retired on her jointure, just as the Thynne ladies each in turn reluctantly vacated Longleat) as well as two of his sisters, Parnell Fettiplace (until her marriage in 1616) and Cecily Covert, whose marriage had not turned out well. Five of Sir Richard's brothers and sisters are mentioned in particularly affectionate terms in his will, among them poor 'Cicill' to whom he left an annuity he could probably ill afford, on

*If this was Elinor Fettiplace's daughter, she must have been a late, possibly even posthumous child of the marriage, having already survived both her father and her eldest brother. The inscription on the church wall at Pauntley is partly missing, but the parish register describes her as the wife of 'Thomas Addis the yonger', and gives the date of her death as April 29, 1630.

condition that 'she shall be reconciled to and dwell with her husband, which I pray unto God to accomplish'.[25]

He also left gifts to his trusted servant, Humphrey Kelsoe, and others unnamed, one of whom was perhaps the John Blackden who contributed a water for sore eyes to Lady Fettiplace's book. A man's family in Tudor and Stuart times meant everyone in his household, not simply his wife and children. The childless Unton establishment at Wadley contained, besides one- and two-bed dormitories for 'Gentlewomen' and 'Maydens', a chamber apiece for steward, butler, porter, 'coke', gardener, hind, and half a dozen serving men. Aubrey reckoned that the Earl of Pembroke at Wilton maintained 'one hundred and twenty family uprising and down lying', of whom all but six or seven were servants and retainers.

Besides the family, even a moderately-sized manor house could expect to feed 'strangers'—travellers, labourers, delivery men, anyone passing on business—as well as the poor at the gates (cottagers at Appleton and Besselsleigh were still receiving Fettiplace bounty at Christmas well into this century). The local big house was a centre for produce: growing, gathering and preserving (the last process described in detail in Lady Fettiplace's book) the harvest from fields, orchards, garden and dairy for distribution again at the great seasonal feasts of Christmas, New Year, Shrovetide and Easter. William Harrison, whose *Description of England* came out in 1587, a year or two before Elinor Poole married Richard Fettiplace, notes that these winter feasts were essential in country parts where the manor house supported a high proportion of the local workforce ('there are commonly forty or three score people fed in those halls'). Meals were elaborate and copious, appetites often prodigious, though the host and his guests ate moderately. The people who overdid themselves, growing tired and emotional—'cupshotten'—were poorer neighbours, unused to plenty, who probably had precious little left—'hard and pinching diet, small drink, and some of them having scarce enough of that'—in their own larders at home by mid winter. The household books of Sir William Petre, secretary to Robert Cecil's father, Lord Burghley, show that he regularly fed round about forty strangers in the winter months at Ingatestone Hall in Essex, two or three times that many at special feasts like Twelfth Night, a family wedding or a royal visit.

It was an age of extravagant consumption, ostentation, dressing-up, showing off and display. High standards were set for the Fettiplaces of Appleton by neighbours like Lady Unton at Wadley, or the Swinbrook Fettiplaces (descended from a younger brother of the Fettiplace who picked up Besselsleigh) twenty miles to the north in Oxfordshire. Sir Edmund Fettiplace of Swinbrook had been knighted, three months after Sir Richard, by the Queen stopping off on one of her progresses to dine with the comptroller of her household, Sir William Knollys, at Caversham: a sumptuous occasion, according to Chamberlain, at which hangers-on like Carleton's brother George with 'his small troop' found themselves 'halfe drowned in the sea of such shewes as the Oxfordshire men made . . .'.[26] Carleton's cousin, plain Master Dormer of Ascot, rode out to this feast at the head of ten or twelve mounted retainers. It seems unlikely that Sir Richard Fettiplace could have matched this sort of magnificence, any more than his wife could have held court on the same splendid scale as her cousin Dorothy. But Sir Richard certainly posted up to London with the rest of the country gentry for King James' coronation in July, 1603, when three hundred knights were dubbed at one go in the royal gardens at Whitehall, a full-scale naval battle was staged in fireworks on the Thames and, in spite of ravening plague, the City exploded in triumphal pageant and spectacle, 'not one conduit 'twixt the Tower and Westminster but runnes wine, drink who wil'.[27]

When the new King and Queen visited Berkshire on their first royal progress that autumn, they spent the nights of September 7 and 8 with Lady Unton at Wadley.[28] An occasion like this probably meant well over a hundred people—including the court and its retinue, local dignitaries, friends and relations, perhaps the Fettiplaces themselves—sitting down to dinner and supper in Wadley great hall. The Unton inventories list the silver and plate, the pewter dishes, diaper napkins and table cloths, sheets, linen, featherbeds and bolsters, the furniture and fittings which would have had to be fetched out, cleaned, aired, polished, perfumed and waxed ready for the royal visit. There were three green carpets (probably for covering tables or seats) with two green cloth chairs and thirteen matching stools, 'iii long cussins of redd satyn laid wth gold lace', 'one black wrought velvet chayre laid wth silver and gold lace' in the Parlour, another velvet chair and 'vi tufted taffetye stooles' in the Great Chamber, a magnificent yellow silk and silver lace bedstead with 'rich taffitye curtains' in the Drawing Chamber, together with more velvet and turkey-work cushions, gilded leather hangings, silk damask testers, canopies, coverlets and bed curtains.[29]

No such list of Fettiplace finery survives but Elinor's book makes it clear that she knew how to look after it: she describes how 'To wash gould and coloured silk', 'To white clothes' and 'To wash Leather ready for perfuming' (this was to be steeped in rosewater, wrung out, dried, rubbed, stretched to make it supple, smoked in the sweet fumes of benjamin, then wrapped close in silk and laid 'betweene the blanket & the bed when you go to bed, & so drie it to keep it from the ayre'). She gives two ways 'To perfume Gloves'—always a popular present for royalty—instructions for scented soaps, pomanders, perfumes, fragrant pot-pourri powders to sweeten a bedchamber or stuff 'sweet baggs' for the linen closet (see p. 230), and several 'sweet waters' distilled from damask rose petals, dried orange and lemon peel, herbs, spices, musk, civet, balsams, precious gums and resins, oil of almonds or jasmine.

Robert May, author of one of the best known seventeenth-century cookery books, gives a famous description of a Jacobean dinner party that ended with the ladies drenching one another with these sweet waters to drown the stench of gunpowder as a pasteboard battleship at one end of the table opened fire on a castle 'with Battlements, Portcullis Gates and Draw-Bridges'[30] at the other. The damask tablecloths would be sodden by this time with claret wine seeping from a great bleeding pastry stag with an arrow in its side and, now that the party had really got going, the lids were to be lifted from two mighty pies, releasing respectively live frogs and birds, 'which makes the ladies to skip and shreek' as the terrified frogs hop up under their skirts while the birds blunder into and snuff out the candles. Lady Unton's party was no doubt too early in the reign for the Stuart court to have got into its full stride for frivolity and rowdiness. But it was clearly the sort of affair for which Lady Fettiplace would have brought out her stores of banqueting stuff, sweetmeats, liqueurs and cordials, perhaps the costly narcotic Tobacca Water given her by Raleigh, and her delectable Spanish Marmalad, enriched with beaten gold and crushed pearls. These were exotic specialities but there were also any number of less outlandish delights—delicate creams, jellies, syllabubs, and rich, fruity confections like The Lord of Devonshire his Pudding.

The Lord of Devonshire was Charles Blount, eighth Lord Mountjoy, who had succeeded the disgraced and treacherous Essex (beheaded in 1601) as Lord Deputy in Ireland. Sir Edmund Fettiplace served under him from the defeat of the Spanish auxiliaries at Kinsale in December, 1601, until the unconditional surrender of the Irish under Tyrone in the spring of 1603, when Mountjoy was recalled in high favour with the new King, who created him Earl of Devonshire at the coronation that summer. Lady Fettiplace must have got the pudding soon afterwards, if not from his lordship himself, then from someone who ate at his table—perhaps Sir Edmund, or perhaps his commander in Ireland, Mountjoy's Lieutenant-General of Horse, Sir Henry Danvers. Danvers, like Mountjoy, was another of Essex's former friends greatly favoured by the new King. He certainly knew Lady Fettiplace, for she identified him—'Sir Henry Davars' (Danvers frequently signed his own letters without an 'n')—in her own handwriting in the front of a book he had given her.*

The Danvers of Dauntsey were an old Wiltshire family related to both Pooles and Fettiplaces.† Sir Henry Poole was one of the neighbours who refused to cooperate in Queen Elizabeth's attempts to raise revenue from the Danvers estates, after the execution of Sir Henry Danvers' elder brother Charles in 1601 for his part in Essex's rebellion.[31] Danvers got his lands back (and sold a substantial portion, including Cirencester and its seven hundreds for £2,600 to Elinor's father), together with a barony from King James, and was afterwards made Earl of Danby by Charles I. He founded Oxford Botanic Gardens, and lived latterly not far from Appleton at Cornbury Park in Oxfordshire. Aubrey, who admired his 'magnificent and munificall spirit', thought that he laid out £11,000 'per annum at the least' on building and doing up Cornbury, allowing another £3,000 a year (in a bachelor establishment) 'only for his kitchin'.[32] Aubrey's sums are not always reliable, but even so this last staggering estimate—at a time when £30 a year would have been reckoned a reasonable living for a clergyman—gives some idea of the scale and splendour of hospitality that was by no means unusual in the circles in which Elinor Fettiplace and her family moved.

Though they could not compete with Danvers at Cornbury, or for that matter with Pooles at Sapperton, the Fettiplaces seem to have made some attempt at modernisation themselves round about

*Charles Estienne, *Maison Rustique, or the countrie farme*, 1600. I am grateful to Elizabeth David for locating Lady Fettiplace's copy (inscribed and dated by her 1624) at Sotheby's, where it was sold in the Astor of Hever Book Sale, June 29, 1983.

†Richard Pole or Poole, Elinor's great-great-grandfather—the Poole who bought Sapperton—seems to have married a Danvers as part of a long and bloody struggle for possession of Dauntsey, which belonged to a fatherless boy, Edward Stradling, claimed as a ward by both Pole and his wife's brother, Henry Danvers. Pole married young Edward's mother as his second wife, but she was murdered at Dauntsey, together with her son, c. 1488, probably by Danvers, whose family finally secured Dauntsey by the marriage of Sir John Danvers to the murdered boy's sister. Their daughter, Dorothy Danvers, married John Fettiplace of East Shefford, Sir Richard's great-great-grandfather.

this time. Appleton is a rarity, a twelfth-century manor house (still moated in Lady Fettiplace's day) with what Pevsner rudely calls Tudor insertions: a new north porch tacked on in the late sixteenth century to the great, round-headed, Norman doorway, a stone fireplace and chimney stack built into the partition which cut down the old mediaeval hall into two storeys.[33] The lower one served probably as an entrance hall and common room, the newly panelled great chamber above being used for entertaining and as a family dining room, with a little private sitting or 'withdrawing' room over the porch: Sir Richard kept his things here, bequeathing to his daughter-in-law in his will 'all such goods and implements of household which shall be at the hour of my death in my closett over the Northwest porch of my house'. In 1604, he and his father founded a local elementary school to educate the children of Appleton and Besselsleigh 'in good manners and learning'; and seven years later, after Bessells had died, Richard endowed a charity for the distribution of bread and relief to the poor[34] (the distribution continued every other Sunday in the church to fourteen good persons at least until the 1920s, when the remainder of the fund was divided between Christmas boxes and a night school, 'Fettiplace's Foundation and Advancement': loaves and green Fettiplace livery coats from a later seventeenth-century charity at Swinbrook were still being given out up till the second world war).

Sixteen hundred and four was a terrible plague year, like the year before when thirty thousand people are thought to have died of it in London alone. Lady Fettiplace distilled bitter herbs and roots in white wine 'To make imperiall water' ('this is very good against the plague, or the poxe, or any other infectious disease'), or boiled them with spices in malmsey for 'Doctor Burges his receipt for the plague' ('bee provided of this medicen in time of Infection'). Both are endorsed in the margin in her own handwriting, the first 'for the plague', the second (which was to be taken night and morning as a preventative) 'prob:' for '*probatum*' or 'tested'. She also gives 'A medicine of King Henry the eighth for the plague or pestilence'. Her grandfather, Leonard Poole, had been gentleman usher extraordinary in Henry VIII's household in the 1520s, her father and uncle had been his gentlemen pensioners, and two of her husband's relations had seen service at his court. The king's medicine is another bitter brew of marigolds, sorrel, burnet, rue, feverfew and the roots of dragonwort, sweetened with sugar candy, and recommended in the encouraging but not over-sanguine terms typical of Lady Fettiplace's practical approach to nursing: 'if this

Drink bee taken before the markes appeare, it helpeth by the grace of god.'

Lady Fettiplace's contemporary, Lady Hoby of Hackness in Yorkshire—sister-in-law to Ann Russell at whose wedding Sir Richard was knighted—kept a diary which gives a vivid impression of what it was like in the country in the long hot summers of 1603 and 1604, waiting for news of the plague, hearing terrifying reports from neighbouring towns of people shutting themselves up in their houses or fleeing before it, while those not yet infected walked in their gardens among the roses and waited for it to come. Like Lady Hoby at Hackness, Lady Fettiplace must have run Appleton as both surgery and dispensary for a substantial section of the countryside round about: fifty-six ways of dressing wounds, nearly four dozen remedies for failing eyesight, two dozen plasters and potions to relieve and comfort the stomach, sixteen different cough mixtures and eleven cures for a bad back suggest some of the commonest afflictions with which she had to contend.

Doctors were few and far between. Lady Fettiplace includes prescriptions from some of the most fashionable practitioners of the day, including Leonard Poe ('A water for a Canker or ulcer in the mouth') whose following among the nobility led to a royal appointment in 1609,* and the learned Thomas Muffet ('Doctor Muffet's Clyster', a harmless external plaster to be applied warm, altogether milder than the syringes and enemas that generally went under that name; and perhaps the two remedies on the same page for the lungs—a soothing syrup and a conserve or cough sweet—marked in her hand 'D.M.'). Both had served the Earl of Essex at the same time as Elinor Fettiplace's father round about 1590: Dr Muffet was an army doctor on the French campaign in which her brother Devereux was killed,[35] and afterwards one of the eminent scientists gathered at Wilton in Wiltshire round the Countess of Pembroke, whose brother, Robert Sidney, was staying with the Pooles at Sapperton in 1604. There is also Dr Stephens' cordial water, a celebrated herbal panacea (Dr Stephens or Stevens is said to have survived ninety-eight years on the strength of it[36]) popularly supposed to cure virtually any complaint from the stone, worms and palsy to barrenness in women: present in every medicine closet,

*Contemporaries blamed the cruelty and violence of Dr Poe's treatment for the death of Robert Cecil, Lord Salisbury, in 1612: 'Thus to king and state he was a great stay/Till Poe with his syringe did squirt him away' (L. Stone, *Family and Fortune*, p. 51).

copied out in every household book for another century and more, it was, in a phrase from Karen Hess's *Martha Washington's Booke of Cookery*, 'the aspirin of the age'. Local physicians practising in the Midlands include a Dr Ashworth (who was a favourite with Lady Unton, as well as with Carleton's cousin Dormer at Ascot[37]), and 'mr Hall a chirurgian', who contributed a cure for nosebleeds: this was John Hall who settled at the turn of the century in Stratford-on-Avon, built up a thriving practice for forty miles round about, married Shakespeare's daughter Susanna in 1607 and remained for the rest of their lives, at any rate in the west Midlands, a great deal more famous than his father-in-law.*

Dr Hall's cure relies on sympathetic magic (a pinch of the patient's dried blood snuffed up the nostrils), reinforced by the application of cloths dipped in plantain and wild tansy juice, astringents that staunch and soothe in much the same way as Lady Fettiplace's own simple first aid for nosebleeds, scrawled in her handwriting at the back of the book: 'robe grounsel betwene your handes and hould et to your Noes et well presently helpe.'† Her remedies stick on the whole to the practical, verifiable healing properties of herbs, roots and minerals, and she pays particular attention to nursing, recommending the sort of gentle, comforting, sensible approach that would have pleased Florence Nightingale. She nursed the very sick or dying with nourishing broths (see p. 191), and she was especially careful with children, dosing them for worms, combing their hair once a week with a nit lotion made from oil of white lilies, prescribing salad oil boiled with green lavender and cumin, to be laid warm to the navel, 'For the fret in a child'.

She treated fevers with cooling juleps, cured insomnia with seven sorts of sleeping potion (one, made from poppy seed, henbane, lettuce juice, opium and the narcotic mandrake apple, worked

*I am grateful to Dr A. L. Rowse for confirming Dr Hall's identity. The Pooles were several times connected to the Lucys of Charlcote, Stratford-on-Avon, in whose park Shakespeare is supposed to have been caught stealing deer as a boy: the incident was first recorded by a seventeenth-century rector of Sapperton, Richard Davies, who identified Sir Thomas Lucy as Shakespeare's persecutor and the model for Justice Shallow (Sir Thomas's sister had married a Tracy of Toddington, his son married Sir Henry Poole's second cousin, and his grand-daughter married Poole's friend Sir William Cooke, see note on p. 121).

†Dr Hall of Stratford left records of two cases of nosebleed, one cured by a fierce emetic infusion, the other by stopping the nostrils with a cloth dipped in frogspawn, then applying a second cloth spread with a soothing, clay-and-vinegar plaster to the temples and neck, a remedy also included in Lady Fettiplace's book and very similar to the one she marked with Hall's name (John Hall, 'Select Observations on English Bodies', case histories nos. 102 and 46, from Harriet Joseph, *Shakespeare's Son-in-law*).

externally, by the patient's inhaling the fumes), relieved the wind colic, or stomach pains, with a variety of ointments and plasters applied in a linen bag, like a hotwater bottle, or under a bread poultice ('warme it in a saucer upon coles, & then anoynt the place so greeved, & take hot trenchers, & lay theirto, which will take away the extremity of the paine within halfe an howre'). Her regime for smallpox patients, who had to wait until the invention of vaccination for more radical relief, is a model of kindness and common sense: 'When you know certainlie that it is the pocks, let them drink some safron & milk, & let them keep their chamber for fear of taking cold, let them keep themselves warme, but not too hot, for that will doe them much hurt, when they [the scabs] begin to drie, anoint them to make them skale of, & as soon as you dare wash your face, wash it with malmsey & butter together . . .' (The anointing mixture, made from pure lard and rosewater, is marked by the friend who supplied it: 'This oyntment is coole & comfortable, proved by my self B:C').

Superstition plays virtually no part. Nor do the frightening cures freely prescribed by professional contemporaries whose brutal purging, vomiting, bleeding, clysters, emetics and glisters must often have done more harm than good. Barely half a dozen out of well over three hundred remedies betray the barbarity of the age, and even then it is not the patients that suffer, but the creatures involved (one fat cat and two hedgehogs flayed alive, a cock whipped to death, fledgeling swallows ground in a mortar with or without powdered earthworms to make the ancient, highly prized, mucilaginous 'oyle of swallows'). 'A gentle purge', 'a cool posset', 'a restoring iellie' and 'a pretious oyle' are typical of Lady Fettiplace's cautious and considerate approach so that—as she said herself of her sinister-sounding Ruberb Pilles—'if it never woork it can not hurt'.

At a time when there were still very few printed medical or cookery books,* a manuscript like Lady Fettiplace's must have come in useful for anyone (provided she could read) running a household. Throughout the seventeenth, eighteenth and nineteenth centuries books like this one were passed down from one wife to another, or from a mother to her daughters, each of whom would take a copy when she married, reproducing the family collection

*A. W. Oxford, *English Cookery Books, 1500–1850*, 2d ed., 1977, lists twenty-four before 1604, of which nine at most might qualify strictly as cookery books (the rest deal primarily with health, philosophy, medicines, menus or manners).

with alterations and additions of her own.[38] Many of the first printed cookery books were based—though men generally took the credit for them—on these manuscripts compiled by anonymous gentlewomen. Lady Fettiplace's is a random accumulation of items, copied out with no attempt at classification, many evidently collected (and afterwards annotated) by the owner herself, others passed down through her family. Hence no doubt the preponderance of Gloucestershire and Wiltshire, or Poole rather than Fettiplace connections. The leather binding is decorated in gold, front and back, with the initials E.F., four fleur de lys (gold fleur de lys and a silver lion rampant made up the Poole coat-of-arms), and a rectangular tracery of leaves. The endpapers are made from those old Latin manuscripts which, according to Aubrey, 'flew about like butterflies'[39] all over the West country after the dissolution of the monasteries, being commonly cut up for book-covers or glove patterns and specially prized by home brewers for stopping up beer-barrel bung-holes.

Nearly three quarters of the text has been copied out at a single sitting or session by a scribe, Anthony Bridges (the last part of the book was completed by someone, perhaps an assistant, with a very similar trained hand), of whom all one can say for certain is that he took pride in his fine, flowing, bang up-to-date Italian handwriting, in the elegant, even laying out of a page, and in the quality of his brown ink (which has faded not at all, unlike the inks used by various later hands adding receipts and an index at the back). He concluded his task—225 numbered pages, followed by a set of blanks and half a dozen or so miscellaneous items at the end—on the penultimate page with 'An excellent medicine to cure any man or Beast that is bitten with a mad dog', letting his pen run away with him in a large, unique flourish under the signature: 'By mee Anthony Bridges.'

He was probably a relation of Grey Bridges, fifth Baron Chandos of Sudeley Castle in Gloucestershire, whose sister Beatrix or Beata married Elinor Fettiplace's younger brother Henry. Anthony was a common name in the Bridges family: Grey had an uncle, Anthony Bridges of Avenynge in Gloucestershire, who was a member of the same circle of West country squires as Elinor's father (the families were already related through Sir Henry Poole's grandmother, Katherine Bridges, sister to the first Lord Chandos). It was standard practice in those days for a young relative at the start of his career to be taken into a great house like the Pooles' at

Sapperton,* where Elinor's book was probably made and written: not only is it stamped with the Poole device, but a note in Bridges' handwriting, written beside her name at the top of the first page and subsequently scored out with a fine nib under a decorative band of cross-hatching, reads 'facto Sapperton 1604'.

II

Sapperton at the start of the seventeenth century reflected the size and splendour of its owner's estate, energy and ambitions. According to the Gloucestershire historian Robert Atkyns (whose father eventually bought Sapperton from the Pooles after the civil war), 'Sir Henry Poole was eminent for his great housekeeping'. Good housekeeping in those days meant keeping house on the most generous possible scale, entertaining all comers, strangers, workmen, carters, carriers, cupshotten cottagers as well as the local gentry: Tracys, Raleighs, Wroughtons, Thynnes, Fettiplaces of Coln St Aldwyns, Knyvets of Charlton, Hungerfords of Down Ampney, Rogers of Dowdeswell, all of whom regularly traded lands, succeeded one another in office and married each other's wives or daughters. Sapperton was also ideally placed for company passing on the Bath road to or from court. The Queen's chamberlain and privy councillor, Lord Sidney, stayed at Sapperton in September 1604, with the court on its progress via Woodstock to Windsor and Hampton Court. Sidney, younger brother to Sir Philip Sidney and Mary, Countess of Pembroke, owned lands bordering Sir Henry Poole's in Longford and Wootton, and found himself 'so well pleased with all that I meane, God willing, to have a further footing in Glostershire . . .'[40] A week later Poole himself wrote to Robert Cecil—now King James' Secretary of State, soon to be appointed Lord Treasurer, newly created Viscount Cranborne after his manor of Cranborne just over the Wiltshire border in Dorset—hoping to intercept him at Bath, 'where I meant to have attended you to my poor house, lying conveniently in your journey to the Court'.[41]

Sir Henry had been looking after a hawk for his patron, and offered at the end of the month to see a 'cast of sore falcons'. He

*A Berkshire neighbour and distant relation of Lord Chandos, Anthony Bridges of West Shefford, left a signature (as witness in 1591 in the case of Richard and Elizabeth Walter *v.* Francis Cotton, P.R.O.) which is not unlike but much shakier than the one in Lady Fettiplace's book; he would have been in his early sixties by 1604. A more likely candidate is his nephew Anthony, who died at Colingborne-Sunton in Wiltshire in 1617 (Cooper Willyams, *History of Sudeley Castle*, 1841).

had been sheriff again the year before and his footing in the county was high (when he fell foul in 1608 of a certain Theodore Newton, Cecil's local agent reported that 'a Gloucestershire jury would condemn Mr Newton in £2,000 damages if the matter went to trial, so great is Sir Henry Poole's credit with them'[42]). Cecil, who had grown up from earliest years in what his latest biographer calls 'an atmosphere of architectural ostentation',[43] was about to succumb to the building mania that had already gripped so many of his contemporaries and would eventually prove almost too much even for his colossal financial resources. When Sir Henry offered to put him up for the night, 'my poor house' was, of course, nothing of the sort.

Sapperton was a princely mansion in the spacious modern style, three storeyed, L-shaped, with a north wing for servants and offices, a battlemented lodge opening onto a paved court before the main entrance, tall windows arranged in three symmetrical bays, and ornamental ledges running the length of the building at ground, first- and second-floor levels on the garden front. The design of the bay windows looks as if it had been copied from Longleat,* and, like his brother-in-law Sir John Thynne, Sir Henry seems to have built little domed and pinnacled pavilions, or banqueting houses, for admiring the view from his flat roof (a century later Alexander Pope praised this view of 'Sapperton's fair dale' up the beautiful valley of the Frome). Banqueters in Sir Henry's day would have looked out over his great terraced garden with its raised walks, rectangular lawns, shady alleys and arbours, walled kitchen garden and espaliered orchard, to parkland and tree-lined pastures beyond. There were two more banqueting houses strategically placed in the garden where guests might adjourn after dinner to drink wine, and toy with an elaborate array of delicacies like the Spanish Marmalad, and the five or six dozen fruit sweetmeats described in Lady Fettiplace's book.

In an age of prodigious showpieces and spectacle, laying out a banquet was as much a branch of display as designing an ornate and fanciful house or garden. Elinor's sister, Anne Poole, married Sir Theobald Gorges, whose father Sir Thomas had practically ruined himself building Longford Castle: moated, triangular, allegorical and so romantic that Sidney took it as the model for his

*I am grateful to Mark Girouard for confirming Sapperton's debt to Longleat, from the double-page engraving in Atkyns' *Ancient and Present State of Gloucestershire*, 1712, and for dating the building probably some time in the 1580s.

castle in *Arcadia*. Even Sir Walter Raleigh had spent his brief spell as a West country squire in the 1590s putting up a new castle for himself at Sherborne, and designing a complicated system of walks, parterres and waterworks. Longleat was generally reckoned to be, in Aubrey's phrase, 'the most august building in the kingdome'; and ''twas Sir John Danvers' (another of the Pooles' Wiltshire neighbours, Sir Henry Danvers' younger brother) 'who first taught us the way of Italian gardens'.[44]

People all over the south of England were furiously building and beautifying and—almost before the decorative plasterwork was dry and the last coat-of-arms gilded—going in for some highly competitive housekeeping. Of Elinor's two other sisters, Frances married a kinsman, Sir Neville Poole of Oaksey, and Dorothy married Sir John Savage of Elmsley Castle in Worcestershire, a relation of the Berkeleys whose feudal fortune—infinitely greater than the Fettiplaces'—was being rapidly dissipated by the current lord and his second wife (Lady Fettiplace gives 'The Ladye Barklyes receipt for an old sore', perhaps from this lady, perhaps from her even more high-handed and rapacious predecessor). Lord Berkeley, who liked to ride round the county with a train of one hundred and fifty uniformed servants on horseback and church bells ringing as he passed, kept open house for his neighbours with baskets of food distributed to the poor three days a week at Berkeley Castle.[45] So did Lord Chandos—future brother-in-law to Elinor, Dorothy and Ann Poole—at Sudeley Castle: a flamboyant figure whose temperament was so liberal, hospitality so lavish and train of retainers so impressive that he was known locally as the 'King of Cotswould'.[46]

This was the style approved by Robert May, looking back wistfully as an old man in the year of the Restoration to his apprenticeship as a professional chef at the time Lady Fettiplace's book was written: 'then were the Golden Days wherein were practised the *Triumphs and Trophies of Cookery*, then was Hospitality esteemed, Neighbourhood preserved, the Poor cherished, and God honoured; then was Religion less talkt on and more practised; then was Atheism and Schism less in fashion...'[47] Conservatives like Chandos and Berkeley (the latter set his face equally against modern methods of farming and estate management) still subscribed to the old Tudor principles of feasting and 'good lordship'. But Lady Fettiplace and her friends already inclined towards the new order beginning to favour smaller and more intimate meals, often served in the new 'withdrawing' or 'drawing chambers', and consisting of the sort of simple but sophisticated food—imaginative, carefully prepared, delicate and decorative but not over-rich—she describes in her book. People who lived in Jacobean country houses, seated in their high airy rooms hung with gold and coloured silks, scented with pomanders and sweet bags, looking over choice views through great casement windows, were no less discriminating when it came to the food they ate. The new homes called for a new kind of home-cooking, and Lady Fettiplace's book gives a glimpse of this cooking at a turning point—like so much else in both private and public life in England at the turn of the seventeenth century—between mediaeval and modern times.

The tradition of the mediaeval feast lived on in the extravagant special effects of professional chefs—naval gun-boats, wounded stags, four-and-twenty blackbirds baked in a pie*—the 'Triumphs and Trophies' May had seen, and longed to try his hand at, as a boy before the civil war ("These were formerly the delights of the Nobility, before good House-Keeping had left *England* and the Sword really acted that which was only counterfeit in such honest and laudable Exercises as these'). May clearly had the ambitious, competitive, masculine approach that sees cooking as a branch of social, and in those days often political, one-upmanship. It had regularly brought subjects entertaining Queen Elizabeth to the verge of bankruptcy, and it led Cecil, in the next reign, to spend as much as £200 on a single royal meal. Its supreme expression was *haute cuisine*, invented and gradually refined from the latter part of the seventeenth century onwards by rivalrous French chefs whose superiority was acknowledged at once on this side of the channel (the French vogue reached London with the Stuart court returning from continental exile in 1660), and has scarcely been challenged since. They were, of course, invariably men, egged on by jealous and exacting masters (these were the days when Louis XIV employed one thousand five hundred full-time cooks at Versailles, and the Prince de Condé's maître d'hôtel killed himself because of a humiliating delay in delivery of a crucial consignment of fish), for whom cooking was an art demanding a sensuous imagination, strict logical organisation and serious intellectual effort. Women had played no part in the running of mediaeval and Tudor households where the cleaning, catering and serving staff were

*May gives elaborate instructions in the preface to his *Accomplisht Cook* for mastering the trick of this pie, which was to bake it with a bran stuffing replaced at the last minute by live cargo.

almost always exclusively male; and they were similarly excluded from the great French professional kitchens in the seventeenth and eighteenth centuries, or admitted only to scrub and chop vegetables.

Lady Fettiplace's book represents an alternative, more modest and durable tradition of good housekeeping, practised and passed down by women to this day. Her allegiances are European at a time before the emergence of *haute cuisine* abroad had bred a sense of inferiority and corresponding insularity at home. The pervasive Arab strain in mediaeval cooking may still be seen in her lavish use of rosewater, dried fruit and spices. She herself acknowledges her debt to continental confectioners in A French Custard, French Biskit Bread (almond tart and macaroons respectively, see pp. 83, 224), and A French Dish (little rice and almond cakes fried in butter, see p. 84). These last are all delicious in a style not noticeably different from her other characteristically simple but subtle sweets and puddings. Her liaisons of egg yolk for thickening sauces (instead of the earlier breadcrumbs, and the later marked English insistence on flour) suggest a thoroughly up-to-date cook. Her instructions for White Biskit Bread (on p. 118) describe how to make meringues getting on for a century before the recipe in François Massialot's celebrated *Nouvelle instruction pour les confitures* (1692), generally cited as the first appearance of meringues in print.

Lady Fettiplace's cooking is essentially straightforward, fastidious and practical, mediaeval still in its fondness for currants and rosewater, but also unmistakeably modern. Indeed, considering the earliest dates usually suggested for the sort of food we should find familiar today, its modernity is one of the most surprising things about this manuscript. It barely mentions saffron, relies little on almond milk or butter, gives none of the thick, bready pottages or spiced meat hashes and hardly any of the syrupy, sweet-and-sour meat dishes popular in the middle ages. Dates of origin are for the most part impossible to establish; but Lady Fettiplace's delicate puddings, her pretty, fresh-tasting sauces for meat, her few but unfailingly elegant vegetable dishes were clearly not meant to be eaten jumbled up in the mediaeval manner, sweet and savoury side by side or together under one cover in the same dish. Though she uses sugar in small quantities to bring out the flavour of meat dishes (as Mediterranean cooks still sweeten a beef stew or a *sauce bolognaise*), and she serves fruit with meat (think of pork with apple sauce, *canard à l'orange*, the American fondness for pineapple with ham), the modern distinction between savoury and sweet is already securely established.

This is food for people who ate well and knowledgeably, and whose taste was by no means unrefined. But it is also everyday food, what Gervase Markham (author of *The English House-wife*, 1615, the most popular cookery book of the period) called a 'Humble Feast, or an ordinary proportion, which any good man may keep in his Family for the entertainment of true and worthy friends', not the frogs and birds and spectacular setpieces of 'the extraordinary great Feasts of Princes'.[48] Lady Fettiplace's recipes, whether she set them down herself or collected them from friends and relations, come from people who knew what they were talking about. There is careful attention to detail and considerable expertise in her directions for thickening a custard, drying out a spinach purée, setting soft fruit to warm gently till the juices run, sharpening a meat sauce with verjuice or slices of lemon: all operations that have remained pretty much unchanged for nearly four centuries. Many of what Frenchmen still think of as our more outlandish native dishes—roast beef and Yorkshire pudding, redcurrant jelly with mutton, bread sauce spiked with cloves and nutmeg for a Christmas turkey—go directly back to her day. So do the nursery puddings which retained pride of place in the English repertoire at least down to the first half of this century: billowing golden bread puddings like the Lord of Devonshire's speciality—stuffed with currants, laced with sherry and puffed up like a soufflé (see p. 213)—custard tarts and cheese cakes, fools, trifles, creams and the shamefully maligned boiled bag pudding.

Lady Fettiplace's food tastes as good as it looks, even allowing for the inordinate pains taken in those days over dressing each dish, both individually and as part of an overall table design that would, as Markham says, 'not only appear delicate to the eye but invite the appetite with much variety thereof'.[49] Markham reckons three courses of thirty-two dishes each to even a humble feast; and there are elaborate directions for clearing away and replacing the dishes, four by four, so as to preserve the symmetry of a table laid as intricately as any Jacobean knot garden. Half of Markham's dishes were extras—salads and vegetables, kickshaws or *quelquechoses*, custards, biscuits and fancy tarts. Admittedly, the sixteen 'full dishes' sound formidable enough ('First, a shield of Brawn with mustard, Secondly, a boyl'd Capon ... Ninthly, a Swan rosted, Tenthly, a Turkey rosted, the eleventh, a Haunch of Venison ... the thirteenth, a Kid with a pudding in his belly ...'[50]). But no one was expected to sample all these. Each guest made his choice from the selection of dishes close at hand, or he might call for a particular favourite to be passed from further away: the nearest equivalent today is probably a restaurant serving different meals to groups of guests, any one of whom may order what he or she fancies from a menu of thirty-two dishes or upwards.

The ancient tradition still lingers on in the north-country or working man's high tea. It flourished in considerable splendour for grand occasions well into this century: 'At one end of the table, which glittered with silver, glass and Longshaw china, was a fowl which had been boiled for four hours; at the other, a hot pork pie, islanded in liquor, which might have satisfied a regiment,' wrote Arnold Bennett, lingering over Anna's betrothal tea in Chapter Twelve of *Anna of the Five Towns* (1902): 'Between these two dishes were ... hot pikelets, hot crumpets, hot toast, sardines with tomatoes, raisin-bread, currant-bread, seed-cake, lettuce, home-made marmalade, and home-made hams.' Accounts like this one, in both fact and fiction, nearly always emphasise something very like Gervase Markham's pride in presentation—snowy cloths, polished implements, heaped plates—together with the same mouthwatering spread and variety of dishes. Recipes for a good many of Bennett's individual items—boiled fowl, hot meat pie, currant-bread, seed-cakes and marmalade—are included in Elinor Fettiplace's book. The same is true of the many real farmhouse teas described in, for instance, Mathena Blomefield's enchanting reminiscences of a Norfolk childhood in the 1880s: 'There was stiff, shiny pork cheese, a plate of pink and white ham, cut very thinly and decorated with parsley; a glass dish of pickled white herrings, also adorned with parsley; a damson cheese, flanked by a jug of thick cream; a dish of rich brown gingerbread, two plates of home-baked bread and butter, stewed pears and custard...'[51] This sort of meal would have been laid out within living memory for a large family (including workers and farm hands) round the long kitchen table to help themselves as they pleased.

It was a practical and flexible system for an age when numbers at table might be expected to fluctuate a good deal. Sir William Petre kept about thirty indoor servants ('no more than was required in a country house of medium size'[52]) at Ingatestone Hall in the mid sixteenth century. Lady Unton had five spits for roasting meat in her kitchen at Wadley, and 'ix houckes to hange the pottes' (for boiled joints and puddings) on a great iron bar in her chimney.[53] Sir Kenelm Digby, writing in the generation after Lady Fettiplace (by which time most people had switched to eating in private, rather than in the hall with the servants), gives Lord Lumley's excellent pea soup in quantities to make 'about a Gallon', and says, of 'My Lady of Portland's Minced Pies', that roughly four pounds of my lady's pie filling 'is enough for once in a large family'[54] (ample by my reckoning for sixteen to twenty persons as a main course, or a great many more if supplemented by other dishes). Lady Fettiplace's own gigantic spiced fruit cakes (see p. 137) must have been made to slice several times round the whole household, yielding perhaps five or six dozen pieces. But, roughly speaking, the pattern of an Elizabethan or Jacobean meal meant that individual dishes were made up in quantities that seem perfectly reasonable today. Lady Fettiplace's pies and puddings, creams and custards, pancakes and apple fritters, generally serve six people or so, and the amount of sauce required for a single leg of mutton has not changed down the centuries.

It is this practicality and moderation that make her book still what it was in her day, a working manuscript. She and the friends with whom she swapped recipes—Mistress Gresham Thynne of Longleat, Mistress Mary Poole and other, unidentified gentlewomen (the Misses Scarlett, Higgs, Walline, Panesfoot, Mrs L.P. and Lady Wentar)—not only knew what they were talking about, but were used to trying and testing things out for themselves. The many corrections in Lady Fettiplace's hand are not confined to the equivalent of proof-reading, and supplying names in the margin. She adds extra ingredients, alters times and quantities (a week's steeping has been change to 'all night', for instance, and 'two or three spoonfulls of water' to '4. E.F.'), suggests in her atrocious spelling how to give a lift to a dull sauce ('you most pot som whit win in to the gravi with the venygar'), or an alternative method of preserving plums ('ef you well have hole freut ly in the gely you most presarve et with out stones and when the gely es redy to be dryed put et in and so drey et').

The tone is matter-of-fact, as far removed from the cookery books of great Edwardian hostesses whose contact with the kitchen was limited to a daily conference with the cook as from the inquisitive, experimental, comparative and cosmopolitan gourmet's approach of an inspired amateur like Sir Kenelm Digby. Digby's *Closet Opened* vividly evokes the world of indigent Stuart courtiers exiled in continental hotels or holed up at home, amusing themselves by rustling up scrambled eggs on a portable stove or *cresme fouettée* or a nourishing broth for the Queen, running in and out of the kitchen to taste a soup or test a batch of apple jelly for set, improving on one another's recipes, comparing notes, criticising, refining, enthusiastically sampling Master Adrian May's potted venison, My Lord of Bristol's Scotch collops, My Lord D'Aubigny's broiled red herrings, the Queen's quince marmalade alongside my Lady of Bath's and Digby's own. Lady Fettiplace and her friends are homely by comparison, competent, authoritative, skilled in the day-to-day management—the 'huswiffrie' and husbandry—of their largely self-sufficient country households. Just as in medicine Lady Fettiplace put little faith in the far-fetched, semi-magical remedies favoured by her contemporaries, so in cooking she is neither extreme nor exorbitant. Many of her meat dishes suggest ways of producing something succulent from the cheapest possible cuts; freshness and delicacy are the point of her plain white creams; she avoids all the artificial colourings—saffron, purple turnesol, red and yellow sanders—so prevalent in the cooking of even a generation earlier. There is no crimping or crenellating in her book, no torturing food into the unnatural shapes and lurid colours popular then as now, no trompe l'oeil pastries, marzipan meat or fake fried eggs (seventeenth-century ancestors of the pink ice-cream foot, the blood-red or poison-green Space Alien ice lolly, the professional caterer's carved tomato basket brimming with sculptural dollops of inedible mayonnaise).

I have called the author 'Lady Fettiplace' throughout (except where a specific recipe is otherwise attributed) partly for convenience' sake, partly because this is so evidently a coherent personal collection, reflecting the empiricism, clarity and confidence of the time, if not of a particular personality. A collection copied out in 1604 goes back through the reign of Elizabeth to her father's day, in places probably well before that. A few of these recipes seem very old indeed. Sometimes the same one recurs at intervals in similar or even identical versions, having reached Lady Fettiplace presumably via different routes from the same original source. Some contributors are more detailed, chattier or more expert than others. From time to time it is possible to pick out an individual behind a particular batch of recipes: someone who sets store by oil of adder's tongue fern, for instance, someone else who calls a frying pan a skillet, a third who specialises in the healing properties of green nutshells and mulberry syrup. Occasionally some sort of rudimentary attempt at classification produces a clump of back remedies or puddings grouped together, four scented powders and perfumes, five ways of candying fruit and flowers. Anyone who has ever collected recipes from friends, jotted down higgledy piggledy on scraps of paper or the backs of old envelopes, will recognise the method or lack of it. The scribe took no interest whatsoever in ironing out discrepancies or repetitions, often copying out the same recipe in different forms separated by no more than a page or two, a few lines, or once (To Boyle Neats Feet) by nothing at all. A seasonal reminder ('Doe green apples at St Jamestide, greene peare plums in the middle of August, greene white plums in the middle of June') has been accidentally slipped between two sections of a single cure 'for a red face'.

But through this hopeless jumble runs a marked preference for clarity, simplicity and discretion (in flavouring as in all else). There are curious omissions: no mention of pork, bacon or ham (except for one sucking pig seethed gently in goat's milk to make a nourishing broth for a consumptive), no duck, geese, game (unless you count rabbits) or venison, no carrots, parsnips or turnips (although Besselsleigh was noted locally for the last), and only a single culinary mention (under stewed oysters) of onion. Beef is restricted to remedies (the traditional raw beefsteak to stop bleeding), although much use is made of both beef suet and marrow. These oddities may be accidental (seventeenth-century cookery books normally include meat—as Lady Fettiplace does—only if there is a special sauce to go with it), or the result of local Berkshire vagaries of harvest and marketing, or perhaps of personal taste. Certainly fruit preserving and confectionery—still a popular novelty, amounting at times to a craze since the first London refineries were set up half a century before to process raw sugar from Brazil and the Barbary coast—were Lady Fettiplace's speciality, judging by the high proportion of recipes, and the great number of annotations in her own hand.

She is a perceptive cook, taking care to specify in apparently unimportant detail the technique for, say, making an omelette ('let yor butter bee scaldinge hott in yor pan and powre in yor Batter, as yt doth begin to bake stirr yt w^{t}h a knife untill yt will frye w^{t}hout stickinge...'), or decorating a leg of mutton with sliced lemon ('you must not stue it w^{t}h the rest, for it will cause yor limonde to tast bitter'). She is unusually precise over quantities and careful to specify oven temperatures. Above all she is reliable: ten years spent following her directions have given me considerable respect for what May called the Golden Days of English House-Keeping.

Strict authenticity is another matter. Chemical fertilisers, pesticides, crop-spraying, gas storage, silicone injections and battery houses, pasteurising, homogenising, food additives, new uniform varieties of fruit and vegetables, all put it out of the question. Twentieth-century, industrially refined sugar and flour bear very little resemblance to even the finest white sugars and flours available in the seventeenth century; milk no longer comes from the cow; commercial dried yeast and liquid rennet are effective but dissimilar substitutes for Lady Fettiplace's ale barm and her scrap of calf's stomach. Even the fuels we use and the stoves we cook on may radically change the character of a particular dish. The great open fire of an Elizabethan or Jacobean kitchen provided a fierce, steady, crudely adjustable flame for roasting or boiling, and embers for long, slow baking and simmering ('keep it in a seethe near al day' is a hard instruction to follow using gas or electricity). For more delicate procedures needing a critical adjustment of heat—pancakes, fritters, sauces, sugar work—there were charcoal stoves, either built in or portable in the form of a metal contraption on legs with a lower pan holding coals and an upper, lidded pan for cooking.

This was the 'chafing dish of coals' specified in many of Lady Fettiplace's recipes, generally installed in a separate stillroom which also contained distilling equipment and specially fitted, lattice-work cupboards, sometimes with their own charcoal heaters, for drying and storing preserves and medicines. Then there was the brick bread oven, heated by kindling a fire inside it which was afterwards raked out and replaced by the bread: coarse household loaves took longest, fine white bread or manchet required a medium heat ('the oven must not be so hot as for Manchet' is a frequent instruction), 'smale bred' went in last of all, and meringues, fruit pastes and candies, anything that needed slow drying out, were laid on papers or a pierced, footed board on the floor of the oven after the bread had been removed altogether.

Meat roasted over a dripping-pan before an open fire had a crisp crust and clear dripping quite different from what we mean by roast meat, baked in a sealed oven, lying frying and fuming in its own juices. The moist retentive uniform heat of the brick oven is said to have produced bread with a crustier outside and finer crumb than a modern metal cooking stove. Though a contemporary kitchen may be incomparably cleaner, cooler and more convenient than its Jacobean equivalent, it would be naive to suppose that technological changes have been all gain. The subtlety of many of the processes Lady Fettiplace describes—seething, smoking, infusing—would be almost impossible to reproduce at home today. The ingenious gadgetry of cooks obliged to rely almost wholly on their own home resources is always enchanting: a section of hollow, dried, fennel stalk, stoppered at both ends, served as a test tube for infusing eye drops; feathers were used for applying the drops, dressing a burn, icing a marchpane, scumming the froth off boiling syrup. The most delicate sugar syrup imaginable was produced by poking powdered sugar with a hollow quill into a cleaned pig's bladder which was then blown up and suspended by a thread in a pan of warm water 'over a verie soft fire' all day (Elizabeth David describes the identical method used for cooking a chicken—'*Poularde en vessie*'—at the Hôtel du Midi, Lamastre in 1958 by Madame Barattero, who said indignantly when told such a thing would be impossible in England: 'What do you mean, why can you not get a pig's bladder in England? You have pigs, do you not?').[55]

Pre-industrial devices like these belong to a world we have lost. So, of course, does the unending drudgery of a Jacobean kitchen. Modern whisks, balloon or electric, are a huge advance on the bundles of rushes or birch twigs, the rod or bat or 'little wooden spatter' used in an age without even forks. Electric mixers, liquidisers and food processors do the mincing, chopping, straining, pounding and pulverising that would have taken hours when everything had to be ground—'brayed'—by hand with pestle and mortar. Electricity enables us to sample the fine textures and flavours, the refinement and simplicity of much of this cooking with comparatively little labour.

On the other hand, one of the pleasures of cooking from Lady Fettiplace's book is the glimpses it gives of an orderly, interlocking, rural economy organised to supply and service most of its own wants. In the Fettiplace household, apples came from the orchard, herbs and flowers from the garden, honey from the hives, 'the top of the mornings milk' still warm—'cow whot'—from the dairy. Bread was baked most days, and beer brewed probably every other week or so. Flea powder, rat poison, weedkiller, soap and toothpaste were all manufactured on the premises. Nothing was wasted. Steel shavings from paring a fowling piece or gun were saved for the Steel Diet (see p. 79); 'smith's water' made a gargle for a dry, scurfy throat ('Take Smithes water that hee cooles his iron in, & as much honie as will make it sweet...'); wool from a black sheep was specially prized for dressing and binding wounds.

I have organised this book as a calendar so as to preserve some sense of this network of supply and demand, and also of the seasonal tides flowing into and out of a Jacobean country house. The year begins with the great feasts of New Year, lasting through January and February, enters the narrows of Lent with its fasting and fish days, emerges to spring flowers—candied primroses, celandine water, balls of violets—and the first spring lamb at Easter, moves on via summer flowers, soft fruit and vegetables to the harvests of autumn ('I take it you gather your apples about Michaelmas...'), picked, preserved and stored for the bleak winter months. Now that the surviving furniture of the period, the jewels, paintings, fabrics, books, musical instruments, household implements, even the houses themselves, have nearly all been turned over to museums, it seems to me that following their domestic round by cooking and eating their food brings us as close as anything can to the ordinary daily life of our ancestors.

III

It was a munificent and welcoming age. Generosity is the prime attribute ascribed to Sir Henry Poole on the great canopied Renaissance tomb put up for himself and his wife in Sapperton church: 'Theise Both loved and lived Together Many Yeares, Much Given to Hospitality, He was Alwayes Faithful to his Prince, and lovinge to his Cuntry, True to his Freindes, and Bountifull to his Servants.' He kneels in full armour and ermine-lined mantle, she wears her richly embroidered gown looped up at the hips, with ropes of pearls (divided after her death between her four daughters) and a high ruff.

Sir Henry died in 1616, leaving £100 (the same princely sum as Sir John Thynne at Longleat) to build this 'comely and convenient tomb', another £100 to his Fettiplace grandson, and £500 to his daughter Elinor—herself a widow by this time, for Sir Richard had died the year before—together with his coach and its furniture, two geldings to pull it, 'one other hackney nag for her own saddle and a hackney gelding to carry a man'.[56] Perhaps Elinor found herself less well provided for than her three sisters, who got no more than their quarter share each in their mother's great pearl chain. The £500 was in lieu of the bequest from Elinor's grandfather, which had served as her marriage portion, presumably in exchange for a reasonable jointure: this would have been an additional charge on her husband's estate, to be reckoned along with all the other grants and leases Sir Richard had committed to the care of his young son and heir, John Fettiplace, praying 'God from ye bottome of my harte to blesse him and his'.

The widowed Lady Fettiplace seems to have packed up and left Appleton, passing control of the household to her daughter-in-law, retiring presumably to her own dower lands and taking her cookery book with her, together with her husband's inlaid cabinet ('I give and bequeath to Dame Elenor my wife my little inlayde cabnott, desiring her to accept it as from one that loved her'). She remained as always within her own family's orbit at Sapperton, making a brief second marriage to a citizen of Gloucester called Edward Rogers, probably one of the Rogers family of Dowdeswell who were part of the Pooles' local circuit of Gloucestershire squires. He died in 1623, leaving forty shillings to the poor of Sapperton, and distributing his cloth cloak, two suits of cloth clothes, his best and second-best swords, his scarf, his seal ring and his best horse ('except that horse or nagge which my Ladye useth to ryde on') among various Sapperton servants, relations and friends, including the landlord of the Crown at Gloucester.[57] He left everything else to his wife, who buried him in Sapperton church under a stone defining his status entirely in terms of her own: 'Here lyeth buried ye body of Edward Rogers, of ye Citie of Gloucester, Esq., late husband unto ye Lady Elinor Fettiplace, daughter to Sir Henry Poole of Sapperton, Knight...'

Elinor's son John had also died before he was thirty in 1619, leaving four small children, the eldest of whom, Edmund, sold Appleton and Besselsleigh fourteen years later, migrating himself to his mother's home at Fernham. What little was left of the Fettiplaces' Berkshire estates was frittered away during and after the civil war in a series of lawsuits between Edmund and his brothers John and Thomas, his son Edmund junior, and the five children of his sister Anne.[58] When Lady Fettiplace herself died, she left her book to another Anne, daughter of her brother, Sir Henry Poole the younger of Sapperton: 'Thes bock I geve to my deare nees and goddutar Mrs Anne Hornar desyring her to kepe it for my sake: 1647.' Anne Poole, who had married George Horner of Mells and Cloford in Somerset, seems to have been, like her aunt, an excellent housekeeper.

At the back of Lady Fettiplace's book someone has made an index in a new and inferior ink, and six or eight later hands—probably one of them Anne Horner's—have added various items, including a clutch of rather frivolous, post-Restoration fruit liqueurs, and the chocolate and barley creams on pp. 232 and 231. A portrait bust of Anne Horner in the church at Cloford (where she was buried in 1678) shows a plump, comfortable matron with pink cheeks, gold chain and matching ear-rings, plain black stuff gown and sleeves rolled up to the elbow. Her husband beside her, holding a book, has a gilt top to his cane and a gilt hilt to his sword. They look a sober, well-liking, thoroughly well-to-do couple beneath their tasselled stone canopy swagged with fruit and rococco cherubs. He died in 1676, leaving his land to his son George together with the carts, wagons and farm implements to work it, his two coaches to his wife ('for the use of herself and Daughters all') and everything else to be divided between wife and children, excepting 'my Books which I intend to give by my own hand or some other writing . . .'.[59]

Whether or not Lady Fettiplace's book was part of this library, or was counted in with his wife's household goods (which were hers to dispose of), it found its way back at some point to the Horners' Fettiplace cousins. Elinor's great-grandson, Edmund Fettiplace the younger, acquired the manor house at Kingston Bagpuize, halfway between Appleton and Fernham, and the male line came to an end when he died in 1711, the year after his only child Elizabeth. Sir Edmund Fettiplace's line at Swinbrook also petered out after the death of his grandson, John Fettiplace, one of Prince Rupert's commanders in the civil war, created a baronet by Charles II at the Restoration. He was followed by four childless sons, each of whom in turn inherited the baronetcy and died, leaving by the middle of the eighteenth century only their great house (pillaged and dismantled after becoming a highwayman's headquarters in the early 1800s), a pair of tourney helmets topped by the Fettiplace griffin, and the extraordinary Fettiplace tombs in Swinbrook church: twin tiers of stone bunks, six in all, each containing a recumbent male Fettiplace propped on his elbow, the first three (put up for Sir Edmund, his father and grandfather) stiffly posed in suits of wasp-waisted armour, the next three (erected by a second Sir Edmund in 1686) more relaxed, lolling on cushions, with cavalier sashes, scarves and ringlets.

The Pooles fared no better. Elinor's brother, the younger Sir Henry, died the year after Charles I spent the night of July 14, 1644, at Sapperton (he had stayed with the Swinbrook Fettiplaces at Childrey the previous April), on his triumphant march over the Cotswolds to Bath, where he received the terrible news of Marston Moor. The King is said to have conferred a baronetcy on the young son of the house, William Poole, an ardent royalist who was fined £1,494 for delinquency after the civil war and died, six years after his father, worn out by unsuccessful attempts to raise this huge sum, by threats of sequestration, arrest, further fines, and by the depradations of unscrupulous lawyers.[60] Sapperton was sold by his son in 1660 to Baron Atkyns, Speaker of the House of Lords. Appleton and Besselsleigh had been sold thirty years earlier to the

Speaker of Cromwell's House of Commons, Sir William Lenthall. It would be hard to imagine a more neatly symbolical, parliamentarian line ruled under the fortunes of two royalist families, one on the way up, the other already in decline, both done for by the time of the Restoration.

Atkyns' son Robert, the historian of Gloucestershire, died in 1711, when his executors pillaged the Poole tombs for the Atkyns memorial in Sapperton church,[61] and sold the great house to Lord Bathurst, who demolished it in the interests of clearing the view. The stones were carted away to put up a folly as part of Bathurst's grandiose plans for landscaping Cirencester Park, and the new owner wrote cheerfully to Alexander Pope (who had his own bower—Pope's Seat—specially constructed in the park), congratulating himself on having access to such a first-rate source of ready-dressed building materials.[62]

Lady Fettiplace's book was handed down until her branch of the Fettiplace family became extinct altogether in both male and female lines at the end of the eighteenth century. Elizabeth Fettiplace, Elinor's great-great-grand-daughter, had married John Blandy of Inglewood, Berkshire, bearing him a son, Fettiplace Blandy, who died a bachelor, and a daughter, Elizabeth, who married William Shaw and whose own daughter, Fettiplace Shaw, wife of the Rev Francis Merewether, died childless in the 1790s. The book passed to her husband's nephew, another Rev Francis Merewether, whose daughter, Emily, married as his second wife in 1864 Dr George Currey, master of the Charterhouse and my husband's great-great-grandfather, on whose family's shelves it remained, as a curiosity, gathering dust, until the invention of the electric food processor turned it back once more into a working cookery book.

Apart from a few Jacobean bench ends, some oak panelling, two chairs and a table in Sapperton church, it is probably all that remains of the mansion built to rival Longleat. A gigantic mound beside the church, levelled off on top in a rectangle, bare terraced sides falling steeply to the river below, marks the site where the Pooles' house once stood with its courtyards, lawns, orchards, gravelled walks and symmetrical, tree-lined approaches stretching in all directions as far as the eye could see. Pope had protested about Bathurst's act of vandalism at the time in the second epistle of his *Imitations of Horace*, Book Two; and it is the sort of irony Pope would have enjoyed that, for all his splendour and state, his great ambitions and noble kinsmen, Sir Henry Poole should be remembered, if at all, nearly four hundred years later by his daughter's cookery book:

All vast possessions (just the same the case
Whether you call them villa, park or chase)
Alas, my Bathurst! what will they avail?
Join Cotswold hills to Sapperton's fair dale,
Let rising granaries and temples here,
There mingled farms and pyramids appear,
Link towns to towns with avenues of oak,
Enclose whole downs with walls, 'tis all a joke!
Inexorable death shall level all,
And trees and stones and farms and farmer fall...

I

JANUARY

January was always the season for party-going and -giving, at its height from Christmas Day to Twelfth Night but often stretching well beyond that. In the reign of Elizabeth I, Sir William Holles reckoned to begin his Christmas at Allhallowstide and keep it up until Candlemas, November 1 to February 2, three solid months of feasting (when, as his grandson bitterly said, the family fortunes might as well have been poured down the privy). December 25 was a minor feast compared with Twelfth Night, January 6, the chief day of the whole year for entertaining and parties. Country houses up and down the kingdom kept open house with a welcome for allcomers so that, what with friends and relations, guests, servants, villagers and 'strangers', a family like the Fettiplaces at Appleton Manor in Berkshire might expect to feed anything from fifty people upwards twice daily for twelve days on end at Twelfthtide.

Sir William Petre of Ingatestone Hall in Essex sat down to dinner on January 6, 1552—half a century before Lady Fettiplace's book was written—with over a hundred people, who consumed between them sixteen raised pies, fifteen joints of beef, four of veal, three of pork (including a whole sucking pig), three geese, a brace each of partridge, teal, capons and coneys, a woodcock and one dozen larks, with a whole sheep and much else for supper that night. Entertaining on this scale was quite normal, and remained so until well into the seventeenth century. It is clear from Lady Fettiplace's book that she spent a good part of each summer and autumn laying in sufficient store of 'banqueting stuff' to stock an ample and hospitable table right through the winter.

She grew winter cabbages, dried or distilled herbs in season, pickled samphire, cucumbers and artichokes for winter salads with bright yellow broom buds and crimson gilliflowers for decoration.

She made and stored fancy biscuits, macaroons, meringues, gilded marchpanes and striped sugar plate. But above all she preserved fruit, beginning with oranges and lemons shipped from Spain to make marmalade at this time of year, going on to soft fruit and green plums from her own garden in early summer, ending with apples, pears, quinces, rosehips and barberries gathered before the first frosts in November. All these reappeared on the winter banqueting tables as part of a last course at dinner which ended with cheese, wine and fruit dried, candied or turned into conserves, jellies, sweetmeats and tarts of many colours—white, red, green, amber, coral pink and all shades between to deepest purple-black.

The first two courses of any meal consisted of meat, pudding, salad stuff and vegetables, cooked and dressed in ways we should often find perfectly recognisable today. Englishmen, then as now, liked roast meat served with nothing but its own pan juices enriched with a little claret wine. The joints, trussed and skewered on spits before a great open fire, had to be ceaselessly turned and the fire carefully adjusted: Gervase Markham gives detailed instructions, in *The English House-Wife* (1615), as to which meats need a gentle heat to be 'pale and white rosted', which a brisk flame, while others (swans, peacocks and bustards as well as more mundane meats like mutton) call for slow, steady, leisurely cooking. Dry meat like venison 'will lie long at the fire and soak well in the rosting'. All must be basted beforehand with sweet oil, butter or cream (Sir Kenelm Digby says that Charles II's Queen, Henrietta Maria, 'useth to baste ... meat with yolks of fresh eggs beaten thin'), and dredged with fine white breadcrumbs to protect them from burning. Both processes were then repeated—'basting upon dredging, and dredging upon basting'—while the meat was tended and turned: hot, greasy, tiring work rewarded with a crisp casing impossible to reproduce in a closed modern oven.

Spit-Roasted Meats

Lady Fettiplace gives very few meat dishes, no doubt because the lost art of spit-roasting was in those days too dull to write about or, in Markham's phrase, 'so ordinary that it needeth not any relation'. The few included in her manuscript are mostly for the local Cotswold mutton or for capons and chickens, the sort of meat becoming increasingly fashionable in France as the old, extravagant fancy for sampling anything that moved, from porpoise to seagulls, fell out of favour. Each dish comes with its own stuffing or sauce: piquant sauces with unexpected and often surprisingly successful combinations of flavour, thickened with egg yolks or puréed vegetables or simply a nut of butter stirred in at the end.

Flour did not come in, let alone take over as the all-purpose English thickener, for another hundred years (though it was well known before that to Digby, who picked up a good many continental cookery tips in exile with the Stuart court, including the Queen Mother's Hotchpot, which is scrag end of mutton stew thickened at the last minute with a roux of butter and flour).

But Lady Fettiplace's meat dishes already show the discriminating simplicity of the new style of cooking that gradually emerged in the seventeenth century. Flavours are separate, not mixed so profusely as to blot one another out, spices are used singly or sparingly, two or three at a time, as in this recipe for mutton with orange sauce. These would have been the bitter Seville oranges shipped in round about the turn of the year then as now, but by no means reserved in those days exclusively for making marmalade. You could at a pinch substitute an ordinary sweet orange (the 'China' orange, not known in England till much later in the century) sharpened with lemon juice. But Seville oranges remain one of our very few still truly seasonal pleasures, so I think this remarkable dish is best kept—like the French *sauce bigarade* to which it is clearly related—for a January dinner party.

TO DRESS A SHOWLDER OF MUTTON

Roast Mutton with Orange Sauce

*Take a showlder of mutton and beinge halfe Roasted, Cut it in great slices and save the gravie then take Clarret wine and sinamond & suger w^t^h a little Cloves and mace beatne and the pill of an oringe Cut thin and minced very smale. put the mutton the gravie and these thinges together and boyle yt betweene two dishes, wringe the Juice of an oringe into yt as yt boyleth, when yt is boyled enough lay the bone of the mutton beinge first Broyled in the dish w^t^h it then Cut slices of limonds and lay on the mutton and so serve yt in**

Half-cooked joints were often sliced so as to extract the meat juices and make serving easier in an age without forks: the meat would have finished cooking in its sauce in a lidded pan ('betweene two dishes') on a charcoal burner. But, failing an open fire with a spit and cob irons, it is perfectly possible to make the sauce in a roasting pan as you would ordinary gravy. In either case, take a five pound shoulder of lamb or mutton, raise it in its pan on a wire cake rack or toasting grid, roast it in a medium oven (Mark 4, 180°C, 350°F) for an hour and three quarters, or until it is still slightly underdone as the French like it. Then either set the joint aside in a warm place while you make the sauce, or carve it and keep the slices hot in a deep dish. Skim the fat off the roasting pan and pour in a glass of red wine, letting it bubble until it is reduced by half. Then lower the heat, add the meat juices (together with a little concentrated meat or vegetable stock, if you prefer to carve the joint at table), a generous pinch of powdered cinnamon, a level teaspoonful of sugar, two ground cloves, two blades of mace, the juice of Seville orange and its peel (previously cut into fine strips and blanched for a few minutes in boiling water). Decorate the meat with lemon quarters, grill the bone or not as you like, and serve the sauce separately—'Sauces are set amongst Roste-mete in sausers', as Comenius explained in his pioneering picture book for children, *Orbis Pictus* (1659).

Green beans or buttered carrots and parsnips go well with this, and so does the purée of spinach on the next page. An alternative recipe for mutton with orange sauce suggests substituting nutmeg for cinnamon, cloves and mace, and adding a dash of wine vinegar. Here is another way of dressing mutton, also doing the rounds at the time: it turns up, for instance, as Digby's 'To make a Shoulder of Mutton like Venison', identical except that he recommends marinading the meat in its own blood for twenty-four hours before cooking it (which would no doubt be an improvement).

TO ROST A SHOULDER OF MOTTON IN BLOOD

Roast Stuffed Shoulder of Mutton

When you kill a sheepe, take some of the blood and mince in sweete hearbes, and a litle suit, and cromes of bread; mingle it altogether and stuffe the motton in every place with it, then spitt the mutton and when you lay it to the fire, rubb it all over with the blood and hearbes, so rost it and bast it with butter, sett a dish under it to save the gravie, when it is rosted put some wine vinigere to the gravie and a litle butter and make it hott and powre it on the mutton and so serve it in

Lady Fettiplace has added sound advice at the foot of this recipe, in her own crabby black hand and villainous spelling: 'you most pot som whit win into the gravi with the venygar'.

Even without the blood, which may prove virtually impossible to get unless you are either a butcher or a sheep farmer (Lady Fettiplace seems to have been both), this is an admirable recipe. Make the stuffing with 4 oz. white breadcrumbs (Digby specifies 'about the quantitie of a Penny loaf' which is generally thought to have weighed roughly this much), 2 oz. beef suet and a generous handful of chopped sweet herbs (marjoram, thyme, parsley, mint, rosemary—use either of the last two sparingly as they tend to overwhelm any combination), moistened with blood if you can get it, or strong meat stock or a beaten egg. Bone the shoulder with a little sharp knife, stuff the cavity, working your forcemeat well down inside; and pin it with skewers, or sew it up with a thick needle and double thread or thin twine (alternatively, wrap it in foil to cook, removing the wrapping and turning the heat up at the end to brown the meat). Roast the meat on a wire rack in the roasting pan for 30 minutes in a hot oven (Mark 7, 220°C, 400°F), then reduce the heat (to Mark 4, 180°C, 350°F) and cook for another hour or so. Be sure to pour off the fat before you add a tablespoonful of white wine vinegar and a glass of white wine to the pan juices; let them bubble, then stir in a small nut of butter.

If you don't want to serve this with potatoes, which were for all practical purposes unheard of in England in 1604, try it with sippets of bread (which are described on p. 92), and this delectable old English dish of spinach:

TO BOYLE SPINAGE

Buttered Spinach

You must boyle yt well wth as little water as you can for the less water the sweeter yor spinage wilbee when yt is very tender part the water from yt as much, as you may, then shred yt very fine and put on verguice, sweete buter, and suger then set yt on the fire and let yt stew, and when yt is stewed neare enough, take the yelkes of two egges and as much Creame as the quantitie of yor egges and somewhat more, beate the Creame and egges together and put yt into the spinage and let them stue together, and when you serve yt strow suger on yt

This careful recipe scarcely needs a gloss. I take 1 tablespoonful of butter, 2 egg yolks and 3 or 4 tablespoonfuls of cream to 2 lb. spinach. A little lemon juice works well if you haven't any verjuice (which was a cider vinegar made from crab apples or unripe grapes); season with salt and a scant teaspoonful of sugar. Add the cream and egg mixture little by little to the spinach, stirring with a wooden spoon over a very gentle heat just long enough to heat the purée. The final strewing of sugar makes a pleasant addition in both taste and texture.

The result, creamy but not over-rich, combines particularly well with the juice of Seville oranges, whether in a wine sauce for mutton or in the buttered sweet potatoes given on p. 193, which make another of my favourite dishes. Here orange juice cuts the cloying blandness of sweet potatoes as successfully as sugar counteracts any bitterness in the spinach, while enhancing its natural sweetness. Of course if you stepped up the proportion of sugar and spice in dishes like these two, you would get a sweet pudding: sweet potato puddings with precisely the same ingredients as Lady Fettiplace's can still be found in American cook books, just as sweet spinach tarts were popular in seventeenth-century England (Robert May gives directions for icing his spinach tarts: John Evelyn's included dried fruit and almond macaroons). But I prefer my version of Lady Fettiplace's Tart of Spinage, served on its own as a vegetable course, either to start a main meal or for supper with cheese and fruit to follow. This was the first of her recipes ever published, so far as I know, by me or anyone else: it appeared in the London *Evening Standard* on August 20, 1976, and turned up shortly afterwards on the enterprising menu of the restaurant decorated by Rex Whistler at the Tate Gallery.

A TART OF SPINAGE

Spinach Tart

Take the spinage & boile it in water till it bee soft, then straine it, & put to it the yelks of vi eggs, & some rosewater and corrance, & sugar, & some sinamon, & ginger & some butter. boile it on the fier, a good while, before you put it in the paste.

The first thing to be said about this recipe is on no account boil your mixture, or the eggs will curdle ('boile' in Lady Fettiplace's usage generally means warm or heat gently: confusingly 'walme' or warm—as in 'give it one or two walmes'—means bring to the boil). You might stir it slowly over the lowest possible heat until it thickens but cooking in the oven is safer, and handsomer unless you mean to eat the tart cold. Quantities for four to six people are 2 lb. spinach; 6 egg yolks or 4 whole eggs (if you use whites as well, it makes the tart lighter), 2 to 3 tablespoons of rosewater, a good handful of currants, 1 scant teaspoon of sugar, 1 good pinch each of powdered cinnamon, ginger and salt, and 4 oz. butter.

Cook the spinach gently in as much water as clings to the leaves after washing, and drain it very thoroughly by pressing and squeezing out the juice in a colander, then returning the spinach to the pan to dry out over a low heat. Put in the butter and stir till it is all absorbed. Beat up the eggs in a basin, and add them to the spinach along with the rosewater, fruit, spices and seasonings. Taste, and tip the mixture into a tart tin lined with puff or short pastry. Bake for 10 minutes in a hot oven (Mark 6, 200°C, 400°F), then turn the heat down (Mark 5, 190°C, 375°F) for 20 to 30 minutes till the middle is well risen and browned.

Rosewater

Rosewater is a self-effacing ingredient in this as in a very great many of Lady Fettiplace's recipes: you can get it sometimes from delicatessens or health food stores, usually from a good dispensing chemist (but make sure it is not mixed with glycerine, and beware the prettily packed, exorbitantly priced varieties sold in tinted bottles as toiletries by cosmetic companies). There is also a triple-strength version which gives an elusive, oriental flavour—almost more of a scent than a flavour—to sweet dishes like the Tart Stuf of Pippins Green on p. 196, or the exquisite fresh cream on p. 100. But this concentrated essence would overwhelm many of the immense variety of dishes from spinach tart to rabbit pie in which rosewater supplies the basic liquid (where we would use tap water) for mixing and moistening. I haven't noticed this so much in other Jacobean or Stuart cookery books. Perhaps conditions were muckier in the country. Whatever the reason, it is noticeable that where water is specified in Lady Fettiplace's book it is nearly always 'fair' or 'running' or 'spring' water, more rarely—perhaps only when the recipe came from a town source—'conduit water'. Ordinary water, fetched from a well or a stream in wooden buckets, earthen pots, leather bags, must often have been dubious, muddy, polluted, twice used. At that time, nobody—not even small children—would have dreamed of drinking it. No wonder a fastidious cook preferred rosewater, bought or distilled from her own garden at home each summer, and put up in nice, clean, stoppered glasses.

Certainly it does no harm in a tart of spinach. If you start with this, follow it with stuffed shoulder of mutton, the buttered sweet potatoes given on p. 193, and a green salad. Alternatively, you could serve either ordinary potatoes or—the great native speciality for at least another two hundred years—a boiled bag pudding.

When good King Arthur ruled this land
He was a goodly king.
He stole three pecks of barley meal
To make a bag pudding.

The sweet or savoury British bag pudding goes back, if not to Arthurian times, at least to the middle ages. As an accompaniment to meat, it would eventually be wiped out by the exotic alien potato, though not without a stout rearguard action fought well into this century when boiled or baked batter puddings were still served in outlying country parts with almost any roast meat (or often before it, to take the edge off people's appetites). Nowadays the sole survivor of a long line is Yorkshire pudding, even that in a sadly enfeebled state since it used to come with mutton, pork, rabbit or hare, not just with roast beef. For the poor, batter puddings with green stuff, and meat if there was any, traditionally provided cheap and sustaining padding. But the country staple is a far cry from Lady Fettiplace's elegant version which turns out something like a pale yellow soufflé flecked with green, tastes as smooth as it looks, and gives no more trouble than peeling potatoes.

TO MAKE A BAGGE PUDINGE

Bag Pudding

Take thicke Creame and make yt somewhat hotter then bloud warme, then take halfe a dossen egges and beate them well and mingle them w[t]*h yo*[r] *Creame then ad to yt a little parsely and winter savory cut very smale and some nutmegges suger and a little salte then put to yt as much Crumes of bread and fine flower as will make yt thicker then Batter for pan-Cakes, then wett yo*[r] *bagge in cold water and put yt in and when yo*[r] *water boyles put him into yt, yt must not bee boyled w*[t]*h meate but alone in fayre water*

The last instruction was necessary because, in old English kitchens, a good many items in bags, cloths or nets were suspended in the great iron cauldron that heated water over an open fire. I use half cream and half milk (or all milk to go with a rich meal), and vary the herbs: parsley and winter savory or mint go well with lamb, chives and a sage leaf or two with pork, thyme and marjoram with almost any meat. To 1 pint of cream or milk take 3 eggs, 2 rounded tablespoons of flour and 4 oz. fine white breadcrumbs. Beat these very well with the eggs before adding the warmed cream, then put in salt, pepper, a large handful of chopped fresh herbs and a generous grating of nutmeg. Leave out the sugar unless you like a sweet taste.

Bold cooks may boil the batter in a floured, closely woven linen bag or cloth, wetted, wrung out, floured and laid in a large sieve or colander for filling (thereafter follow Hannah Glasse's careful directions from *The Art of Cookery*, 1755: 'If a Bread-pudding, tie it loose; if a Batter-pudding, tie it close; and be sure the Water boils when you put the Pudding in, and you should move the Puddings in the Pot now and then, for fear they stick'). But wooden bowls were already a possible alternative in the seventeenth century, and a greased china pudding basin is easier still. Don't fill it by any means full as the pudding will rise. Cover the basin with two layers of buttered paper or foil, securely tied; lower it into a saucepan containing enough boiling water to come half way up the sides; simmer it gently for about an hour and a quarter; and serve it at once, or the pudding will flop. This makes a delicate, light, sweet pudding if you leave out the savoury herbs and take a sprig of rosemary instead, or half a bay leaf and a twist of orange peel.

King Arthur's speciality was, of course, sweet, solid and exceedingly rich ('A bag pudding the King did make,/And stuffed it well with plums,/And in it put great lumps of fat/As big as my two thumbs'), designed for huge feeders like Lancelot Gobbo in *The Merchant of Venice*. Here is a gigantic Arthurian pudding which sounds (from its inclusion of saffron, let alone its ancient cooking technique) one of the oldest recipes in the whole book. It may well go back pretty well unchanged to the middle ages, and it certainly reaches forward to the plum puddings we still eat exclusively at this time of year. We tend to think of Christmas pudding as a Victorian speciality, if not a nineteenth-century invention, but Lady Fettiplace made hers from virtually the same ingredients—eggs, breadcrumbs, suet, dried fruit and spices—in the same hospitable quantities as Mrs Beeton.

FOR A PUDDING

Plum Pudding

Take twelve eggs & breake them, then take crumbs of bred, & mace & currance & dates cut small, & some oxe suet small minced & some saffron, put all these in a sheepes Mawe, & so boile it.

The sheep's maw is its stomach bag or paunch. Florence White, in *Good Things in England*, gives instructions for boiling haggis in a mutton paunch which must first be washed, turned inside out and loosely stuffed so as to allow the filling to swell (there is a grim warning postscript to this eighteenth-century recipe, contributed by a Mrs MacIver of Edinburgh, daughter of a Highland laird imprisoned in the cause of Bonnie Prince Charlie: 'Be sure to put out all the wind before you sew up the bag'). I haven't tried Lady Fettiplace's recipe, and I don't know how big a sheep's maw might be, but standard Victorian and Edwardian cookery books suggest that, for twelve eggs, you need something like 2 lb. breadcrumbs, the same of suet, 5 to 6 lb. dried fruit (raisins and candied peel in place of Lady Fettiplace's dates), and 8 to 10 hours' boiling time. In old recipes, right down to Mrs Beeton's day, the dried fruit supplied sufficient sweetening: adding sugar to plum pudding is a comparatively modern innovation to suit the ubiquitous twentieth-century sweet tooth. According to Dorothy Hartley, who includes a recipe in *Food in England* said to have been used by the Royal Family since the time of George I, half the amount above will feed twenty to twenty-eight people. Anyone mixing a pudding in these industrial quantities might be well advised to take a tip from a later age, and moisten it with half a pint of brandy and a good deal of beer.

Hard sauce—equal quantities of butter and sugar beaten to a cream with sack (or sherry: we would use brandy or rum)—was the correct accompaniment to plum pudding, then as now. Here is an altogether more manageable alternative for the smaller household:

TO MAKE A PUDINGE

Baked Batter Pudding

Take Crumes of bread and wheatne flower of each a like quantity the yelkes of 4 egges and the whights of 2. some Nutmegge, Curans, and Reasons of the Sun the stones pulled out, mingle all theise together w[th] *good Creame, make yt somewhat thicker then bater, then put yt in a fat Calle, and so set yt in a dish and bake yt, when yt is baked slipp yt out of the dish and sarve yt on a pye plate*

I make a light, spongy version of this pudding using roughly ½ pint of thin cream (or creamy milk) with 3 oz. each of flour and fine breadcrumbs. Put the last two ingredients in a bowl, make a well in the middle, drop in the beaten eggs and gradually work into a batter with a wooden spoon. Add the cream little by little, beating well, then stir in 3 to 4 tablespoons of dried fruit and a grating of nutmeg. Failing a fat cawl (this is the membrane encasing a lamb's or pig's intestines—'wherein the bowels are lapt' in Cotgrave's phrase), line your dish with very well buttered grease-proof paper if you mean to try turning it out, and bake it for about 45 minutes in a moderate oven (Mark 4, 180°C, 350°F), till it is well risen and browned.

Some modern adaptors assume that sugar has been forgotten in a recipe like this one and correct the mistake, but I think that, after a rich dinner, plainness is the point of this pudding. It comes out palest primrose yellow with a fine, flower-petal texture, what cooks of the period called 'tenderly firm'. I add salt but no sugar and serve it instead, as Sir Kenelm Digby advises, with a foamy little sauce made from brown sugar and melted butter, thickened by beating and flavoured with a tablespoon of rose or orange-flower water or sack (sherry), 'a little of any of which may also go into the composition of the pudding'. This sauce may be melted in the bottom of the hot dish that receives the pudding, poured over it or served with it. Whatever you do, the pudding should be piping hot and (as Mrs Beeton said of another unsweetened, boiled batter

Sir K. Digby's Sherry Sauce

pudding three and a half centuries later) 'it must be sent quickly to table'.

The extraordinary thing about bag puddings is their longevity: they were hardly new inventions in 1604, and they retained a central position in English home cooking right up to the time of my mother and grandmother. Their virtual disappearance from the current repertoire seems to have coincided with the revival of interest in food in England in the last twenty or thirty years: there are none, for instance, in Susan Campbell's otherwise excellent *English Cookery New and Old* (1981) and only three (one suet crust, one sponge and one Christmas pudding) in Jane Grigson's immensely influential *English Food* (1974). I suppose that what finally did for them was the nauseating slatternly meanness of school and institutional food in wartime, and in the years of austerity that followed. People old enough to remember that time still have vivid memories of greasy, grey slabs of suet crust, slimy cloths ('If you boil it too long, the Milk will turn to whay in the body or substance of the Pudding, and there will be a slimy gelly all about the outside': Digby), and congealed white fat on cold plates. But a properly made bag pudding—batter, suet or sponge—is remarkable for lightness, subtlety and richness in that order, a combination which has surprised and delighted Frenchmen at least from the time of the seventeenth-century traveller, Henri Misson (whose rhapsody on puddings may be found on p. 214). Here is one that combines to perfection all three qualities. Again, it looks back to the middle ages, when almonds were consumed in astonishing tonnage, and forward at least to the nineteenth century, being in essence a much simpler version of Eliza Acton's Publisher's Pudding (which, unlike The Poor Author's Pudding, 'can scarcely be made *too* rich').

TO MAKE ALMOND PUDDINGS

Steamed Almond Pudding

Take a pound of almonds blanch them in cold water, then beat them verie smale, then put to them some crums of white bread, and the yelks of six eggs and some rose water and some sugar, and some mace, cut smale, & some thick creamed warmed, & some biefe suet, cut smale, mingle all these together, & fill the gutts, & so boile them.

Presumably this pretty, pale, cream-coloured pudding was to be turned out in a long roll and sliced (sheep's guts or intestines supplied the traditional casing for sausages, plain, savoury or sweet), but it does very well in an ordinary pudding basin. Almonds were a staple ingredient in the mediaeval kitchen, used for thickening sauces and stews where we would use flour, and as a substitute for milk and dairy products on fast days. They give a nice fine firm crumb, something like Madeira cake in texture, but if you like a more almondy taste add a few bitter almonds or some drops of their essence. The combination of almonds with rosewater goes back to the Arabs, and is a particularly fine one.

To ½ lb. ground almonds (I find that half quantity is generally enough for four to six people), add 2 rounded tablespoonfuls of sugar, 3 of breadcrumbs, 3 level tablespoons of beef suet, and mix to a smooth paste with 3 egg yolks and 3 tablespoons of rosewater. Blend the paste in a mixer if you have one, and slowly pour in ½ pint or more of warm cream. It makes a fairly stiff mixture which will need hard beating (and probably rather more liquid) by hand. Flavour with a blade or two of fresh mace (hard to come by, and in any case generally stale in the shops, so I use nutmeg instead). Pour it into a greased basin, tie down securely and boil for an hour, or slightly longer if you follow Lady Fettiplace's full quantity. Serve a sherry or rosewater sauce (p. 48) with this pudding, which is even better next day warmed up in butter according to good King Arthur's recipe for leftovers:

The King and Queen did eat thereof
And gentlemen beside.
And what they could not eat that night
The Queen next morning fried.

Fruit Marmalades

A seventeenth-century dinner party wound to a close, after meat and pudding, with a banquet laid out to enchant the eye in patterns of glistening, gaily coloured sweetmeats, chief among them the thick fruit pastes, known as 'marmalades', that must have occupied Lady Fettiplace and her maids for a good part of the late summer and autumn. They make excellent presents—Karen Hess gives a recipe from *Martha Washington's Booke of Cookery*, a household book much like Lady Fettiplace's, for 'a Marmulet that was presented to Ye Queene for a New Years gift' (the Queen in question was the Catholic Mary, who died half a century before the book was published in 1608). Tudor and Jacobean marmalades still survive in country recipes for Apple Butter and Damson Cheese, Quince Paste and Apricot Leather (the longer you keep these pastes, the chewier they get). All these and a great many more may be found under the appropriate month for harvesting the fruit. Orange marmalades and preserves are in Chapter Two. Here I give a single princely sweetmeat compounded of beaten gold and powdered pearls, all the piratical plunder of the Old World and the New, the sort of thing that must have been served at the lovers' aphrodisiac banquet—'a sumpteous supper . . . furnished with sondrie sortes of delicate dishes'—in the story of Apolonius and Silla on which Shakespeare based *Twelfth Night*.

TO MAKE SPANISH MARMALAD

Spanish Marmalade

Take five sponfulls of rose water and seaven sponfulls of suger finely beaten, make yt boyle you must have redy by you two handfulls of almondes blanched and finely grownd, w^t^h 15 or 16 dates ye stones and whights taken out, and yor dates cut smale and beaten in a morter, then mixe yor dates and almondes well together, then put yt in your Sirrope stirringe yt well together, then take on sponfull of pouder of sinamond, halfe a sponfull of ŷ pouder of pearles, three sheetes of Golde, stirr all theise well, but you must take yt first from the fire or else yt will bee to stiffe that you can-not mingell yt, before yt bee through cold put yt upp into a marmalad boxe

Powdered seed pearls are called for twice elsewhere in this manuscript: one optional ounce in 'Mr John Knights pills & powders for the back' (the powder was compounded from ground amber, red coral, red oak bark, bole armeniak and terra sigillata, sweetened and spiced, to be taken at night beaten up with a raw egg); and quarter of an ounce in Mistress Scarlet's powder of steel shavings ('that cometh of the paring of a gun or [fowling] piece, which you may buy at the Apothecaries') for the Green Sickness. Gold leaf, commonly sold for gilding pills and pastries, cost sixteen pence for quarter of an ounce in an Ingatestone Hall shopping list for a wedding feast in June 1552 (ten dozen eggs were 3s. 10d, and even imported luxury goods like currants and almonds were only 4d. a pound). Clearly both ingredients were to be used sparingly, and strictly by the wealthy. I have tried Spanish marmalade without pearls or gold, and it comes out a sweet crumbly fudge, dark brown and datey if you take Lady Fettiplace's spoonful as the equivalent of a modern tablespoonful, paler and more delicately flavoured with almonds and rosewater if you take it (as I generally do in this book, following Karen Hess's expert advice) that a Jacobean spoon held roughly the equivalent of two level tablespoons, or one fluid ounce of liquid. Either way, a whole spoonful of cinnamon is fairly overpowering to the modern palate, so I use a good deal less.

Quantities are 10 tablespoons (just over $\frac{1}{4}$ pint) rosewater and 14 tablespoons sugar to 2 handfuls of almonds (which I take to be round about 6 oz.), 15 or 16 dates and 1 teaspoon cinnamon.

General principles, in so far as I have managed to deduce any from Lady Fettiplace's other marmalades, suggest that you boil your syrup for a few minutes without stirring, after the sugar has dissolved, till three or four drops in a glass of cold water will form a soft ball, like a glass bead, between your thumb and forefinger: this temperature will register 240°F, 115°C, on a sugar thermometer. Have ready your cinnamon, ground almonds and dates—fresh ones if possible—very finely chopped by hand or in a mixer, together with the gold leaf and pearls if you can get them. Stir them in quickly off the fire, beat hard and pour out at once onto a greased tin, or straight into a shallow, lidded, greaseproof-paper lined 'marmalade box' (a sandalwood cigar box does very well, or one of those oval matchwood cartons still used by the French for storing biscuits and candied fruit). Mark it in squares or lozenges, and store in a dry place.

Lady Fettiplace must have had scores of these marmalade boxes stacked on racks in her stillroom cupboards, ready for the winter banqueting season. She also had a well-stocked cellar, and probably a special brewing of beer organised at Christmas and Twelfth Night, sufficient to dispense hospitality to a fair portion of the countryside roundabout. The Petres at Ingatestone Hall, running a moderately-sized country household not unlike the Fettiplaces' at Appleton in Berkshire fifty years later, laid in forty kilderkins of beer—twenty barrels, or nearly six thousand pints—for the Twelfth Night festivities in 1552. The corresponding figure kindly supplied by Messrs Whitbread for a modern Berkshire pub (The Pineapple, just outside Newbury) was twenty-one barrels of beer sold over the twelve days of Christmas, 1984–5. The Petres also got through a fair amount of cider, wine and spirits just as the Fettiplaces must have done, judging by the copious quantities of Rhenish wine, claret, malmsey and sack called for in Elinor Fettiplace's recipes, and by her many receipts for home-made liqueurs. Here is a warming, well-fortified mulled wine, designed to be drunk a few spoonfuls or a tot at a time by people with no external system of central heating in a cold northern climate:

TO MAKE CLARETT WINE WATER

Claret Wine Water

Take a Quarte of stronge aquavitae, as much of good Clarett wine, a pound of the best suger, beate yor suger smale then powre the wine and the aquavitae to the suger and stir the wine and the suger together untill yor suger bee disolved, then ad to it whight pep, ginger, nuttmegge, large mace, Red jylloflowers the whights cut of and two dayes dryed as many as will give it a good couloure you must cut yor ginger and nutmeggs in greate peeces, and yor peper must bee devided in the midest shake it well together and put some brused cloves therein when you put in the other spices

Aquavitae was neat spirit, generally distilled in the stillroom at home by Tudor and Stuart housewives (the physician Thomas Cogan reckoned, in *The Haven of Health*, 1584, that it took a gallon of strong ale or wine to produce a quart of 'reasonable good Aqua vitae'). A rough country marc or brandy will do nicely, though for a Christmas party it might be wise either to dilute this sweet and exceedingly potent drink with liberal amounts of hot water, as for a nineteenth-century punch, or to reduce the proportion of spirits from equal parts to one part per four or five parts red wine. Heat the alcohol gently with the sugar until it is dissolved, before adding the spices. Crushed 'whight pep' or white peppercorns give a delicious aroma (so long as you avoid the ready-powdered variety which will almost inevitably be stale); the ginger which was to be sliced 'in greate peeces' means green ginger root, and it should be peeled first; the hard, dry nutmegs sold nowadays are more easily grated than cut up, though this can be done with a small, strong, sharp knife. Add a blade or two of mace if you can get it, adjusting all quantities to suit your taste. The dried petals of 'red jylloflowers', or clove carnations (see Chapter Seven, which covers the month of July), commonly used to 'give a good couloure' to alcoholic drinks, make a pretty but inessential addition.

Sir William Petre entertained his Twelfthtide guests with minstrels, mummers, tumblers or a clown most years. January 6 itself was celebrated with a specially baked, spicy fruit cake containing a bean and a pea for the King and Queen of the Revels. Shakespeare's *Twelfth Night* was written for this sort of party probably two or three years before Lady Fettiplace's book. Just over a century later, Pepys had his own Twelfth Night cake ('cost me near 20s of our Jane's making'), which cut up into slices for twenty people, including gate-crashers. The difference in scale between Pepys' small London household—already much more like a self-contained, modern, urban, nuclear family—and Lady Fettiplace's country hospitality may be gauged from the fact that her version of one of these great cakes (the recipe is on p. 137) would cut up, by my reckoning, into one hundred and sixty slices or upwards.

Twelfth Night Cakes

Pepys served sack posset (see p. 87 for Lady Fettiplace's version) with his cake, and, after a thoroughly satisfactory Twelfthtide during which he had spent more than he could afford, eaten and drunk more than he meant, entertained his friends lavishly and danced till two in the morning, concluded his entry for January 6, 1688, with a philosophy of parties that holds good to this day: 'and so away to bed, weary and mightily pleased; and have the happiness to reflect upon it as I do sometimes on other things, as going to a play or the like, to be the greatest real comforts that I am to expect in the world, and that it is that that we do really labour in the hopes of; and so I do really enjoy myself, and understand that if I do not do it now, I shall not hereafter, it may be, be able to pay for it or have health to take pleasure in it, and so fool myself with vain expectations of pleasure and go without it.'

2
FEBRUARY

Pies were an ancient standby, literally so in the days when salting was the only alternative means of preserving and tenderising tough meat. 'Red deer, Venison, wild Boar, Gammons of Bacon, Swans, Elkes, Porpus and such like' went into the great, cold, standing pies described by Lady Fettiplace's contemporary, Gervase Markham: highly seasoned, moistened lavishly with butter or lard, sealed inside a coarse, rye-flour paste and baked in the bread oven very slowly for six or eight hours at a time, sometimes overnight. We use the same method today for ham baked in a flour-and-water casing. Chicken, turkey and game pies were cooked, then as now, 'in a good white crust, somewhat thick', made from wheat flour and meant to be eaten, rather than serving simply as a disposable container. By the time of Sir Kenelm Digby, a generation later, the pastry crust was sometimes discarded, the finely chopped meat filling being cooked instead in a tightly stoppered pot, afterwards sealed with clarified butter to produce an early potted meat 'which . . . will keep a quarter of a year', where the standing pies, sent up to table time and again, must often have grown high before the diners were through. This was presumably why Digby so often uses the heels of old venison pasties, as we might add mushroom ketchup, to give a tang to beef stew; also the point of Mercutio's joke about the nurse in *Romeo and Juliet*—'a hare, sir, in a lenten pie that is something stale and hoar ere it be spent'.

But before the invention of canning, freezers or vacuum packs, pies were convenient and relatively durable portable food, easily packed and eaten without implements in lodgings, under canvas or on the road. Gentlemen in chambers commonly kept a pie on the sideboard for anyone who cared to drop in, and country people sent them as presents to friends or patrons in town. Right up to the coming of the railways, the roads must have been full of parcels of game and venison, with or without pastry crusts, trundling round the country or over the Channel (Lady Lisle shipped partridges, 'either baken or raw', whenever she could find a carrier, to her husband who was governor of Calais in the 1530s). Robert Cecil's papers, preserved at Hatfield House, include a note from Elinor Fettiplace's father, Sir Henry Poole, sent 'With a present of a brace of bucks' and dated 'My house of Sapertoune, 22 May, 1606'. Nearly half a century earlier her grandfather sent round a lamprey pie to Queen Elizabeth's favourite, the Earl of Leicester (who tipped 'Sir Giles Poole's man' a handsome twelve shillings and fourpence). Perhaps Elinor herself sent similar presents to her kinsman, Sir Edmund Fettiplace of Swinbrook, commanding a company of foot in Ireland in 1604. Here is her simple but succulent recipe for a cold, raised rabbit pie:

TO BAKE A RABBET

Raised Rabbit Pie

Take the flesh of two rabbets, and a piece of the leafe of a hog, and lay them both together, then with a woodden pestill beat them well together, then season it with some nutmeg & pepper and salt, & some sugar, & then beat it well with the meat, then bake it in a pie, & when it is cold serve it.

This is first cousin to Digby's Excellent Hare-Pye in which the hares are boned, hashed, beaten to a paste in a mortar, seasoned and thoroughly larded, then packed into an earthen pot with a double layer of brown paper tied over the top. When the 'pie' was baked, the meat juices were to be poured off (otherwise the whole thing would go mouldy, like Mercutio's hare) and claret wine poured in while the filling was still hot, a technique much the same as we still use today for a raised pork or game pie.

Lady Fettiplace's rabbits, if not precisely wild, would have come from the home coney warren; add extra seasonings if you have to make do with frozen, imported or hutch rabbit. The 'leafe of a hog' is the layer of pure fat round a pig's kidney, called flare (or flead in some parts) and generally rendered down as lard. It is what gives crispness and flavour to lardy cakes, ideal for lubricating a dry meat like rabbit, but a mixture of streaky bacon and pork fat (there should be one third fat to two thirds lean meat) will do instead.

Two rabbits, with half a pound each of streaky bacon and pork fat, make a handsome raised pie which will feed eight to ten at one sitting and keep well, if there is any left over, being designed to furnish a cold sideboard for large numbers of people as an adjunct to the roast meats. First prepare the filling: it is easier to strip the flesh of the rabbit joints if you simmer them beforehand for half an hour or so in just enough water to cover (keep this water to make stock with the rabbit bones). Blend or finely chop the meat and fat together, and season well with salt, pepper, a teaspoon of sugar and a generous grating of nutmeg. Add a few scraps of finely pared lemon peel and more spices—say, cinnamon and cloves—or some thyme and marjoram if you are using comparatively tasteless bought rabbit.

When I first made this pie, I baked it in a pie dish under an ordinary short-crust pastry lid which works quite well, and is indeed what Markham recommends for hot pies (increase the amount of bacon to about three quarters of a pound, leave out the pork fat, add a cupful of the reduced cooking liquor, and bake for two hours in a slow oven, protecting the top against burning with a sheet of paper). But a raised hot-water pie crust is handsomer, not hard to make, and undoubtedly what Lady Fettiplace had in mind. Take 1 lb. plain flour, add 1 level teaspoon salt, and work it into a smooth paste with an absolutely boiling mixture of 6 oz. lard melted in ⅓ pint hot water. Knead the dough by hand as soon as it stops being too hot to handle. Bold cooks raise the pie without outer walls round a wooden mould or floured, two pound jam jar (tie a double strip of brown paper round the pie wall for support when you remove the mould), but I do it inside a greased, warmed, round cake tin with a removable base. Coax the dough up the sides of your tin, keeping back a quarter for the pie lid; mound the filling up inside; roll out a lid and put it on top, wetting and crimping the edges together. Make a small hole in the lid, decorate with leaves, birds, beasts or a Tudor rose, brush the top with beaten egg and bake in a slow oven (Mark 3, 160°C, 325°F) for two hours or so, turning the heat up at the end to brown the pie if you like.

The problem with this pie is that it is extremely dry, unless you greatly increase the proportion of fat (which was probably what Lady Fettiplace intended—see her recipe for mutton pies on p. 220). The risk of pouring liquid even at the very last minute into an unmoulded, freestanding, raised pie is—then as now—that the crust may turn sad, or spring a leak, or at the very worst tumble down. One ancient solution was to add a syrupy wine sauce sharpened with vinegar (see below) for the hot filling to soak up as soon as it came from the oven: modern practice prefers a jellied stock made from the rabbit bones simmered, while you are making the pie, in white wine or cider and water with a carrot, onion, celery stalk, a few peppercorns, bay leaf, parsley and thyme. When the pie is nearly done, strain the stock, reduce it by fast boiling to about half a pint and pour it gently down a small funnel, or tube of brown paper, through the hole in your pie 'as long as it will receive it'. Leave it to set overnight (add a little gelatine if you feel at all nervous).

Here is another, probably more nearly mediaeval version:

TO BAKE A RABATT

Hot Rabbit Pie

Take two Rabetts divide the flesh from the bones, season yt w^t^h Cloves mace and nuttmegge, put a good deale of butter to yt and so bake yt, when yt is baked enoughe take the yelkes of three egges and some rose-water wine vinegere and suger, beate yt well together, then warme yt and powre yt into the pye, stirr yt well together, and then set yt in the oven a little while and soe serve yt

You will need at least half a pound of butter, perhaps more (think of the proportions in potted meat), if this pie is not to be unpleasantly dry. Bake it under a shortcrust lid for 1½ to 2 hours at Mark 3, 160°C, 325°F. Make your syrup with 2 tablespoons wine vinegar (or half vinegar and half white wine), 1 teaspoon sugar and 2 tablespoons rosewater, simmered together for a few minutes, then mixed little by little with the beaten egg yolks. I find you need a cupful of meat stock as well to dilute the eggs, otherwise if you are not careful they will simply scramble instead of thickening the sauce, and you need to allow quite a while for what Digby calls 'baking and soaking': twenty minutes at least in the lowest possible oven (the plate warmer is ideal) for the meat to take up the liquor.

This is a dish for anyone interested in seeing what our ancestors did with sugar and spice to meat that was often, in the Victorian phrase, only fit to be curried. But the same technique works so well in a fruit pie that I don't know why it ever fell out of favour. Here is one that makes a rich, warm, winter alternative to cold apple pie with a jug of cream poured over.

TO MAKE A CREAMEAPPLE PIE

Creamapple Pie

Take your apples, & slice them, & put some butter & sugar to them, & so put them in the paste, & bake them, when they are baked cut open the pie, & put in a good deale of sweet creame, & stir it well togither, & then let it stand a little, till it bee somewhat cold, & so serve it to the boord.

 Choose an absorbent apple like a Bramley (introduced two and a half centuries too late for Lady Fettiplace), the kind that puffs up in cooking, and slice it very thin so that it soaks up the buttery juices. To 2 lb. apples in a pastry-lined pie dish, take 4 rounded tablespoons brown sugar and a good-sized knob of butter, dotted over the top in little chips or flakes. Put on a pastry lid and bake for 45 minutes in a moderately hot oven (Mark 5, 190°C, 375°F). Pour in between ⅓ and ½ pint of warmed cream when the pie is baked, and don't let it get more than somewhat cold or the butter will congeal ('Set into the Oven again for a little space, as while the meat is in dishing up, and then serve it,' is Gervase Markham's advice for his Pippin Pye).

Here is another warm, fragrant, winey fruit pie for a dank February day. It comes in a little clutch of spicy pie recipes probably all from the same source, including the mugget and eel pies in Chapter Eleven, and the minced mutton pies in Chapter Twelve which were the direct ancestor of modern Christmas mince pies. This is also a close relation:

TO MAKE A MARROW PIE

Fruit and Marrow Pie

Take the bottomes of artichocks, & marrow & reasins & currance & dates & whole mace, & nutmeg & sugar, & bake it all together, when it is baked, take the pie out of the oven, & take some sack, & gynger, & a little butter, & sugar, & warme it all together, & put it in the pie, & set the pie into the oven againe, & let it stand there a little while before you draw it; before you put the things in the pie put a little butter in the bottome of it, when you put in the sack beat the yelks of two eggs into it, & stirre it well together before you put it in the pie.

Artichoke bottoms, a favourite titbit in both sweet and savoury pies until at least the eighteenth century, were still a comparative novelty in England by the turn of the sixteenth century. Lady Hoby noted in her diary that 'Hartechokes' bore a second crop in her Yorkshire garden in the exceptionally warm autumn of 1603. Lady Fettiplace preserved them for winter pies (her recipe is on p. 143), but unless you have a glut in the garden, it seems such a waste to use precious artichokes in a dish where they are intended to soak up other, much stronger flavours that I use apples instead. Marrow (from beef marrow bones) was another favourite enricher of sweet pies and puddings, thick and oily, highly nutritious, not unlike peanut butter in texture, bland and curiously earthy in taste. Increase the quantity of butter if you can't get marrow or prefer a vegetarian dish.

I use ½ lb. of peeled, cored and sliced apples, 3 oz. each of chopped dates, currants and stoned raisins, 1 rounded tablespoon of brown sugar, and the marrow from 1 beef marrow bone. Line a shallow pie plate or shallow dish with pastry, put in the filling, dot it with butter and put on the lid (don't forget to leave a hole in the middle, covered with a removable pastry rose). Use flaky or puff paste: Jacobean and Stuart cooks were expert at both, giving any number of variations on what have remained essentially unchanged techniques for trapping air between the layers of their meltingly light and fragile sweet pastries. Bake for 30 minutes in a hot oven (Mark 6, 200°C, 400°F). Have ready your sauce made from a heaped tablespoon each of butter and brown sugar, dissolved in a tablespoon of sherry, flavoured with ginger and beaten, little by little, with 2 egg yolks. Pour this very slowly into the cooked pie, 'shake the Pye well' as Markham advises, and return it to the lowest possible oven to soak while you are eating the first course. This pie is not large but rich, and you can of course make it richer still by increasing the proportions of dried fruit, sugar and/or butter.

Comforting food and reviving hot drinks naturally go with the miseries of freezing fog, rain, wind, sleet and drizzle so vividly evoked by the poets of this period, never better than in Spenser's February threnody from *The Shepheards Calender*:

But eft, when ye count you freed from feare,
Comes the breme winter with chamfred browes,
Full of wrinckles and frostie furrowes:
Drerily shooting his stormy darte,
Which cruddles the blood, and pricks the harte.

Lady Fettiplace knew all about the ancient art, afterwards beloved by the Victorians, of making a northern climate bearable in the long winter evenings with cinnamon toast browned at the fire, apples or pears roasted in the embers (see p. 88), buttered beer, mulled wine, the almond cakes or buns given in the next chapter, and these little buttered loaves, part cheese cake, part hot buttered scone. Contemporary recipes often suggest cutting the tops off the loaves as soon as they are done, pouring in melted butter and setting them briefly back in the oven as you might put a plate of buttered crumpets to steep for a few minutes in a warm place. Lady Fettiplace adds melted butter before cooking, and mixes her dough with cheese curds on the same principles as you use sour milk for the lightest and best risen scones.

TO MAKE BUTTERD LOAVES

Buttered Loaves (1)

Take the top of the mornings milk, warme it, & put therto three or fowre spoonfulls of rose water, then run it, & when it is hard come take some flower, the yolkes of two eggs, the white of one, & some melted butter, & some sugar & some nutmeg, then temper all this together with the milk, & mould it up into loaves, then set them on papers, & so bake them, if you make five loaves as big as manchets, you must put half a pound of butter to them, when they are baked, straw some sugar upon them, & so serve them.

I reckon 'the top of the mornings milk' for the purposes of this recipe at about one quart or two pints, yielding between ½ and ¾ lb. of cheese curds if you set it with rennet, which is what Lady Fettiplace meant by 'then run it' until 'it is hard come' (see p. 101 for how to do this; alternatively, use bought curd or cream—*not* cottage—cheese, sieved and beaten with rosewater). Mix the curds with the beaten egg, not forgetting an extra yolk, 4 oz. sugar and ½ lb. melted butter. Add enough flour to make a stiff scone dough, 12 oz. will probably be enough, with well-drained curds. Season with salt (see next recipe) and nutmeg. Divide the dough into five equal pieces, and shape each loaf like a manchet, 'round and flat, scorcht [scored] about the waste to give it leave to rise' in Markham's phrase. Manchets were rather large, fine, white bread rolls, roughly the size and shape of a modern bap or tea cake. This amount of dough will make five large manchets, or two dozen small scones. Bake in a hot oven (Mark 5, 190°C, 375°F) for 25 to 30 minutes, split the loaves, and eat, plain or with honey, while they are still warm. They are good toasted next day for breakfast, if you have any left over, with one of the orange marmalades given at the end of this chapter.

Lady Fettiplace also gives a second version, enriched with eggs rather than cheese curd, clearly the ancestor from which our tea-time scones and splits evolved with the invention of commercial baking powders in the nineteenth century.

TO MAKE BUTTERD LOVES

Buttered Loaves (2)

Take a pinte of fine flower, & three eggs with one of their whites, & some warme water, & a piece of fresh butter, put in your butter unmelted, & some sugar cloves & mace, & a little salt, so worke it up into little Loaves, & set them in the oven upon papers, & when they are almost baked take them out & roule them in butter, & rose water melted together, then strowe on some sugar on them, & set them in the oven againe, & when they are baked inough serve them.

For half quantities, proportions are 2 oz. butter and 1 rounded tablespoon of sugar rubbed into crumbs with 8 oz. plain flour (there were sixteen ounces to the pint in the seventeenth century), ½ level teaspoon salt, and ½ level teaspoon each of ground cloves and mace. Mix it with a beaten egg and enough warm water to work it into a firm dough. Divide the dough into 8 or 10 lumps and roll them out between your fingers into little loaf-shapes, or cut them into rounds with a scone cutter, and bake the loaves for 15 to 20 minutes in a brisk oven (Mark 6, 200°C, 400°F) until they are risen but not brown. Remove the tray from the oven, cut a deepish cross in each loaf, dip them first in melted butter and rosewater, then in soft brown sugar, and return them for another 5 minutes to the oven for this topping to harden. Serve them hot with more butter at table.

There is the same crunchy crust with a quite different texture underneath in the next recipe. Don't be put off by the name: sops are quick, simple, encouraging, convenient food, ideal for anyone in a hurry, tired, chilled or dispirited, coming in from shopping or school or a wet walk. They must also be one of the oldest dishes in Lady Fettiplace's repertoire: the Anglo-Saxons comforted themselves with sops, and so did the lord in *Sir Gawain and the Green Knight* (1135) who 'Ete a sop hastyly, when he hade herde masse'. Their memory survives in the sweet-smelling, old-fashioned clove pink—dark red with white speckles—called 'Sops-in-wine'.

TO MAKE COURT SOPS

Court Sops or Cinnamon Toast

Take ale and sugar and nutmeg and boile it together, and then have manchet cut like tostes and tost them browne, and then put them in the ale one by another without breaking of them, then boile it till the sops bee drie, then put some butter in it, and straw some sugar and nutmeg on it, and so serve it when it is somewhat cold.

For three or four people, heat half a pint (or one can) of brown ale with nutmeg and a tablespoon of sugar, stirring till it has dissolved. Take three or four slices of white bread, cut half an inch thick, toasted as slowly as you can and laid side by side in a baking dish. Pour over the ale (it would be at least half an inch deep for the bread to soak up), and leave the dish in a slow oven, plate warmer, on the Aga hob or any other warm place 'till the sops bee drie': ten minutes is enough but the beauty of this dish is that you can leave it almost indefinitely, toasting on top and steeping below. Add more liquid if necessary and serve your sops buttered, with more sugar and nutmeg. Robert May suggests claret wine and cinnamon, and I think a sprinkling of cinnamon improves these Court Sops no end.

Country households in those days brewed their own ale and beer (regularly once a fortnight or so at Ingatestone Hall, weekly in thirsty seasons like haymaking, harvest and the winter festivities). 'Water is not holesome sole by it selfe, for an Englysshe man,' wrote the Tudor physician Andrew Boorde, a view still held in some quarters today, and widely endorsed by Boorde's contemporaries: the average consumption of small beer at Ingatestone Hall was one gallon per head on normal days. For special occasions or more important company, Lady Fettiplace brewed her own strong, spicy bragget from ale and honey, as well as copious amounts of the potent, honey-based meads and metheglins that were the native British alternative to imported wines. 'It is marvellous to see how Welshmen will lie sucking at this drink,' reported another Tudor dietician, Dr Thomas Cogan (who was obliged to withdraw this offensive remark about metheglin from his *Haven of health* after the first edition in 1584, on account of complaints from Wales). Lady Fettiplace's mead is on p. 105. The Orange Water at the end of this chapter is one of many recipes, all currently illegal, for home-distilled liqueurs, 'strong waters' and 'uskebaugh' which was Gaelic for water of life—*eau de vie, aquavitae*—Englished as 'whiskybae', and later shortened to whisky.

Liqueurs and Spirits

Lady Fettiplace's Irish Aquavitae adds liquorice, raisins, aniseed, cinnamon and cloves to neat spirits (Dorothy Hartley, in *Food in England*, 1954, gives a current recipe for a very similar, brandy-based 'Drogheda Usquebaugh'). Three more elaborate uskebaughs add sugar to the basic infusion, and many more spices; one has saffron; another musk and ambergris; 'little baggs' of powdered spice 'to be put into any aquavitae' include bitter aloes, yellow saunders (sandalwood, for colouring), cardamums, galingale, red rose petals and Indian spikenard. She also gives two versions of Aqua Mirabilis, two Imperial Waters, three sorts of Cinnamon Water and 'a pretious drink': decoctions of wine or spirits flavoured with spices and seeds, herbs, flowers, sometimes sharpened with rhubarb or the juice of celandines. All were strictly speaking medicinal (Imperial Water was a protection against plague, Aqua Mirabilis offered to cure anything from ulcerated lungs to heartburn, melancholia, poor circulation and failing memory), though perhaps chiefly in the sense that any strong, comforting, alcoholic stimulant might be said to do good. Imperial and Cinnamon Waters were both on Richard Hakluyt's list of provisions, set down a few years earlier (and quoted in *Food In England*), for a trading sea captain hoping to entertain potential customers at banquets on shipboard, 'to be had with you to make a shew of by taste, and also to comfort your sick on the voyage. With these, and such like, you may banket where you arrive the greater and best persons.'

There seems to have been no hard and fast line in those days between drinks meant for hospitality, to please and impress the best persons, and those intended to heal. Delicious concoctions came out of the cupboard at this time of year to soothe swollen tonsils ('Take a quart of red wine, roses three handfulls, pills of twoe pomgranats ... '), quinzies, 'Cold Rhumes', 'aking bones', running eyes and sore throats. If you couldn't fancy red wine with roses and pomegranate peel, there was barley water with mulberry syrup and honey of roses; oil of sweet almonds beaten with sugar candy; elicampane root infused with liquorice and honey ('to make it sweet, or more to take away the taste [of] it in eating'); and, 'For an Extreme Cough', another barley water flavoured with herbs, brown sugar candy, red rosewater and syrup of green ginger. Lady Fettiplace gives in all eleven cough syrups, four gargles for throat-washes, a chestrub for the cold and five sorts of cough drop. The book is full of practical tips: sage, hyssop and pepper, for instance, laid 'on a hot tylestone' for a bronchial patient to inhale the fumes, or a 'Cap for the rewme' made from spices and frankincense strewed upon flax, which was then sewn between two layers of brown paper and worn on the head. One nourishing herbal meat broth for the lungs comes with a modest testimonial from its supplier, perhaps Lady Fettiplace herself: 'This did help mee when I was extreme short breathed'. Her remedies could, as she says herself, be relied on to cheer and comfort, if not necessarily to cure the sufferer. Her egg nog is a case in point:

Cough Syrups

FOR A GREAT COLD

Egg Nog

Take the yolk of an egg, & one spoonfull of aqua vitae, & foure spoonfulls of goats or cowe milk, hot from the cow, beat it all together, & then drink it fasting & last at night.

Whatever its miseries, February was still—at least until the onset of Lent, generally towards the end of the month—part of the festive season, when foul weather ensured that there was not a lot to do save enjoy the flowers and fruits of the field preserved from the year before in pots, glasses, jars, bottles and barrels. But February was also, then as now, the time for making marmalade. Lady Fettiplace's orange-and-apple preserve on p. 67 was to be made 'at the beginning of Lent': Sir Kenelm Digby gives a very similar recipe to be done in November when 'Pippins are in their prime for quickness'. The Seville orange season in the seventeenth century seems to have lasted from Allhallowstide (November 1, when the first ripe oranges were landed) to April or later, nearly half the year, not the measly month or two that is all modern merchant shipping can manage; moreover you could eat oranges in the other seven months preserved in a variety of ways—dried, crystallised, candied, stuffed, bottled and floating in syrup or jelly, or boiled to a thick sweet paste called 'marmalade'.

Orange Marmalades

The word was originally Portuguese *marmelado*, from *marmelo* or quince, so meaning a preserve of quinces. But it was promptly applied all over Europe to other fruits, indeed it seems to have been only in Britain—and then only comparatively lately—that it came to mean exclusively jam made from oranges (there are several 'jammes' in a MS receipt book dated 1683, belonging to Elizabeth David, although the Oxford English Dictionary identifies the word as an eighteenth-century coinage derived, according to Bailey's dictionary, from nursery French, *j'aime*, I love it). Mrs Beeton still lists quince and apricot as well as orange marmalades. Lady Fettiplace gives eight different sorts of what we should call orange marmalade (three including apples), besides marmalades made from cherries, grapes, raspberries, plums, gooseberries, pears, almost any fruit cooked gently by itself till it is soft, then boiled fast in a syrup made from one pound of sugar to each pound of fruit pulp. But where we pot our marmalade as soon as the syrup reaches setting point, Elizabethan and Jacobean cooks boiled theirs on till the mixture stiffened and candied and could be eaten neat as a sweetmeat, sliced or cut into squares, not spooned from the pot and spread upon bread. 'Or with the gift of these Marmelades in small boxes, or small vials of sweet waters you may gratifie by way of gift, or you may make a merchandize of them', was Hakluyt's advice to the enterprising Elizabethan sea captain. Here is one to be made at this time of year with the first oranges shipped from Spain and the last English apples stored from the autumn before. People who find strong dark bitter marmalade altogether too much of a good thing will like this pretty, delicately flavoured, pale golden preserve flecked or speckled with bright orange peel.

TO MAKE ORINGE MARMALAD,

Orange and Apple Marmalade

Take yo[r] oringe Rindes pare them and boyle them untill they bee very softe, then take them out of the water and bray them very smale in a morter, then take faire water some suger & the Juice of 3. or 4. oringes boyle and scum yt, then put in yo[r] oringe stuffe, let yt boyle a quarter of an hower them poure yt out and let yt stand, to a pound of oringes you must take a pound of pipines pared and cored and to every pound of pipines a pound of suger & a pinte of water, let the water and suger boyle and bee scumed and then put in yo[r] pipines and boyle them till they are very tender then breake them to peeces and put yo[r] oringe stuffe to them, let them boyle together still stiringe of yt until yt will cut

It is not entirely clear to me whether the quantity of sugar and water given in this recipe is to be divided between the two fruits for the initial stage of cooking, or whether you need extra sugar for your orange stuff. I have tried both methods and, though I prefer the taste of the first and more extravagant of the two (which produces less marmalade much less sweet), the second keeps better and is probably authentic. You will need 2 lb. sugar* for 3 or 4 Seville oranges, weighing probably round about 1 lb., and 1 lb. apples (Cox's orange pippins will do very well). A pint, in this and Lady Fettiplace's other recipes, means the original English pint measuring 16 fluid ounces, or four fifths of the modern imperial pint, which was introduced in 1826 and contains 20 fluid ounces (the American pint remains unchanged: in practice, except in a few tricky operations where exact measurements are crucial, it doesn't always matter a great deal which measure you use).

Halve the oranges, squeeze out their juice, and simmer the hulls with sufficient water to cover them for about three quarters of an hour, or until they are soft enough to pierce with the end of a wooden spoon or blunt wooden skewer. Mince the peel into fine

*I have made all Lady Fettiplace's marmalades, preserves, jellies and conserves with ordinary, white, granulated sugar, which makes it unnecessary to follow the instructions given in many of her recipes for clarifying the sugar with egg whites. But even the finest white sugar loaves (which had to be crushed as well as clarified at home) available in Jacobean England would have been darker than ours, less uniform in texture and better flavoured. C. Anne Wilson, author of *Food and Drink in Britain*, suggests that a more nearly authentic solution might be 'to try mixing equal parts of white sugar and a pale muscovado (from a health food shop, *not* Tate and Lyle sugar which is browned with caramel)'.

strips by hand, grind ('bray') it in a mortar, or whizz briefly in an electric mixer. Make a syrup from 2 lb. sugar dissolved in 32 fluid oz. water, or 2 U.S. pints, and set half of it aside. Bring the rest to boil with the orange juice, scum it, put in the peel and boil fast for fifteen minutes.

Slice the apples and simmer them in the other half of the syrup till they are transparent and tender. I find this preserve sets almost as soon as the orange stuff is put to the pippins but for an authentic solid, seventeenth-century marmalade, you must boil it on, stirring incessantly towards the end for fear of burning, till the stuff begins to thicken, coming away from the sides of the pan and holding the tracks of the spoon. Now pour it quickly into a box or tin, following the instructions for Spanish Marmalad on p. 52. This is perhaps the finest—and certainly at the time one of the most popular—of all these rich, sticky Elizabethan and Jacobean fruit sweetmeats: an early attempt to preserve the exquisite flavour and perfume of Seville oranges which were later, and even more successfully, captured in curaçao, Cointreau and Grand Marnier.

But, if you prefer something more liquid, you can of course pot the marmalade in the usual way as soon as it begins to set, leaving the apple slices whole and the orange peel suspended in clear apple jelly which is what Digby recommended on aesthetic grounds for his highly ornamental Apples in Gelly. Here is Lady Fettiplace's own, somewhat similar orange-and-apple jelly, particularly decorative if you have any small keeping pippins or eating apples stored from last year (they must not be too shrunken or shrivelled, nor the watery kind that disintegrates in cooking, above all not the glossy tasteless, imported jobs you can buy in the shops at this time of year). They are to be peeled, but not sliced, and preserved whole with the sliced orange rind.

FOR WHITE PIPPINS

White Pippins or Orange and Apple Jelly

Take to everie pound of pippins a pound of sugar & a pinte of faire water, & rose water together, then put the sugar & the water together, & let them melt on the fire, when it begins to boile beate the white of an egge into it, then let it boile a prettie while with the egg, then scum it, pare your pippins & put them in, & have the pill of oringes readie watered & boiled, cut them in small slices & put them in with the pippins, so let them all boile, till the syrup be gellie. These Pippins must bee doone about the beginning of Lent.

Proportions are 1 lb. sugar, 16 fluid oz. water (including a few spoonfuls of rosewater) and the peel of 1 or 2 Seville oranges per pound of apples. There is no need to scum the syrup with egg white, which was for clarifying the juice and collecting impurities, if you are using modern, factory refined sugar. The orange rinds (use the flesh for the little orange cakes at the end of this chapter) must be previously soaked, boiled in several waters till soft, and cut into matchstick slices. Lady Fettiplace gives excellent practical instructions on how to test for set in another recipe, To Make Iellie of Oringes, using sugar, water and fruit pulp (not rind, which was candied separately): 'so set it over the fire, and let it boyle apace, till you perceve it stif inough, by setting some to coole in a spoone'. As soon as your drop of syrup is quite cold (try the freezer compartment of the fridge, or an outside windowsill for quick results), push it with your finger and if it wrinkles, the jelly will set. Leave it to cool a little before potting it, to stop the apples rising to the top.

'White' as opposed to 'red' pippins refers to the colour of the finished preserve, not the type of apple you chose in the first place. Cooks of this period took particular pride in their skill at preserving colourless fruit like apples and pears in almost any shade, from a red so dark it is almost black (see Lady Fettiplace's red wardens on p. 180 or her red and white quince marmalades on p. 202 through cornelian and amber to palest lemony green like this one. Here is something closer to a strong, dark, well-soaked, Oxford marmalade, which is made by much the same method today. Substitute Seville oranges, as Lady Fettiplace suggests, if you can't get pomecitrons or citrons, which were the earliest of the citrus fruits to reach Europe from the Orient.

TO PRESERVE POUNE-CITERONES

Preserve of Pomecitrons or Oranges

Take yor Citterons and scrape them well with a Knife then lay them on night in stronge brine made of cold water & salte, let them boyle an hower in that brine, then have a pan of water boyleinge and change them out of the brine into that water, and let them boyle halfe an hower, then put them in another hott water and let them boyle untill they bee very tender, then cut them in quarters and take out the meate, and way to every pounde of yor Citterones a pound and quarter of suger smale beaten put as much water to yor suger as will wett yt, then boyle and clarrifie yt very well, then dry yor Citterones in a hott cloath very dry, so put them into yor sirrope then boyle them halfe and let them stand two dayes then boyle them upp, then take out yor Citterones and boyle yor sirrope very thick, and then put yt to them this way you may doe Oringes and Limondes

The pomecitron has a specially thick rind, which is why it had to be first scraped with a knife, not simply scrubbed, then soaked overnight in salt brine, precautions which may safely be left out if you are using ordinary Seville oranges. Wash the fruit, leave it to soak overnight, and bring to the boil in the morning, changing the water three times (Mrs Beeton recommends the same thing) to lessen the bitterness. What Lady Fettiplace seems to have had in mind was a translucent orange jelly with quarters of citrus rind suspended in it, a typically elegant conceit of the period. Weigh one and a quarter pounds of sugar to each pound of fruit, and dissolve it in as little water as possible, say half a cupful per pound. Carefully quarter the fruit, and discard the pulp, keeping the rind which is to be thoroughly dried (the 'hott cloath' is another characteristic touch) before being boiled briefly in this syrup and left to stand forty-eight hours. The mixture is then brought to the boil again, the rinds removed and the syrup reduced by fast boiling till it will set (it needs to be thicker than usual at this stage, as the moist orange peels will dilute it). Later recipes often recommend several days soaking and standing, interspersed with boiling and re-boiling, but they nearly all keep the pulp (leaving out only the pips) which gives the thick lumpy texture favoured today.

Lady Fettiplace includes two further recipes for preserving whole fruit, bright orange globes in clear golden jelly. In both, the fruit is to be thoroughly soaked, then boiled till tender in several waters. The later recipe (added at the end of the book, perhaps as late as the eighteenth century, in a new hand and different ink) advises you to 'tye e'm in peices of Tyffany' (muslin) so as to keep their shape. The flesh is then to be scooped out—a tricky operation—through a little hole in the top, and replaced by sugar in which the fruit is drenched overnight; next day you add water and boil 'till the oranges be clear', then leave them to stand a further day before the final boiling, 'then put e'm in glasses and fill em up with jely'. In the earlier recipe, the flesh is to be extracted from the raw oranges before they are soaked, and their juice added to the syrup half way through the final boiling. Proportions in each case are a pound of sugar to a pound of fruit (weighed after the preliminary soaking and boiling) and a pint of water.

Orangeadoes

These must have been the fashionable 'orangeadoes'—orange peel candied, preserved in syrup or stuffed and stuck with herbs—which went into sweet pies, or were used to flavour and decorate a variety of creams and fruit fools, or (in their dry, crystallised form) carried about in courtiers' pockets to eat at the theatre or offer to friends. Confectioners did the same thing with sugar plums, candied eringo roots or sea holly (see the note on p. 179), candied stalks of mallow or lettuce: what they called 'wet suckets' as distinct from the dry suckets which were taken out of their syrup and hardened off in the bread oven. The nearest thing to a wet sucket nowadays would be a jar of ginger in syrup; candied angelica, marrons glacés and other crystallised fruits are dry suckets. Lady Fettiplace's recipe for candied peel—To Candie oringe pilles—is almost identical to her preserved oranges, except that the soaked, boiled, softened and carefully dried peel is first candied by fast boiling in syrup, then removed and laid 'on a sheete of paper to drye by the fire'.

She gives all sorts of other dry suckets or 'orange cakes', little crystallised pastilles or lozenges packed in boxes, some made from the orange rind only, some from the pulp, some from both. One charming recipe is for uncooked orange sweets, nice for children to make as well as to eat:

TO MAKE CAKES OF ORENGES

Orange Cakes or Sweetmeats (1)

Take some oringes & take out the meat of them, then pick them cleane from the white skins, & stamp them in a stone morter, very fine, then take away the iuice that is too much, & wey to a pound of the orenges a pound of the finest white sugar beaten very fine, & put it to your orenges, beating them all together a good while till they bee throughlie mingled, then take it out, & lay them upon plates, of what fashion you best like, but they must bee very thin, then set them to drying, & when they bee half dry, turne them, they wilbee soone dry.

Bitter, finely-flavoured Seville oranges are essential for this recipe, which would be insipid and far too sugary with ordinary sweet oranges. Peel the fruit carefully, removing all the white pith, and discard the peel (which may be candied, dried or used in the recipe for White Pippins on p. 67). Remove the pips, reduce the orange flesh to a paste in a stone mortar or electric mixer, and strain off any surplus juice. Weigh this paste and pound it again with an equal weight of white sugar. Pour out the mixture onto a large flat plate or tin baking tray and set it in a warm place, turning it as soon as the top has dried out, so as to harden off the underside. These sweets probably don't keep long—mine have never had a chance to—but taste delicious, especially if you dry them off in a slow oven till they begin to brown and caramelise, when they can be rolled by hand into little balls or drops with a dark, burnt-orange taste to serve after dinner with coffee.

Another recipe—To Make Orenge Cakes—mixes pippins and oranges in a preserve essentially the same as the Oringe Marmalad with which I began, except that the syrup is made with rosewater, a definite improvement. In fact, as Lady Fettiplace explains in her directions for plum cakes on p. 176, the only difference between these fruit cakes and marmalades lies in the method of drying. Here is another nice dry sucket:

TO MAKE CLEARE ORINGE CAKES

Orange Cakes or Sweetmeats (2)

Take very good Oringes ffull of meate Cutt them and take the meate cleane forth of the whight Skinne, Crush it w^t^h a spoone that all the Juce may not bee in it, then take as much sugger as the waight of the meate of yor Oringe boyle the sugger untill it come to a hard Candy, then putt the meate of yor Oringe to it, stirringe it well but lett it not boyle. When it is allmost cowlde powre it in little deepe plates and sett it where ffire is to dry, when it is candied on on side turne it on little peeces of Glass, and soe lett it stand untill it bee through dry

The fruit in this recipe needs de-pipping and chopping, or a brief whizz in the liquidiser, to break up the fibres. Warm the sugar gently with a little water (I wet it with the surplus orange juice) till it dissolves, then boil fast without stirring to the soft ball stage, what Jacobean cooks called 'candie height' (240°F, or 115°C, if you have a sugar thermometer), when a few drops in cold water will cohere into a soft ball. If you beat the sugar hard at this point with a wooden spoon, it will crystallise into a pan of 'hard Candy' which melts when you put in the meat of your oranges. Lady Fettiplace doesn't say that the fruit should be ready warmed, but other recipes do, and it certainly helps. Stir over a very low heat to melt the candy, which may take some time.

This technique—crystallised sugar liquified by the addition of raw fruit or a hot, dry fruit purée—is not one I have found in post-seventeenth-century cookery books, though it was clearly well known in Lady Fettiplace's day. It produces a semi-solid preserve which sets loosely when cold, like a rather runny modern jam, and may be put up in jam jars or dried off on tins or plates 'where ffire is'. Lady Fettiplace would have had a stillroom cupboard, specially fitted with pierced lattice shelves and heated by a slow-burning charcoal brazier, but a hot airing cupboard will do instead, or a plate warmer, or at a pinch the oven itself, switched to the lowest possible heat with the door left open. Box it as soon as it is thoroughly dry—whole, or cut into squares, or moulded into fancy shapes according to the instructions on p. 185—between layers of greaseproof paper in an airtight container.

Oranges were all the rage, and not only at seasons when other fruit was hard to come by. Sir Hugh Plat (who published his *Delightes for Ladies* in 1602, two years before Lady Fettiplace's book was written) gives directions for keeping orange juice all the year round to make sauces and cooling drinks, together with a labour-saving tip for snapping it up at bargain prices when the first shiploads arrived in November: 'if curteous Ladies you will lend eares and followe my direction; I will heere furnish a great number of you . . . with the iuce of the best civill Orenges at an easie price: About Alhallowstide or soone after you may buy the inward pulpe of civill Orenges wherein the iuce resteth, of the comfetmakers for a small matter, who doe only or principally respect their rindes to preserve and make Orengadoes withall . . .'*

At the end of Lady Fettiplace's book, copied out in a delicate, flowery, unknown and much later hand, there is a recipe for orange liqueur, one of those deceptively strong fruit cordials that gave eighteenth-century ladies' tea-and-card parties such a bad name. I include it for curiosity's sake, to show the sort of thing country ladies once produced in their stillrooms at home to the consternation of husbands like Mirabell, in Congreve's *Way of the World*, who made it a condition of marriage that his wife should not serve her friends orange brandy at tea time:

TO MAKE ORANGE WATER

Orange Water or Brandy

Take 2 quarts of Orange peels dried & beaten to 2 Gallons of Brandy; an ounce of Cinamon, half an Ounce of Cloves & as much Mace, & about an Ounce of Ginger all grossly beaten. Let it stand 2 or 3 days, then distill it.

*I am grateful to Elizabeth David for passing on Plat's tip.

3
MARCH

The forty-six days' fasting of Lent, enforced more or less strictly by church and state, meant that for two months the whole country dieted, giving up meat—sometimes eggs, milk, butter and cheese as well—eating fish twice daily, and going without supper altogether on Fridays. This penitential regime was preceded by a last fling at Shrovetide with carnival games, masques, parties and a great deal of drinking. Shrovetide Cocks were set up to be pelted by revellers in country market places, and mayhem was let loose in London: 'By the unmanerly maners of Shrove-Tuesday Constables are baffled, Bawds are bang'd, Punckes are pillag'd,' wrote James Taylor, a poet, Thames waterman and Gloucestershire contemporary of Lady Fettiplace. Her friend Dudley Carleton, writing on March 6, 1598, described the festivities laid on by his cousin Dormer at Ascot, 'where their entertainment was very royal, according to the custom of the place. Their Shrovetide guests were no more than Mr. Allen, myself and Mr. Ashworth, who enjoyned the lady of the house a very unseasonable fast in this time of feasting ...' This was the same Dr Ashworth, evidently a popular figure in the district, who gave Lady Unton 'a silver cann' (which rated special mention in her will), and presented her cousin, Lady Fettiplace, with the recipe for his Dyet Drinke (which she incorporated into her book on the flyleaf).

Shrove Tuesday was Pancake Day, then as now, when dinner at mid-day culminated in great mounds of pancakes and apple fritters—spiced, rose-flavoured, mixed with ale or sherry, enriched with butter, cream and a great many eggs. Each house had its own speciality, and hostesses under the critical appraising eye of bachelor guests like Carleton faced stiff competition to outdo one another and themselves from one year to the next. Some of these recipes are closer to continental frivolities like Salzburger Nockerl, or the

Edwardian Crêpes Suzette, than to today's comparatively frugal English Shrove Tuesday pancakes, made from the plainest possible batter and served simply with lemon juice and sugar. Here is Lady Fettiplace's version of a light, fluffy omelette soufflé, spiced and stuffed with apple purée:

FOR FRITTERS

Apple Fritters or Omelette Soufflé

Take the whites of eggs & beat them very well, then put to them some creame, & a little flower, & some cloves and mace beaten smale, & some sugar, & the pap of two or three boiled apples & stir it well alltogether, then fry it in a frying pan with some sweet butter, & when it is half fried, break it in pieces like fritters & so fry it.

First stew gently 2 or 3 small pippins (or 1 large modern cooking apple), peeled, cored and sliced, in a very little water to a soft pulp. Beat 2 egg whites stiffly, then fold in with a metal spoon 2 rounded tablespoonfuls of sugar (more, if your apples are tart) mixed with one of flour, 2 ground cloves and ½ teaspoonful of cinnamon. Now add 4 tablespoonfuls of cream, and the apple pap. Melt a good ounce of butter in a large, deep, thick bottomed, preferably iron frying pan. Make it very hot before you pour in the mixture and cook it over a moderate flame for 3 or 4 minutes on each side. It takes both skill and nerve to toss a soufflé omelette, but anyone who follows Lady Fettiplace's directions can turn it. These quantities are enough for two people. For anyone who keeps batches of stewed apple pulp in the freezer, this is one of the quickest and simplest as well as the most elegant of puddings. Egg yolks left over from this recipe, or from the White Bisket Bread given in Chapter Five, or December's Marchpane and Maccaroonds, might go into a traditional pancake batter like this one:

TO MAKE FRITURES AND PANCAKES

Ale-based Apple Fritters and Pancakes

Take good ale, make yt bloud warme, put to yt some fine wheatne flower, the yelkes of 4 or 5 egges some Cloves, mace, and smale quantity of ginger, with some salte, and a qter of a pound of beefe suett shred very smale, temper yt all well together, then pare yor apples, Cut out the Cores & slice them round into yor batter, and bake them in beife Lard as other fritures of the same bater make yor pancakes leavinge out yor suett and apples, and let yor ale bee halfe sacke, fry yor pancakes either in butter or beefe lard

These are the fritters Pepys loved, and seems to have made a point of sampling at a different house most Shrove Tuesdays. To make a great pile of them—enough for eight people or more—you will need a ½ pint can of light ale, 8 oz. plain flour seasoned with 1 level teaspoonful of ginger, 2 or 3 ground cloves and a pinch of powdered mace, 4 or 5 egg yolks, 4 oz. shredded beef suet and probably 2½ to 3 lb. of apples. Make up a batter, taking care not to mix it too thin: Lady Fettiplace directs elsewhere that you should, in the charming phrase of the period, 'put in ... as much flower as will make it thicke enough to hange uppon yo[r] apples'. Beat it well and leave it to stand for an hour or so while you peel, core and slice your apples into rings.

These should be pippins or sweet eating apples, which contrast well with the unsweetened, light, crisp, beer batter, while the suet gives richness and texture. Drop the apple rings half a dozen at a time into your batter, heat a good-sized lump of butter or pure beef dripping (the kind butchers sell, not the dripping mixed with meat juices left over from a roast joint), in a large frying pan, '& when it is very hot drop in y[r] apples one by one with y[r] fingers as fast as you can' (this is a contemporary instruction from *Martha Washington's Booke of Cookery*, messy but practical). Fry them over a moderate heat for two or three minutes on each side, drain them on kitchen paper and keep them warm on a dish in a low oven while you fry the next batch. Strew with sugar and spices, and serve with more sugar in a bowl and a canister of powered ginger or cinnamon.

Ale and Sherry Pancakes

Spiced pancakes made, as Lady Fettiplace suggests in the recipe above, from the same basic ale batter, minus the suet and apples, are also very good. You will need a much thinner batter than for fritters: say, 4 oz. plain flour, 2 or 3 egg yolks (or a whole egg), salt, 2 crumbled cloves, a generous pinch each of powdered ginger and nutmeg and just under ½ pint light ale. Add 2 tablespoons sack or sherry, which will probably be quite enough of any of the modern fortified sherries. Have ready a thick-bottomed frying pan—an omelette pan is ideal—well greased and sizzling hot. Pour in a tablespoonful of batter which should be thin enough (about the consistency of single cream) to spread and cover the pan by tilting and tipping. Toss the pancake, or loosen and turn it with a spatula—what Lady Fettiplace calls 'a little wooden spatter'—as soon as the batter bubbles and sets. Stack these fine, light, lacy pancakes on a hot plate, strewing brown sugar liberally between the layers as you go, with a little butter and perhaps an occasional sprinkling of cinnamon. Put the plate in a low oven to keep warm as soon as the stack is high enough, and cut it into wedges, like a cake, to serve at table.

Pancakes are generally much improved by the addition of alcohol. Try gingering up an ordinary, milk-based batter with spices and a little sherry or sack: 'as much sacke as milcke' is Lady Fettiplace's advice (which may be altogether too much of a good thing) in one of two more recipes for apple fritters. Alternatively, serve them with the same wine sauce as bag pudding, made from butter, sugar and sherry beaten to a froth over a fierce flame for a minute or two in the pancake pan: you could, if you prefer to prepare them beforehand, reheat your pancakes folded into parcels in this sauce as you would Crêpes Suzette. Mrs Raffald, more than a century and a half after Lady Fettiplace, served her common fritters (the fritter batter above, with apples, dropped by spoonfuls into a pan of boiling lard) 'with Sugar grated over them and Wine sauce in a boat'. Here is a sweet pancake batter, excellent with sugar and lemon, stuffed with apple pap or with one of Lady Fettiplace's runnier orange-and-apple marmalades, or in any of the ways suggested above:

TO MAKE PANCAKES

Rosewater Pancakes

Take the yelks of eggs, & rose water, & some flower, & a little cloves, and mace, and some sugar, & beat it well togither, make it somewhat thin, and so frie them.

Quantities are a cupful of rosewater to 4 egg yolks and 4 oz. flour, with a tablespoonful of sugar and spices to suit your taste.

Shrove Tuesday was named from the Catholic custom of going to church to be shriven, or absolved by a priest after confession, in preparation for Lent. The next day was Ash Wednesday when penitents were sprinkled with ashes, a black day in the kitchen of any household that kept strict observance: *dies cineris*—day of cinders—is the heading for March 3, 1552, in Sir William Petre's household book. For the next forty-six days, the scribe records a monotonous diet of fish, salt, dried or pickled, relieved from time to time by 'a piece of green [i.e. fresh] fish', and once by a salted salmon which turned up at successive meals over a week. The Petre household in Lent consumed a barrel a week of white or pickled herrings, and half a cade or barrel of fresh red herrings from the North Sea. Fresh fish from both river and sea was plentiful at Newbury market in Berkshire, according to the traveller Thomas Baskerville who made a leisurely journey from Abingdon to

Southampton in 1641, including splendid descriptions of the countryside and paying particular attention to local facilities for shopping. 'Gloucester lampreys' were among the delicacies he listed along with 'trout, jack and excellent crawfish'. Oysters were also cheap and plentiful, growing more expensive as they travelled further from the coast, but still sold at inland markets by the peck or bushel from barrels packed with seaweed. One of the ingredients in Lady Fettiplace's remedy 'for a lame or withered hand' is 'the green sea weed that the oyster wives lay upon the oysters'. Here are her directions for scalloped oysters:

TO STEW OYSTERS

Stewed Oysters

Take the water of the oisters, and one slice of an onyon, and boile the oisters in it, when they are boiled put in some butter and an oringes peel minced, & some lemon cut verie smale, and so serve it. (You must put some whight wine in yͤ stewinge.)

The last instruction has been added in a neat hand, not belonging to Lady Fettiplace or to her secretary Anthony Bridges, and it is an improvement. Open the oysters by inserting a short sharp knife at the hinged end, over a bowl so as to catch 'the water of the oisters'. Now stew them in their own juice with a slice of grated or very finely chopped onion and a tablespoonful of white wine in a covered pan over a medium heat for two or three minutes. It is perhaps wise at this stage to remove the oysters and strain the liquor before finishing off the sauce with a knob of butter, a generous grating of orange zest (Lady Fettiplace would have used the sharp, fragrant Seville orange, still obtainable with luck in March) and a thinly sliced lemon for decoration.

If there is plenty of sauce, serve the oysters in the Jacobean manner on strips of toast, or sippets, in a deep dish with the liquor poured over. Or else eat them with fresh brown bread and butter, salt and pepper, and more white wine to drink. Oysters shrink a lot and grow tough if overcooked so this dish is difficult as well as expensive to prepare nowadays for more than two or three people at a time. If you want the sort of generous, heaped platter served in the seventeenth century, you might try using mussels (also available to Lady Fettiplace, who coloured one of her ointments with the scrapings of black mussel shells), in which case you would need a good many more—say one pint per person—and there would be no need to open the shells before cooking.

Diet Drinks or Spring Tonics

Six solid weeks of a meatless diet, enforced as much to strengthen the navy by encouraging ship building as for spiritual reasons, might also be expected to cleanse the system weakened by the alternating hardship and plenty of winter. If dieting was a legal requirement, its effects were reinforced by spring tonics made from the first sharp, fresh, green leaves, administered to purge the blood and skin in much the same spirit as women's magazines still recommend astringent lotions, herbal teas and slimming regimes at this time of year. Lady Fettiplace gives getting on for two dozen different drinks 'for the dropsie or shortnes of Breath', for constipation, liver complaints, bad breath and a sluggish digestion. Lack of fresh fruit and vegetables in winter meant, at any rate among the poor, the swollen limbs, sore gums and blotchy skin that were the first signs of scurvy, to be treated with a variety of mildly diuretic and antiscorbutic preparations made from herbs like agrimony, betony, scabious, wild cresses, brooklime and scurvygrass.

These annual tonics were made up in quantities sufficient to dose the whole Fettiplace household night and morning in spring. 'Doc^{tr} Ashworth dyet drinke, to clerifie ye bloud & ye Liver' calls for the usual bag of herbs, augmented by senna and sliced dock root, suspended in two gallons of ale and topped up with the juice of watercress and scurvygrass. It was to be taken three times a day, at seven and nine in the morning and four in the afternoon: 'When it is almost spent put in a gallen of new ale into the barrel or pott where ye bagg is' was his final thrifty instruction for a supply that seems, by the standards of this manuscript, relatively modest. The diet drink Elinor Fettiplace herself singled out—endorsing it 'of note' in her own handwriting in the margin—was mixed on a basis of 'three gallons of rennish wine'. Her friend Lady Tracy based hers on 'five gallons of neaw ale', while her cousin Gresham Thynne of Longleat made up hers six gallons at a time.

Some of these drinks were taken neat, others included aniseed, fennel seed, sliced liquorice and sugar candy to disguise the bitter taste. One—'for the sciatica or French pox' (syphilis)—was accompanied by a strict diet which casts interesting light on the kind of regime considered normal for a gentleman not suffering

Special Diets

from the pox: 'At dinner your meat dry rosted, little salt or basting either of mutton, Capon, Chicken, Rabet or fresh fish, the bread stale, or bisket ... All wine, women, salt meats, shellfish, liquid things, butter, eggs and tart things, are hinderers to this dyet ...' The treatment Dr Ashworth prescribed at Shrovetide for poor Mistress Dormer ('she hath been in diet these two weeks') was for the Mother, a blanket word covering women's troubles from gynaecological disorders to palpitations, nervous hysteria and melancholy, the sort of thing we should now call depression and treat indiscriminately with sedatives. Green sickness was another specifically female complaint, afflicting young girls who grew moody, pasty-faced, anaemic, refusing food and sometimes showing obsessive cravings for chalk, lime and dirt, a widespread early form of anorexia nervosa. It was thought to be caused by lack of iron, and Lady Fettiplace dosed it with four different mixtures, all but one based on steel shavings or powder (the powder was to be taken in rose petal jam), again backed up by dieting and exercise: 'Take so much at a time as you can take upon a sixpence, eat it dry first at morning, & fast two howers after it, & walk upon it ... the gentlewoman that shall take this pouder, must eat no milk, cheese, vinegar, salt meats, nor fruits ...'

The very old or young, the sick and anyone already following a medical regime might be excused the Lenten fast. Others had to get by as best they could by exploiting loopholes in the regulations. Strictly speaking, the prohibition of meat included—as it still does for stern vegetarians—cheese made in the usual way with rennet from a cow's stomach, a technical difficulty solved then as now by vegetarian rennet (extracted, according to Charles Estienne's *The Countrey Farme*, from thistles, artichokes, ginger or the green rind of fig trees: 'with these it is usuall to make Cheese to be eaten in Lent'). In mediaeval times, when milk itself and all its products were forbidden, a single household consumed a staggering annual bulk of almonds (28,500 pounds went to feed king and court in the year 1286 alone), which were laboriously ground, seethed in water, strained, churned or curdled to make substitute milk, butter and cheese. The ingenuity of mediaeval cooks was responsible for a whole repertoire of sweet and savoury almond dishes, still strongly represented in Lady Fettiplace's many delectable almond puddings, cakes, biscuits and blancmanges, including this ancient recipe for something surprisingly like a light, sweet cream cheese or *crême fraiche*:

TO MAKE ALMOND BUTTER

Almond Butter

Take a pound of Almonds, blanch them in cold water, then grinde them in a mortar verie finelie, straine them with a good deale of faire water, & set them over the fire, & put theirin a little rose water, & a little salt & sugar, stir it over the fire, till it begin to break, then take it from the fire, & put it into a cloth, so that all the whey may run from it, then put it together with a spoone, & so let it hang upon a staff untill all the whey be run out, very cleane, when the whay is run out, beat it againe in a morter, & then put it into dishes.

This is one of those dishes worth reviving only if you have an electric liquidiser or food processor, which eliminates the prohibitive drudgery of reducing the nuts to a paste by hand. One pound of almonds would yield about a gallon of milk (and between one and one and a half pounds of butter), a quantity probably unmanageable without special equipment, so I make a small but rich dish of butter from four ounces of almonds. First blanch and skin them (which is easier if you dip them in boiling, not cold water). Grind them in the food processor with a little cold water, adding more until they have absorbed about half a pint. Now lay a double layer of clean damp muslin or cheesecloth, or a muslin bag, in a colander over a bowl, and pour the almond milk carefully into it. Gather up the drawstring of the bag, or knot the four corners of the cloth, hang it from a hook over the bowl, and leave it for a quarter of an hour or so to drain. Repeat this process three more times, adding a fresh half pint of water each time until the almond pulp has given up all its oil. You should have two pints of creamy white liquid.

Almond Milk

Put it into a large, enamelled saucepan (if you use a small one, it may bubble up and over like cow's milk) with a level teaspoonful of salt, two tablespoonfuls of rosewater and two rounded tablespoonfuls of sugar, and heat it gently, stirring from time to time, until the milk first thickens, then begins to 'break' or separate into curds and whey. Leave it to cool, then strain it in the rinsed and wrung-out bag or cloth suspended from a staff, or a convenient hook. When it has finished dripping, beat the butter briefly in the liquidiser to improve the texture, adding more salt, sugar or rosewater as you like.

Serve this smooth, milk-white butter or curd in a little glass or silver dish with a plateful of Lady Fettiplace's crisp finger biscuits (see Bisket Bread in Chapter Five). Students may prefer Nicholas Culpeper's suggestion, which is prettier still: 'This kind of butter is made of Almonds with sugar and rosewater which being eaten with violets is very wholesome and commodious for students, for it rejoiceth the heart and comforteth the brain, and qualifieth the heat of the liver.' March violets were trebly precious on account of their rarity, beauty and healing properties, 'The flowers of March Violets applied unto the browes, doe asuage the headache which cometh of too much drinking, and procureth sleep', according to

March Violets

Charles Estienne's *Countrey Farme*, a copy of which Lady Fettiplace certainly possessed by 1624, and may well have consulted before that: perhaps she served her Almond Butter with candied violets (the recipe is in the next chapter), as a snack to rejoice the heart, cure hangover and relieve mental tension.

Almond milk is a pleasant drink, soothing to the stomach whether drunk on its own or used as a basis for the creams and custards below. Lady Fettiplace treated indigestion, any weakness in the bladder or kidneys, with a bowl of mild, almond-flavoured, chicken broth or ('To make almon milk for them that have the Flix') an infusion of herbs heated to blood warm with a red-hot poker ('let the patients drink be warmed with a gad of steele'). For a frail or invalid constitution, the milk was to be made with barley water, which stabilised the emulsion, and drunk an hour before supper with mace, sugar candy and a blob of the morning's cream. A similar mixture, thickened respectively with isinglass (a gelatine made from the sturgeon's bladder), wafers, egg yolks, or ground rice and veal jelly, supplied the fresh, light, creamy puddings so popular at this period to wind up a rich meal.

TO MAKE WHITE LEACH

White Almond Leach

Take thick creame & put sugar & hole mace into it, & a pretie peece of Isinglas, as much as you think will make it stiff, & so let it boyle, a good while, then have your almonds readie blanched & pounded, with a little rose water, then take the creame from the fire, & straine the almonds into it, then set it over the fire againe, & let it boyle a pretie while longer, & when it is all boyled, put a little more rose water into it, so put it into a cleane dish, & let it stand without iogging, till it bee through cold; you must remember to lay your Isinglas in cleane water an hower or two before you goe to make your Leach.

The term 'leach' came from an old French word for slice but, though a stiff mediaeval leach was indeed turned out and served in slices, by the seventeenth century it meant something altogether less solid, and invariably sweet. Take 1 pint of cream, which will be ample for six, and heat it gently in a double boiler with 2 rounded tablespoons of sugar and a piece of mace (use nutmeg if you can't get mace). Meanwhile prepare your almond milk from 2 oz. of almonds, ground and strained with ¾ pint of rosewater, well diluted with ordinary water (I find it impossible to extract the essential oil from the almonds in less than this amount of liquid, and neat rosewater is too strong), squeezing and wringing the muslin hard until only a flavourless debris is left. Combine the almond milk and cream, and leave over a low heat while you dissolve ½ oz. of powdered gelatine in 4 more tablespoons of dilute rosewater. Mix the two together, and don't forget to strain out the mace as you pour the leach into its clean dish to set 'without iogging'. I use a square, willow-pattern china bowl, and decorate the leach with a wreath of tiny violets or primroses, or the first soft green leaves of lemon balm, or simply a few split toasted almonds.

The special characteristic of these almond creams and curds is not so much their flavour (the taste and fragrance of almonds is barely noticeable, unless you emphasise it with a few drops of real almond essence) as their suave, slippery texture, wonderfully digestible and refreshing to the palate. It comes from the emulsion of water with almond oil, which is lighter and much less rich than the egg-and-olive-oil emulsion in a mayonnaise, but has the same seductive smoothness. Lady Fettiplace gives a decidedly plain Lenten blanchmane—part way between a mediaeval blancmange, usually a chicken dish with almonds, and the modern nursery version—made from sweetened, spiced, rose-flavoured almond milk boiled, like semolina pudding, with ground rice. The result closely resembles the simple Greek pudding called *risogála*, which used to be sold in bars and cafés all over Greece in the summer instead of ice cream. Like blanchmane, *risogála* is a rice pudding set firm as a jelly, not wobbly as a custard, made from the thin local cow's milk (its characteristic gelatinous texture is clouded and spoilt by creamy English milk, unless you dilute it with water), poured out thin on round flat dinner plates to set, chilled and eaten with a sprinkling of cinnamon. Both dishes go back by different routes to the Arabs, and both have preserved the simplicity, delicacy and cooling properties of so many Arab sweets.

TO MAKE BLANCHMANE

Almond Blanchmane

Take rise & beat it then search it, then take the clearest gellie of a leg of veale & almonds blanched, then straine them with the gellie, then put to it the rise flower & rosewater & sugar, & ginger & synamon & so boile it a good while, & when it is cold serve it.

Quantities are 2 oz. ground rice to 1 pint almond milk, 2 tablespoons rosewater, 2 to 3 level tablespoons sugar with a pinch each of cinnamon and ginger. Make a thin gruel by mixing the ground rice with a little cold almond milk, bring the rest to the boil, combine the two and return to the heat, simmering and occasionally stirring for 5 to 10 minutes. Add sugar and flavourings (with if you like ¼ oz. powdered gelatine dissolved in rosewater to replace the veal jelly for an authentically stiff blanchmane). Serve it strewn with cinnamon and very cold on hot summer days, or with whipped cream on top for a richer pudding in winter.

Lady Fettiplace's blanchmane comes in a clutch of five consecutive sweet puddings, all presumably from the same source, including a rice bag pudding, an almond Creame and a Creame Called a Foole (p. 158)—both early versions of what we should now call trifle—and also this custard, which is in fact a rich almond tart with nothing Lenten about it at all:

A FRENCH CUSTARD

French Custard or Almond Tart

Take almonds, blanch them & beat them single, then put to them the yelks of eggs, then straine it with thick creame, then season with rosewater, sugar & synamon & nutmeg & some dates cut in smale peeces, harden your cofen, then put in your stuf, & so bake it.

Take ½ pint thick cream and set it to warm very gently in a thick-bottomed pan with 6 oz. almonds, blanched, skinned and coarsely ground: bought, ready-ground almonds give a nice, firm, moist consistency but less flavour. Line a 10-inch tart tin with shortcrust pastry, fill it with shells or haricot beans, and bake it blind—'harden your cofen' (coffin was the current word for any sort of container)—for 10 minutes or so in a hot oven. Now beat up 4 egg yolks and add the almond cream, a spoonful at a time to start with to prevent curdling. Lady Fettiplace seems to have strained her custard to extract the almond oil or milk, leaving the debris behind, but I prefer it left in for the sake of both texture and flavour. Add 2 tablespoons of rosewater, the spices, and 2 oz. of chopped dates. Pour your stuff into the pastry coffin, and bake it for half an hour or so (Mark 5, 190°C, 375°F), until the top is nicely puffed and browned. This tart is excellent eaten warm right away but, like many other rich almond sweetmeats, pastries and cakes, it keeps well, and will last a surprisingly long time in an airtight tin as a standby, which must have been a great point in the days when a hospitable and well-stocked sideboard served instead of tins or a freezer.

Lady Fettiplace gives three examples of the French confectioner's art, all very different, all almond-based, all closely related to contemporary practice in England. Her French Bisket Bread is a classic almond macaroon—the kind still occasionally served in France with a glass of wine at mid-morning—so I have counted it with other 'maccaroonds', marchpanes and marzipans as part of the Christmas preparations in December. My favourite of the three is this dish of little fried rice cakes:

A FRENCH DISH

Fried Rice Cakes

Blanche almonds in cold water, then beat them verie smale, then take boyled rice, & beat them together with sugar, and rosewater, then mould them in flower like flat cakes, then frie them in butter & then put sugar on them, and serve them.

For 4 oz. ground almonds and 4 oz. boiled rice, you will need 2 tablespoons rosewater and 1 or 2 rounded tablespoons of sugar, which makes a paste easily shaped into small round flat cakes for frying. I like these cakes the plainer the better so as to increase the contrast of sweetness and texture under a thick strewing of sugar at table. They are better still served with one of Sir Kenelm Digby's frothy little sauces, made from sherry, sugar and butter beaten up in the pan as soon as you have finished cooking the last batch of cakes.

For all its French name, this is one of those dishes that exemplifies Lady Fettiplace at her best. It is simple but not mean, clever in its own modest way (for only a perceptive cook would have thought of lightening the cloying marzipan richness of ground almonds with plain boiled rice, which is the cunning point of this recipe), and it has the characteristic delicacy of English home cooking in the seventeenth and eighteenth centuries before it was spoilt by the coarse, dull, bland frugality of the industrial age. Mrs Beeton's version of these rice croquettes fakes the special taste and texture of expensive ground almonds by boiling the rice in cow's milk instead, with a few drops of cheap almond flavouring, a relatively harmless and wholesome subterfuge compared to the synthetic miracles of modern technological confectionery.

The last of these Lenten delicacies is an almond cake or homely British bun, the sort of thing almost unobtainable nowadays unless you make it yourself. In Lady Fettiplace's day, too, spice cakes and buns had to be made at home because commercial bakers were forbidden by law to make or sell them except on special occasions like Good Friday and Christmas. This almond cake is first cousin to the traditional Good Friday Hot Cross Bun, and should be eaten hot-buttered, split and toasted, or best of all still warm from the oven.

TO MAKE ALMOND CAKES

Almond Buns

Take one peck of flower, one pound of sugar, one pound of almons, beaten & strained with as much ale as will stiffen your paste, put theirto three spoonfulls of barme, & a few annisseds, then woork it well together, then make it in little cakes, prick them thick for rising & bake them.

One peck of flour, generally calculated as twelve and a half pounds, would make between a hundred and fifty and three hundred good-sized buns, so I reduce the quantities to 1 lb. flour, 1½ oz. each sugar and ground almonds (it would do no harm to double this last quantity), 1 oz. fresh yeast or ½ oz. dried (ale barm was the rather more troublesome Jacobean equivalent), round about ½ pint or a small can of ale, salt and a few crushed aniseeds. If I understand this recipe right, the ground almonds were to be first infused in warm ale, then strained out, but, unless on grounds of strict authenticity, there is no need to do this: the oiliness of the almonds enriches the bun dough and so does their crumbliness, giving a nice, firm, soft texture, like the layer of almond paste baked in the centre of the Simnel bread or cake traditionally eaten on the middle Sunday—Mothering Sunday—in Lent.

Cream the yeast in the warmed ale, and leave it to froth up (or if you are using dried yeast follow the manufacturer's instructions, bearing in mind that they usually advise using twice as much as is needed). Mix the flour, sugar, ground almonds and aniseed with a heaped teaspoonful of salt in a big bowl, and make a well in the middle. Pour in the ale, 'work it well together', cover it with a cloth and leave it in a warm place to double in bulk. Now knock down your dough, knead it again and shape it into, say, ten large or twenty small buns. Leave them to prove for another 20 minutes or so, and bake them for 10 to 20 minutes in a hot oven (Mark 5, 190°C, 375°F). Their looks are much improved if you paint them with a glaze of sugar dissolved in rosewater as they come from the oven.

These plain, plump, only slightly sweet buns were often eaten with a dish of cheese melted in ale or wine—an ancient Welsh Rabbit—and they go exceedingly well, as Elizabeth David points out in *English Bread and Yeast Cookery* (1977), with slices of crumbly Cheshire or Lancashire cheese. Mrs David suggests that the aniseeds used to flavour Lenten buns probably symbolised the spring sowing of wheat. Certainly, Lady Fettiplace's almond cakes belong to the same family as the wedge-shaped wigs or spiced buns, the simnels (originally a yeast bun or cake, enriched with currants and ground almonds) and cracknels popular at this time of year from mediaeval times. These were the cakes and ale Sir Toby Belch dreaded doing without in *Twelfth Night*. Pepys reckoned wigs and ale a good Lenten supper (he also recorded his Lenten dinner menus on Good Friday, 1663—'only sugar sopps and fish'—and 1664—'an excellent Good Friday dinner of pease porridge and apple pie').

Lenten Suppers

On Fridays in Lent supper was missed out altogether, or replaced by something described in the respective household books of Sir Wiliam Cecil and his secretary, Sir William Petre, as 'Drinking at night'. Dishes of butter and half a dozen eggs were regularly supplied in Petre's household for these drinkings, which suggests buttered beer and the kind of alcoholic posset drink, spiced and thickened with eggs, that must have made a nourishing meal in itself, with or without a dish of seed buns. If the Fettiplaces, like the Cecils and Petres, followed the convivial custom of serving cakes and ale, or drinking at night, it might explain the quantities in which Lady Fettiplace made up her almond cakes. Although you can make them last several days, by toasting or re-warming them in the oven, they must have gone stale just as quickly then as now, and you would only get through a whole peck if fifty people broke their fast night and morning by eating up to half a dozen apiece.

Cracknels

Lady Fettiplace calls for another peck of flour in her recipe for cracknels, a kind of high-baked, dry biscuit made from a yeast dough mixed with white wine, flavoured with aniseed, saffron and spices, and dropped in spoonfuls into a great kettle of boiling water over the fire. The cracknels were to be fished out as they rose to the surface, dunked in cold water, dried on a napkin, pricked all over and cooked a second time in a very hot oven: a technique that goes back, according to Karen Hess, well beyond the middle ages to Roman cookery. Cracknels were one of the presents (early fruit was another) with which the pederast Hobbinol wooed Colin Cloute in Spenser's *Shepheards Calender*. They were associated from very early times with drinking in Lent, much as we now put out crisps and Twiglets when people drop in for a drink.

There are also a number of Fettiplace caudles and possets made from warm milk or cream, eggs and butter, beaten with sugar and grated nutmeg, then curdled by pouring in ale and sherry. These were semi-solid drinks, supped from a bowl, designed to revive people coming in chilled to the bone after travelling or working all day in the fields: one of Elinor's is called 'a Cawdle for restoritie'. P. C. D. Brears, in *The Gentlewoman's Kitchen*, quotes Henry Best of Elmsworth, a seventeenth-century Yorkshire farmer, boiling up a hot posset at noon to encourage his men sheep-dipping in waist-high, ice-cold water in June. Substantial, strengthening drinks for people often too exhausted to digest a full meal developed into more sophisticated stimulants like the nineteenth-century nightcap and negus, egg flip, milk punch and the charmingly genteel, port wine based pick-me-up, given in Dorothy Hartley's *Food in England*, called Spinster's Blush. In the seventeenth century they were served in specially shaped, earthenware or silver posset pots, sometimes with a tube running from the base of the pot to its rim, like a straw, so that the drinker might suck up the liquid from the bottom without dipping his beard in the froth on top. Lady Fettiplace's cousin, Dorothy Unton, had a 'little silver cawdle-cupp', which she left in her will to Elinor's sister Frances. Here is a posset which should be approached warily, bearing in mind Miss Hartley's warning that 'a caudel was served *before* a meal, a posset was taken *instead* of a meal':*

TO MAKE A POSSETT

Posset Drink

Take the heade of yor milcke, boyle it then take the yelkes of 4 egges and beate them mingleinge them w^t^h some cowld milcke, then put grated bred, Nutmeggs, and sugger, into yor milcke, when yor milcke boyles on the ffire putt it all in, stirringe it once Rownde *then powre it into A Bason, sett it on the fire till it boyle, then put in yor Secke and ale, and stirr it once aboute to the botome, and soe lett it stand untill the Crudde* Riseth

The head of the milk I take to be the foamy 'top of the mornings milk', probably a couple of pints which is the most an ordinary posset pot could conveniently hold. The mixture, heated and stirred and left to stand for half an hour before the fire, would set like a custard, or it might be stirred again to make curds and whey. The 'crudde' or curd rising to the top was as highly prized in this warming winter drink as the froth on summer syllabubs (see p. 115), made from rich creamy milk spurted into, or beaten up with, sherry or white wine. Contemporary recipes for both include instructions for pouring the liquid in from a height, at arm's length,

*Also Mr Brears' cautionary tale in *The Gentlewoman's Kitchen*: 'The first time I served a posset at the end of evening meal, the effects were quite surprising. Conversation ceased entirely, as fifteen guests succumbed to its potent richness from which they barely recovered throughout the remainder of the evening ...'

so as to trap the air and bring up the foam. This is what is meant, I think, by 'brew it together' in the following instructions to make a simple hot buttered posset 'for the cold': a cupful of mixed ale and sack is to be heated up in a pan, poured onto the beaten egg in its shaker (use a screw-topped glass jar), then poured backwards and forwards between the two containers as in A Drinke to Strengthen, on p. 217.

Hot Buttered Posset

Make a posset of half ale, & half sack & take of the curd, then take an egg shell & all, & put it in a pot with some sugar & butter & a nutmeg grated, shake it all together till the egg bee all broken, then put the posset drink to it, and brew it together, and so drink it.

March was the month for brewing the best beer: 'they [the English] have March beere, Household beere and smal beere,' wrote Charles Estienne in *The Countrey Farme*, going on to explain that a quarter of good barley malt would produce at the first brewing a hogshead of March beer, at the second a hogshead of thinner household beer, and at the third a barrel of the thinnest small beer: 'the first is for strangers, the second for the Master, Mistress and the better sort of the familie, and the third is for plowmen or hinde servants'. Lady Fettiplace calls for a quart of 'march beere' to be distilled with three quarts of sack and a pound of bruised cinnamon into a potent Cinnamon Water (still, among other things, a highly effective cold cure). She also roasted apples and hard warden pears in brown paper parcels, tightly twisted and wetted to prevent the paper from catching alight, a method still worth trying with an open fire or in the embers of a charcoal barbecue when meat is being grilled on the grid above (these baked pears are an aside in a prescription for headache powders, made by drying the pounded leaves, flowers and seedheads of the *Carduus benedictus* or blessed thistle: 'put it in a paper, hard together, & wet the paper as you doo to rost wardens, & so lay it on a clean herth, & a good many charcole on it, & so let it burn as long as you perceive it to smoke, & when it leaves smoking take it out ...').

Roasted Apples and Pears

It is pleasant to think of strangers at Appleton manor, or Besselsleigh, sitting round the fire with bowls of March beer, eating cracknels and almond cakes, roasting wardens and waiting for the curd to rise on a newly mixed sack posset in the hearth. Sir Francis Bacon regularly drank a good draught of March beer last thing at night, according to Aubrey, to calm his mind after writing and help him sleep. His distant kinswoman, Elinor Fettiplace, treated strain, tension and palpitations in her household with a whole range of soothing and sedative nightcaps like this one:

FOR THE PASHION OF THE HARTE

Boyle Marigoldes, Egremonie, and Burage in Possett drinke, sweeten it w^t^h suger and let the patiente drinke it goeinge to, bed

Medicinal Posset

4
APRIL

The Berkshire traveller Thomas Baskerville, making a journey to Bristol after the civil war, stopped off to see Lady Fettiplace's great-grandson, 'Mr. Fettiplace, my loving friend', in the manor house 'beautified with fine gardens' at Kingston Bagpuize. The Fettiplaces had by this time sold Appleton and Besselsleigh to the Speaker of the House of Commons, Sir William Lenthall, whose grandson was also busy enhancing his estates with another fine garden, which Baskerville managed to glimpse from the road as he rode by towards Burford: 'As for the town of Burford, 'tis seated by a river on the declivity of a hill in a delicate air, having such rare hills about it for hunting and racing that it tempts gentlemen far and near to come hither to take their pastime. These hills are adorned with many flowers and plants, among the best the Paschal, or Pulsatilla, flowers in the Easter time do very much adorn these downs.'

Easter, when the downs beyond Appleton were carpeted by pasque-flowers or wild anemones, meant an end to the punishing Lenten diet with fresh young spring greens, spring lambs, calves and the very first sweet, grass-fed mutton. Dinner on Easter Day, after six weeks of boiled mudfish, salt cod and pickled herrings, must have been one of the gastronomical high points of the whole year. The Ingatestone Hall menu for Easter Sunday, April 17, 1552, included two roast and three boiled joints of beef, a whole hindquarter of veal, a capon and eight pigeons with more veal, pigeons and four joints of mutton for supper. Here is Lady Fettiplace's recipe for boiled mutton. Don't be put off by the widespread English horror of boiled meats which must, I suppose, be another folk memory of degenerate institutional cooking in schools, hotels and boarding houses haunted by the dreadful smell, and even more dreadful sight, of overcooked cabbage sitting in thin greasy broth with cheap cuts of meat boiled to rags for far too long in far too much water with nothing to flavour or enrich it. Lady Fettiplace's recipe goes back long before that to the same European tradition as the much romanticised French *pot-au-feu.* Properly cooked, a boiled leg of mutton should be moist, tender and succulent. This one is served not with that comparative upstart, mint sauce—not even with redcurrant or rowanberry jelly—but with a sauce made from the meat juices and a glass of white wine, thickened with egg yolks, and sharpened with lemon and a dash of wine vinegar. The result is not unlike the pleasant French custom of serving a *sauce béarnaise* with lamb.

TO STEW MUTTON

Boiled Mutton with White Wine Sauce

*Take a legge of mutton boyle it in water and salte untill it bee allmost boyled, then slice it in prety bigge piecces, put it in a dish save the gravie w*t*h the muton, and put some white wine and a little grose peper unto it, soe let it stew till it bee allmost redy, then beate the yelkes of three egges w*t*h some wine vinegere and put to it stir it still after you have put in yo*r *egges, then serve it uppon sippets and slice a limond smale the meate and rinde & stir it amonge it, but you must not stue it w*t*h the rest, for it will cause yo*r *limonde to tast bitter.*

You will need a cooking pot with a lid, just big enough to hold your leg of mutton (which, unless you are lucky at the butcher's, may well have to be spring lamb) comfortably. Add a tablespoonful of salt and enough cold water barely to cover the meat. Bring it very slowly to the boil, removing the scum which rises to the top with a slotted spoon. Cover the pan and leave it to simmer on the lowest possible heat so that the water never does more than barely tremble in the middle. Two hours should be long enough for a trimmed, medium-sized leg of lamb weighing round about four pounds. But, to follow Lady Fettiplace's instructions exactly, you must stop the meat cooking before it is done—say, after one and a half hours—carve it in thick slices, and leave it to finish cooking gently in its own juices with pepper and a glass of white wine in a shallow covered dish in the oven for half an hour or so. A second, very similar recipe for stewing a shoulder of mutton includes at this point 'some of the broth wherein he was boyled wth . . . a hoale mace and a bundle of smale hearbes' (parsley, thyme and marjoram with perhaps a sprig of rosemary or mint).

When you are ready to make the sauce, strain off the meat juices, make them up to half a pint if necessary with a little of the broth, add a tablespoonful of white wine vinegar and boil the mixture for a few minutes. Now add this gravy, little by little for fear of curdling, to the three beaten egg yolks in their bowl. Gradually thicken the sauce over a very gentle heat, in a double boiler if you have one, stirring it still after you have put in your eggs, until it will coat the back of your wooden spoon. Pour it over the meat in its dish, and decorate with a whole, finely sliced lemon.

An alternative method, which may be more convenient if you haven't a big enough pan or feel safer with roasting techniques, is simply to roast the mutton in the usual way (1½ hours at Mark 4, 180°C, 350°F for a medium-sized leg). Pour off the fat at the end and use the meat juices in the pan, with a small glass of white wine, a tablespoon of vinegar and a cupful of added stock, as a basis for your sauce. This was what I did the first few times I tried this dish, being thoroughly apprehensive at the thought of boiled meat, and it was excellent.

Whichever method you choose, the result will be a jug or sauce-boat full of well-flavoured sauce thick enough to pour over the meat in the modern manner, either before or after it comes to table. Seventeenth-century cooks seem to have preferred on the whole a runnier sauce that could be served, as in this case, 'upon sippets'. Sippets were slices of dried or toasted bread laid in the bottom of a deep dish to soak up any sauce, soup, gravy or juice poured over them. The custom went back to mediaeval trenchers or plates, made from thick coarse bread and meant to be eaten (or gathered up in baskets for distribution to the poor) at the end of a meal. It still survives in the pieces of pale yellow dried bread or *croutes* served in France in a bowl of onion soup or *garbure*. French onion soup is invariably eaten this way. Even in England, the habit has not died out altogether. It lingers on at one end of the social scale in the triangles of fried or toasted bread served under any sort of game bird and, at the other, in the national fondness for hot snacks on toast.

Sippets

Lady Fettiplace served nearly everything from poached carp to eggs—'To potch eggs'—on sippets. Anyone accustomed to baked beans or sardines or for that matter poached eggs on toast will easily get the hang of this technique, which is simple enough provided you pay attention to one or two tricky points. Sir Kenelm Digby, addressing the subject with characteristic thoroughness, specifies that sippets should be made from the best bread ('Take light spungy fine white French-bread . . .'), sliced, dried before the fire to a pale biscuit colour, then laid in a warm dish over a gentle heat and moistened with gravy, or broth, a single ladleful at a time, 'no more than the bread can presently drink up'. The process was to be repeated two or three times, care being taken not to overdo the liquid ('None to swim thin over'), or leave the sippets to soak and swell for more than a quarter of an hour ('if it be too long, it will grow glewy and stick to the dish'). Digby's precise instructions show the importance he attached to taking trouble with even the homeliest dish, something well understood by Lady Fettiplace and observed in her final caution about adding the sliced lemon only at the last minute for fear of bitterness.

When I first tried this recipe for the sake of the sauce, it took me a long time to overcome my prejudice against boiled meat, longer still to trust Lady Fettiplace sufficiently to experiment with sippets. The results were remarkable, both for flavour and—quite as important to Jacobean and Stuart cooks—texture. Don't cut your bread too thick, or take too much. One small square or triangle per person is enough. Use some of the mutton broth (this is Lady Fettiplace's own advice in her second recipe for stewed mutton), reduced if you have time by fast boiling, and follow Digby's directions. The sippets will generally drink up between a half and a whole pint, ladled into the serving dish every so often while you are making the sauce: the same principle still applies to the making of a traditional bread sauce, spiced with cloves and nutmeg, to serve with chicken or turkey at Christmas, an old English survival that always amazes the French. Serve the meat on its bed of sippets in a deep oval or rectangular platter with a border of the thinnest possible lemon wheels.

Bread Sauce

Boiled mutton is especially good—some say even better—next day, eaten cold with salads and perhaps some chopped capers or Lady Fettiplace's own pickled cucumbers and artichokes (pp. 143–4). Hot, it is nice with the buttered spinach on p. 43, or with almost any other fresh green vegetable boiled, as Digby advises, separately, fast and very briefly in a little of the meat broth. He suggests turnips (first fried lightly in butter), cabbage or chicory in winter, sorrel with lettuce, borage and bugloss or new green peas in early summer. If Lady Fettiplace and her contemporaries seldom give individual vegetable dishes, it is perhaps because this ancient and admirable custom of serving boiled, buttered greens or 'potherbs' with meat was too familiar for anyone to bother writing it down.

The broth left over from a boiled leg of mutton makes a good basis for soup, thickened with vegetables or with the egg-and-herb mixture described below:

TO MAKE BROTH

Mutton Broth with Egg and Herbs

Take mutton & boile it in water, then scum of all the fatt, then take small herbs, & chop them small, then take the yolks of ten hard eggs, & chop them with the herbs, then put them to the mutton and some pepper and salt, & so let it boile togither well, when it is well boyled put in some sweet butter, and so serve it.

Leave the stewing liquor to stand overnight or until it is thoroughly cold, when its lid of white mutton fat (particularly good for cooking) can be lifted clean off. The amount of broth will vary, depending on the size and shape of your pan, the size of the mutton and the speed at which you cooked it, but it will almost certainly need to be somewhat reduced by fast boiling to improve the flavour. Chop a generous handful of small herbs—parsley, thyme, marjoram and anything else you can lay hands on, chervil, winter savory, chives, perhaps a little mint. Pound them to a paste with the hardboiled egg yolks (four or five is enough for a medium-sized tureen of soup, say one and a half pints), and gradually incorporate a ladleful of broth until you have a thick sauce that can be added to the rest of the broth in its pan. Reheat the soup—'boile' in this context means simmer at most—taste for seasoning, and don't forget the final knob of butter. A splash of white wine or sherry, often included in contemporary recipes, would do no harm either. This is a simple and excellent way of making soup from any well-flavoured meat or chicken stock, especially good with the rich liquor from the next recipe.

Another, very ancient way of using up leftover mutton broth is to cook a chicken in it. Here is Lady Fettiplace's version of the mediaeval method of boiling a chicken with potherbs and dried fruit, a technique still going strong in Scotch cockie-leekie where leeks and prunes take the place of Lady Fettiplace's lettuce and raisins:

TO BOYLE CHICKENS

Boiled Chicken with Egg and Verjuice or Lemon Sauce

Take a peece of mutton and boyle in water and salte, scum it cleane then put into it a peece of sweete butter and a handfull of the best Lettuse you can gett w^t^h some large mace, and Reasons of the Sunne, then put in the Chickens and lett them boyle well therin, when you dish it upp take the yelkes of 3 eggs and a little vergis w^t^h some sugger, beate it well together and put it into yor Chichen broath, Lett it boyle noe more after you have put in these thinges, but serve upe yor Chickens on sippets

Simmer one reasonable-sized chicken, weighing three and a half to four pounds, or two small ones, very gently indeed in the mutton broth with a handful each of raisins and well-washed lettuce leaves, a few blades of mace or a scrap of nutmeg, and a knob of butter (this last might be omitted unless you are using a lean, stringy boiling fowl). About an hour is usually long enough for a roasting bird, at least twice as long for a boiler, but be sure not to overdo it or you will end up with a superlative broth and no flavour to speak of left in the chicken.

The careful instructions for dishing up at the end of this recipe explain how to make the sort of basic sauce that will go with almost anything: the Greeks call it *avgolemono* and still serve it, made exactly as Lady Fettiplace describes, with chicken, fish or little fried meatcakes. The French elaborated and refined on it in the eighteenth century to make *sauce hollandaise*, *sauce béarnaise* and a whole range of variations on the same reduction of white wine or vinegar ('vergis', or verjuice, is the sharp, slightly fermented juice of sour grapes or crab apples), thickened with egg yolks and butter. The English simply forgot all about it which is a pity since, even in this plainest possible form, it makes a pleasant and very easy sauce for boiled meats.

Lemon juice is generally the most convenient modern substitute for verjuice in Lady Fettiplace's recipes, and for this dish you will need the juice of half a large lemon. Beat it up in a bowl with the three egg yolks and a teaspoon of sugar, gradually incorporate a cupful of the hot broth, and thicken the sauce, stirring all the time, over a gentle heat—'Lett it boyle noe more after you have put in these things'—in a double boiler. A nut of butter is a decided improvement: cut it up and stir it in at the end, instead of adding it first to the broth. A remarkable soup may be made from any remaining stock, crushed with the lettuce and raisins through a mouli or sieve, then finished off according to Lady Fettiplace's instructions To make Broth.

Chicken Broth

Don't be alarmed by the mention of sugar in this sauce, or by the raisins which sweeten, darken and enrich the broth, giving an emphasis surprisingly different from the herb-and-onion or garlic-based stocks and soups we are used to today. For other, equally unfamiliar ways of serving chicken, see the lemony, pale green, herb-and-gooseberry sauce, on p. 124, and the rich, dark, spinach sauce on p. 190. Sugar, still an expensive novelty in the early seventeenth century, was used a great deal less lavishly than it is now: Lady Fettiplace, who put little or no sugar in her fruit cakes, pancakes and some of her puddings, added it sparingly to savoury dishes as a seasoning, much as you might still stir in a pinch of sugar to bring out the sweetness in a dish of carrots or peas, a Provençal beef stew or a tomato soup. Here is that prolific man of letters, Gervase Markham (who boiled his chickens with a parsley stuffing that was minced small at the end to thicken the sauce), elucidating principles that hold good to this day for sharpening, sweetening and generally adjusting the flavour of a soup or sauce: 'And when a broth is too sweet, so sharpen it with verjuyce; and when too tart, so sweeten it with Sugar; when flat and wallowish, so quicken it with Oranges and Lemons; and when too bitter, so make it pleasant with Herbs and spices.'

Vegetables or Potherbs and Salads

Herbs included anything on the long lists of greenstuff frequently included in books like Markham's *English House-Wife*, where vegetables were not treated separately but subsumed, as in Lady Fettiplace's book, under soups, sauces, potherbs and the extraordinary profusion of salads eaten summer and winter, raw or cooked, pickled or plain, dressed with olive oil and vinegar. Garden produce, judging at any rate by contemporary writers on household and estate management, was not only a vital part of the everyday diet but available in far greater variety than any greengrocer—or any but the keenest amateur gardener—could hope to supply today. John Evelyn's famous salad calendar (first published in 1664, reprinted in 1979 in Jane Grigson's *Food with the Famous*) is a planting scheme organised to provide the cook with fresh green leaves, stalks or roots in every single month of the year.

Kitchen Gardens

Lady Fettiplace herself, who had a copy of Charles Estienne's *Countrey Farme* given her by Sir Henry Danvers, must have known Estienne's substantial section on planning, planting, watering, weeding and tending the herb and vegetable plots (which included at least four sorts of lettuce—the curled, the round-headed, the cabbage or Roman, and the little lettuce). The kitchen garden with its flower borders, its separate beds or 'floores' each assigned to a different vegetable or sweet herb, its camomile seats and rose arbours, was as crucial to the network of supply and demand as the brew-house or dairy, and demanded as much of the housewife's attention. Lady Fettiplace's contemporaries at Longleat grumbled about it ('I confess ... it is true my garden is too ruinous, and yet to make you more merrier you shall be of my counsel, that my intent is, before it be better to make it worse ...', wrote Maria Thynne to her mother-in-law round about 1605: 'I intend to plough it up and sew all variety of fruit trees at a fit season. I beseech you laugh, and so will I at your captiousness'). Even the pious Lady Hoby—sister-in-law to Elinor Fettiplace's cousin, Dorothy Unton—interrupted her devotional round to record gardening as one of the pleasures of spring in her diary on April 4, 1600: 'this day I performed my accustomed exercises, I praise God, and was allmost all the after none in the Gardene sowinge seed ...'

Elinor Fettiplace devoted a whole page of her book—'To set or sow all manner of herbs'—to the question of successive plantings, pricking-out, earthing-up, feeding, pruning, cutting and harvesting, so as to be able to pick something fresh all the year round:

The best moneth is aprill in the wane of the moone, at Midsomer in the wane of the moone sow all manner of potherbs, & they wilbee greene for winter; Also Lettice seeds sowne at this tyme and removed when they bee of a prettie bignes at the full wilbee good and hard Lettice at Michaelmas [29 September] ... Sow red Cabage seed after Allhallowentide [October 31], twoe dayes after the moone is at the full, & in March take up the plants & set from fowre foot each from other, you shall have faire Cabages for the Sumer: then sow some Cabage seeds a day after the full moone in Marche, then remove your plants about Midsomer, & they wilbee good for winter ...

Lettuce and Cabbage

Radishes, cucumber and artichokes were part of this plan, as well as flowers, all of which reappeared on the dinner table in salads dressed on their dishes in patterns as beguiling as the plats, beds and borders in which they were grown. John Nott, in his *Cooks and Confectioners Dictionary* (1726), gives a 'grand Sallad for the Spring' which must go back at least to Lady Fettiplace's day, if not before. Lettuce, spinach, watercress and other greens, alternating with pickled samphire and broom buds, capers, olives, raisins, currants and nuts, were to be arranged in a series of concentric rings or shallow circular steps rising, like the great terraced gardens at Sapperton, to a castle in the centre of the mound, carved from a turnip and gilded with egg yolk, containing a little green tree stuck with spring flowers. Markham advised laying out salads for a special occasion to look like bunches of flowers— 'some full blown, some half blown and some in the bud'—using crystallised flower petals with stalks and sheaths of green purslane, and finely cut cucumber foliage.

A Grand Salad for the Spring

Spring flowers were the first of the year's seasonal harvests to be gathered in, dried, powdered, squeezed, infused or distilled into medicinal oils, ointments and healing waters. Perhaps nothing illustrates more vividly the gulf between us and our pre-industrial ancestors than their lavish harvesting of the wild flowers we are forbidden by law to dig up, in some cases even to pick at all. Lady Fettiplace's Aqua Mirabilis calls for a quart of the juice of celandines, 'this water must be stilled in Aprill, before the sallendine goeth to seede'; her violet syrup for between four and six pints—getting on for a gallon—of flower petals. You could no more attempt these preparations nowadays than you could make cowslip balls, or Lady Fettiplace's own Balles of Violetts ('Take the best blew Violets that you can get . . .'), which were mauve, scented cachous for clearing the head, following Pliny who recommended a garland of violets for hangover headaches. Shakespeare's son-in-law, Dr Hall of Stratford-upon-Avon, a town famous for its violets, prescribed a cooling violet syrup as part of his treatment for the poet Michael Drayton suffering from a tertian fever. Lady Fettiplace gives four separate versions of what must have been a pretty and refreshing spring drink, well worth trying as a basis for sherbets and sorbets if you cultivate your own violet beds. Alternatively, it would work just as well, if not better, with garden violas or purple pansies, or with the flower-sellers' deep dark double Parma violets.

TO MAKE SIRROP OF VIOLETTS

Syrup of Violets

First make a thicke sirop of suger and clarifie yt well, then take blew violetts and picke them well from the whights then put them in the sirrop, let them lye in yt 24 howres keepinge yt warme in the meane time, then straine these violetts out and put in fresh, so do 4 times then set them on the fire, let them simper a good while but not boyle fast put in some Juice of limonds in the boyleinge then straine yt and keepe yt to yo[r] *use.*

Quantities for the syrup are a pint of water to a pound of sugar (no need to clarify factory-refined sugar), and one pint at a time of stripped flower petals (another, similar recipe advises replacing the petals six, not four times). Important points are, first, to nip off the stems and base of the petals, and use only the blue or purple parts of the flower; second, to reheat the water each time you change the flowers, and to keep it in a warm place, close covered, in the intervals; third, to let the syrup 'simper' but never boil in the final stage.

Markham takes it for granted that any competent housewife proposing to garnish a salad 'for better curiosity and the fine adorning of the Table' would have pots of colours to hand in the stillroom ('First, if you set forth any Red-flower, that you know or have seen, you shall take your pots of preserved Gilliflowers ... And if you will set forth yellow Flowers, take the pots of Primroses and Cowslips: if blue Flowers then pots of Violets or Bugloss Flowers'), just as she would have coloured silks for winter embroidery. Lady Fettiplace undoubtedly did. Her instructions for preserving gilliflowers are on p. 146, and she gives four, more or less complicated ways of crystallising flower petals, of which the simplest is perhaps best for the fragile flowers of early spring:

CANDIE FLOWERS

Candied Flowers

Take your flowers, & spread them abroad on a paper, then clarifie sugar as you doo for rock candie, let it boile till it bee more then candie height, then put in your flowers with the stalks upward, & the flowers downeward, as soone as they bee through wet in the syrupe take them out, & with a knife spread them abroad on a pieplate, & set them where they may dry.

Take a pound of sugar for the syrup with just enough water—say quarter of a pint—to moisten it (again modern refined sugar makes the preliminary clarification unnecessary). Heat gently, stirring occasionally, until the sugar has dissolved, then boil hard until the syrup passes 'candie height' (240°F, 115°C, on the sugar thermometer), which is when it will form a soft ball in cold water, or a short thread between your thumb and forefinger. Lady Fettiplace gives admirably clear directions for gauging this stage of the syrup in her recipe for Rock Candie: 'let it boile till it bubble up in great bubbles, then dip your finger in it, & pull them asunder, & when it drawes out in a string betweene your fingers, & breaks in the middle, & shrinks upward like a worme, it is inoughe.' Let the syrup cool before you dip the flowers if you want them to keep their shape.

There are other recipes for rose or violet sweets—To Make Cakes of all Kind of Flowers—and for a more elaborate process involving special confectioner's equipment, 'an earthen pan' fitted with wire trays to hold the flowers immersed for twenty-four hours in syrup. This primitive Jacobean version of a modern crystallising tin belongs with a whole range of hot and cold water stills, stoppered pots, grinding stones, drying racks and pierced boards, presses, mortars, limbecks and charcoal braziers called for in Lady Fettiplace's manuscript. She must already have possessed the nucleus of that traditional country-house paraphernalia discovered by Florence Nightingale's sister, Parthenope, when she married a Verney of Claydon in 1858, and set about sorting the family papers, routing out their portraits and rummaging among 'the remains of queer tin vessels of many shapes, with spouts at all angles, in the ancient cupboards of the Claydon stillroom'.

The family letters at Claydon contain several references to hot and flustered Verney women in the seventeenth century toiling over their stoves in the soft fruit season, endlessly potting up fruit and flowers for the winter, for salads and to decorate the dishes of curds and cream Lady Fettiplace herself liked so much. Her Fresh Cheese with cream poured over it is the classic French *fromage frais à la crème*, still now, as it was then, one of the simplest and most exquisite of all spring and summer puddings. Here is the recipe for what is, with the Barley Cream on page 231, almost my favourite thing in her whole book:

TO MAKE A FRESH CHEESE

A Fresh Cheese with Cream (1)

Take a quart of Cream boile it in some mace, then beat the whites of 4 egges, & put into it, & a little rennet, let it boile & stir it still till you see it turne, then put it in a cloth, & hang it up, when it will drop no more, beat it with rose water & sugar, then make it like a fresh cheese, & put cream about it & serve it.

The point of this dish—as Elizabeth David pointed out in *An Omelette and a Glass of Wine*, describing an almost identical fresh cheese eaten twenty years ago on the banks of the Loire—is the contrast between the cheese itself and its veiling of cream: 'not too thick, not rich, not yellow, appearing cream-coloured only because the cheese it half-concealed and half-revealed ... was so muslin-white and new'. For the sake of this contrast, I prefer to make the cheese itself with milk rather than cream. You could of course use bought cheese curds (*not* cottage cheese), which should be fairly moist and not too stiff, but it would be a pity to leave out the egg whites which seem to stabilise the curd, and in any case the taste is never the same. The success of a dish like this, which depends on its simplicity and absolute purity, can be ruined by the faintest hint of chemical preservative in the background. But, contrary to popular belief, it is perfectly possible—and not at all difficult—to 'turn' ordinary pasteurised (*not* Longlife) milk with commercial junket rennet. I have made this recipe both ways, using the pasteurised milk commonly sold by supermarkets and newsagents in bottles or cardboard boxes, and, when on holiday, using fresh, untreated, 'cowe hott milcke' begged from the farmer down the lane. The only difference I could see between the two was that raw milk sets solid, or 'turns', much quicker and more firmly: there was no discernible difference in taste, and both in the end yielded the slippery mass of curds and whey needed to make a fresh cheese.

To Turn Milk with Rennet

Warm two pints of milk to just over blood heat with mace, if you can get it, or a fag end of nutmeg (don't on any account forget to remove this when you put the cheese in the electric mixer). Whip four egg whites till they are frothy but not stiff, and amalgamate them with the milk in its pan off the fire. Add two teaspoons of rennet, cover the pan with a clean tea towel and leave it in a warm place to set solid. I don't advise you to 'let it boile' again; Lady Fettiplace's untreated farmyard rennet may have been more robust than the stuff we buy in little bottles from the chemist today (Mrs Beeton in the nineteenth century was still using 'a small piece of rennet', or calf's stomach procured from the butcher, to set her junkets). She seems in any case to be using the word 'boil' in a much gentler sense than it has now. As soon as the curd has set, hang it up to drain in a cheese cloth or muslin bag according to the instructions for Almond Butter on p. 79. Do this in the morning if the cheese is to be eaten at night, and don't leave it longer than three or four hours or it may turn out too firm and dry.

Now, either sieve the cheese (there may not be much—probably about half a pound), and beat it with a pinch of salt and one or two tablespoons each of rosewater and sugar; or blend the whole lot in an electric food processor. This last process is essential to get rid of lumps and produce a silky smooth finish. Taste as you go, but remember that the cheese should be only faintly rose-flavoured and barely sweet so that you can serve it with more sugar to strew on at table. Spoon it out into a small glass or china dish, leaving room to put cream about it. You will need about half a pint, which should be plenty for four people. Alternatively, if you have a heart-shaped cheese mould, line it with damp muslin and leave the cheese overnight, turning it out next day onto a flat dish with the cream poured over.

A second fresh cheese, supplied by a different source and separated from the first by nearly a hundred pages, is very similar both to the one above, and to the version offered to Mrs David by a French café proprietress in 1965. I include it to show the sort of tinkering that overtakes a recipe as it is passed from hand to hand through space and time. This one is produced in much larger quantities, and beaten up with yolks rather than whites of egg. The result is creamier, no longer pure muslin white, perhaps less subtle, though the spicing of cinnamon is excellent and remained a precious flavouring for creams and ice creams right down to Victorian times (Mrs Beeton used it in her Devonshire junket), when it fell out of favour for reasons I don't understand.

TO MAKE A FRESH CHEESE & CREAME

A Fresh Cheese and Cream (2)

Take a pottle of new milk, a quart of creame, put therin a stick of cinamon, & set it on the fire, have in readines the yelks of twoe eggs beaten, when it boiles up put them in, then take it from the fire, & let it stand, then put in as much rennet, as will turne it, then put it in a cloth, & let it hang will it bee drie. then season it with rose water, & sugar, & serve it.

A pottle is two quarts or four pints (exact quantities are not important in recipes like these, so it makes no odds whether you go by the English or U.S. pint), making six pints in all with the cream, so I generally make half quantities. Use powdered cinnamon if you haven't a cinnamon stick (a one inch length is probably enough). Mix the beaten egg yolk—one yolk to three pints of combined milk and cream—with several spoonfuls of the hot milk first, before adding it to the rest, and leaving the panful to stand till it is no more than tepid before adding the rennet. Follow the instructions given for the first of these fresh cheeses, and don't forget a seasoning of salt at the end.

In so far as I can make out the whole vexed question of curds and whey—cheese curds, 'wild curds', buttermilk, clabbered milk, and yoghurt cultures, all now hopelessly bedevilled by commercial standardisation and government regulations—the term 'wealcruds', or veal curds, in the next recipe means curdled milk from the stomach of a sucking calf or veal. I use ordinary cheese curds instead, made as in the two recipes above. Creame of Wealcruds is a somewhat unappealing title for a highly appealing, suave, rich cream, to be eaten with a teaspoon from small cups or glasses, by itself, or, if you like, with fingers of the fine Bisket Bread on p. 119.

TO MAKE A CREAME OF WEALCRUDS

A Cream of Curds

Take the thickest wealcruds three or fowre spoonfulls of rosewater, two spoonefulls of Sack, the yolks of two egs, & some sugar, beat it all well together with a spoone, & so serve it.

Quantities for a small helping—say a coffee-cupful—each for four people are ½ lb. moist cheese curds, 4 tablespoons of rosewater, 2 of the best sherry, 2 egg yolks and 1 rounded tablespoon of sugar.

Beat the eggs with the sugar till they are thick and frothy, and gradually blend in the sieved cheese curd, rosewater and sherry, beating hard, a process that takes no time at all in an electric mixer.

The distinction between drained cheese curds and the much runnier 'wealcruds' (which might need stiffening with breadcrumbs) is clear from Lady Fettiplace's Cheese Cakes, her only version of a very old English favourite as popular today as it was in the middle ages.

TO MAKE CHEESE CAKES

Cheese Cakes

First make the crust with warme water & good store of butter, put the butter in cold & so mould it together, then take weal curds & yolks of eggs, & crums of bread, & rosewater, & currans & a nutmeg & some sugar, temper it well together & so bake it, in the crust; if you will make them with cheesecurds put in no crums of bread, but temper the curd with good store of butter; Before you make the cheese Cakes hang the curds up in a cloth, that the whey may drop out of it, if they bee made with whey curds.

The initial instructions for making pastry suggest some sort of cross between a hot-water crust (which would have produced a sturdy, long-lasting, probably free-standing pie case), and short or even puff paste made with cold butter. All three techniques were already familiar to Elizabethan cooks. I generally use a deep shortcrust tart shell, about 10 inches across, baked blind for 10 to 15 minutes in a hot oven. While it is cooking, beat 3 egg yolks little by little into ½ lb. of well-drained curds, sieved or blended with 3 oz. of butter. Now beat in 3 tablespoons of rosewater, 2 rounded tablespoons of sugar, another 2 of currants and some grated nutmeg. Pour the filling into its pastry case and bake for 30 to 45 minutes in a medium oven (Mark 4, 180°C, 350°F), bearing in mind the classic caution from Elizabeth Raffald's eighteenth-century cookery book: 'As to Cheese-cakes, they should not be made long before you back them ... for standing makes them oil and grow sad, a moderate oven bakes them best if it is too hot it burns them and takes off the Beauty and a very slow oven makes them sad and look black; make your Cheesecakes up just when the oven is of a proper heat, and they will rise well and be of a proper Colour.'

Beauty in a cheese cake, as indeed in any other pudding, was always a cardinal point. Lady Fettiplace's creams and sweet cream cheeses, leaches, fools and trifles may be garnished with candied cowslips, violets, rose petals, or perhaps with fine slices of the dark red raspberry, rosehip and plum cheeses preserved the autumn before. All these were, as Markham said, 'both for show and use, for they are more excellent to taste, than for to look on'. This decorative sense, so vivid in English cookery books of the period, was still running strongly three hundred years later in fantastic confections of hothouse fruit and spun sugar flowers at the Edwardian dinner table. But it also persisted on a humbler level in the unselfconscious, 'old-fashioned', country farmhouse garnishes described by Dorothy Hartley in the early years of this century: 'A perfectly plain white shape would be turned out on a dish as white, and garnished with scarlet geranium. Maidenhair fern was popular for jellies (being very light and tremblingly appropriate). A sturdy brown chocolate mould would have queer little sticks of cinnamon stuck into it with bay leaves at the ends ... "Dish creams" (i.e. soft creams that had to be ladled out with a spoon) would be poured into a glass dish, which was set down on a circle of tiny flowers or bright leaves.'

Decorating White Creams

The wide range of drinks traditionally made at home seems to have lasted almost as long, lingering in country farmhouses sometimes right up to the 1940s. 'When English workers *made* their drinks, they made strong beer and good wine,' wrote Miss Hartley, recalling the brewing copper still in regular use in her own home in her childhood: 'now they *buy* weak beer and gas waters.' Home-made apricot, gooseberry, currant, raspberry and cherry wines are given in Chapter Six, and Chapter Seven includes Lady Fettiplace's Cooleinge Julepp—barley water flavoured and coloured with lemons, red roses and violets—which makes a nice change from fizzy lemonade, coke, tonic and other gas waters. Stronger stomachs may care to experiment with the meads which varied in type and strength as much as home-made, West country farm ciders still do today. Mead, like beer, was brewed on the premises all the year round, enriched with the first honey taken from the hives in early autumn, spiced with gilliflowers or clove carnations in high summer, flavoured at this time of year with spring flowers and herbs or, as in Lady Fettiplace's recipe below, with imported citrus fruits.

Meads and Metheglins

Her instructions are for small mead, made from eight or nine parts of water to one of honey, to be drunk at meals like small beer, and ready for consumption quite soon. Stronger meads might keep for years. Sir Kenelm Digby, an expert on the subject, collected from his friends and acquaintances altogether one hundred and ten meads and metheglins (there seems to have been no sharp distinction between the two in the seventeenth century, though 'metheglin' nowadays means something more like a spiced, herbal, honey-based liqueur), ranging in strength from eighteen parts water with one of honey ('Hydromel as I made it weak for the Queen Mother') to the headiest brew of all, which was half honey, half water. Lady Fettiplace made a strong dark metheglin, twenty-four gallons at a time, thickened with vast quantities of honey – 'make it so strong of the honie that it will cover an egg to the breadth of two pence' (a silver Jacobean penny had no breadth to speak of). This was Falstaff's ruin, according to the Welsh parson in *The Merry Wives of Windsor* who called him a butter belly, 'given to fornications, and to taverns, and sack, and wine, and metheglins . . .'

Someone at the back of Lady Fettiplace's book has copied out two recipes for mead, five pages apart, identical in method and very similar in content except that the small mead given here uses slightly less honey and three times as many lemons. It is a good deal stronger than it sounds, mellow and full-bodied, with a fresh, faintly lemony aftertaste which lessens with time, and it is extremely simple to make.

TO MAKE LEMMON-MEAD

Lemon Mead

Take ten quarts of water & one of Honey, three pound of ye best powder'd sugar; mix these together & set y^m on ye fire; Boyle y^m three Quarters of an hour; keep them continually skimming, then add Six Penniworth of Cloves & Mace, one Race of Ginger sliced, & a bunch of Rosemary; *then let y^m boyle one Quarter of an hour longer. for double ye Quantity of y^t take 12 Lemmons & cut y^m just in two; put them into a Vessell of a fit bigness, then take ye Liquor boyling from ye fire & pour it into your Vessell, w^n tis almost cold take 2 brown Toasts, spread y^m with good yest; & w^n it hath done working stop it up, & in a weeks time bottle it with a lump of Sugar in each bottle, ye week after you may drink it.*

Instead of ye 3 pounds of Sugar, put 2 Quarts of Honey.

Ten quarts, or two and a half gallons, of water may be too much to handle unless you have special equipment. For half quantity, easily made in a preserving pan, you will need 10 pints of water to 1 pint, or 2 lb., clear honey and 1½ lb. sugar (alternatively, double the amount of honey and leave out the sugar). The quantity should reduce by a quarter in the boiling. A whole race or root of green ginger weighs probably round about five ounces; use half that amount, peeled and sliced, with a dozen cloves, a few good-sized strands of mace (which is the nutmeg's filigree outer casing) or half a nutmeg, a branch or two of rosemary and three lemons.

Honey from the comb, with 'bee bread' and broken comb in it, contains wild yeasts, but commercially refined modern honey is so pure that, though it will probably not require much skimming, it may need some help to start fermenting. Dorothy Wise of the *Farmer's Weekly* (*Home Made Country Wines*, 1955) recommends adding a solution of a quarter of a teaspoon each of tartaric acid, yeast extract and ammonium phosphate, dissolved in a little sugar and water. But I have found the recipe works quite well with ordinary wine or mead yeast, if you follow the directions on the packet. The traditional method was to float a slice or two of toast, spread with brewer's yeast, on the warm liquor in a barrel or earthen vessel which was to be loosely plugged or covered with a cloth for a week or so, until the mead stopped whispering to itself. The sugar lumps were, I think, bound down under the tightly-stretched bladders used to seal the bottles, so as to allow scope for further fermenting: don't fill the bottles too full if you use corks, or they may pop out. In the second recipe from Lady Fettiplace's book, the mead was to be 'tunned up' (use a glass fermentation jar with an airlock) and left for two or three months before bottling; and in my experience it certainly needs a month or two before it is fit to drink, and improves steadily thereafter.

A good, clear, pale amber-coloured mead should not be especially sweet since the sugar content is what the yeast feeds on. According to Digby, who learnt how to make it from a Mr Webbe who brewed the King's mead, many people drank nothing else. Digby's Antwerp Meath comes with a recommendation from the chief burgomaster of that city who attributed his longevity to it, together with his remarkable virility, not to mention his trim figure: 'And though He were an old man, he was of an extraordinary vigor every day, & had every year a Child, had always a great appetite, and good digestion; & yet was not fat.'

5

MAY

May Day was the signal for a mass outbreak of spring fever. Anyone who had it put on a green spring livery, children were allowed to shed hot, itchy winter head-dresses, their elders ordered new suits, Pepys left off wearing a waistcoat in bed and dolled himself up in gold lace for the May Day Parade in Hyde Park. Country people were up half the night in the woods and fields to bring home the May, chasing and tumbling one another, cutting green branches to build bowers and shelters, picking nosegays to tie to their Maypoles or, like Spenser's Arcadian shepherds, coming home before dawn to decorate the church pillars

> *With Hawthorne buds and swete Eglantine,*
> *And girlonds of roses and Sopps in wine.*

Lady Fettiplace brought home the flowers of May to make sugar plate, or candy, and there is a breath of the Elizabethan lyricists' springtime exuberance in her instructions for rolling the sugar paste up into sticks, twists and curlicues, striped in the fairground colours and spirals of the maypole itself:

TO MAKE SUGAR PLATE LIKE MARBLE

Marbled Sugar Plate or Candy

First make a piece of white sugar plate, then with the iuice of Violets colour a piece blew, then with colour of Cowslops colour another piece yellowe, then roule out the white the blew and the yellow, but roule the white thickest, then lay the white first, lay the blew on the top, then lay another piece of white, & then the yellow, so lay it one upon another, then turne it up round, like a loaf. then roul it in your hand in a long round piece, then cut it out in thin pieces, & make it into what fashion you will, & so dry it.

Sugar plate is a kind of uncooked fondant, simplicity itself to make, a great delight to children since even the smallest can roll fancy ribbons, buttons and bows from the multicoloured crumbs of leftover paste. For Tudor and Stuart cooks, sugar-plate confectionery was as intricate and inventive as Venetian spun glass. They would model a whole first course at dinner—birds, beasts, pigeons, rabbits, bacon and eggs and sometimes the plate they sat on as well—to serve as the final banqueting course of sweets. Sir Hugh Plat, whose *Delightes for Ladies* came out two years before Lady Fettiplace's book was written, describes how to make a complete sugar-candy dinner service ('sawcers, dishes, boawls, &c'). Even Lady Fettiplace, running a relatively modest country household, gives five distinct recipes, including sugar plates made with almonds and quinces, and a plain 'whight suger plate' that was to be pressed round shaped moulds—perhaps Plat's saucers and bowls—then peeled off, gilded and dried. Edible crockery must, as Karen Hess pointed out, have been an irresistible novelty to people only comparatively lately accustomed to breakable glazed earthenware in place of metal, wood or bread trenchers.

Plain Sugar Plate

But marbled sugar plate was for fancy work, not *trompe l'oeil.* To make Lady Fettiplace's 'piece of white sugar plate' (she gives the recipe elsewhere), you will need powdered gum dragon, or gum tragacanth, a tasteless vegetable gum from Persia which you can get at a chemist. Put a heaped teaspoonful of the powder to steep for a few hours in two tablespoonfuls of rosewater. Now add this paste to a pound of icing sugar (a less insipid, more nearly authentic, pale, powdered sugar would be the muscovado sold in health food shops) mixed with an ounce of wheat starch (cornflour will do as a substitute). Work it in with a wooden spoon, gradually adding more rosewater, till you have a smooth pliable modelling dough. An alternative family recipe—'M^ris^ Mary Pooles receipte to make suger plates like marble'—directs you to 'beate it so longe untill it come like dowe from the morter'. Other seventeenth-century cooks advise kneading with your fingers, which I find works best.

Now divide the dough into one half and two quarters, colouring the smaller portions blue and yellow respectively. You will probably have to substitute vegetable food colouring for the flower juices, unless you have a large and unusual wild garden (buttercups, though not actually poisonous, are not a possible substitute for precious cowslips because their juice is said to provoke sneezing and blisters). Roll it out in broad strips—about four inches by three inches is easiest for a beginner—as thin as you can, an eighth of an inch or so, on a smooth surface lightly dusted with cornflour.

The tricky part is to prevent drying out and crumbling, so keep the lumps of dough covered with a clean damp cloth, and lay the first strip, which should be a white one, on another damp cloth while you roll out the blue and the yellow. Four or five strips, laid one on top of another—'and betweene every Culler lay a whight one'—is Mistress Mary Poole's advice; and indeed any more would be both difficult to manage and clumsy to look at. Daintiness is the point of these baubles which should be as frail, bright and gaudy as the flowers that colour them.

Striped Sweets

Roll up the whole pile from the narrow end like a Swiss roll, pulling the damp cloth out from under with one hand while you roll with the other, for fear of cracking. Slice it crosswise in whorls of white, blue and yellow. Mistress Poole's marbled plate was coloured with crushed red roses and spinach juice, making red, white and green whorls. These may be left as they are, rolled out thinner still 'w^{t}h a Roleinge pin', or cut into strips and twisted like brandy snaps round the handle of a wooden spoon. All these are authentic seventeenth-century practice, and so is the use of a crinkled cutter, or 'jagging iron'. The trimmings, made up into tiny rolls, may be sliced, moulded into streaky sugar marbles or stamped out with cutters as you please. 'Lay them to drye on papers', which may take several days depending on wind and weather (ventilation is important), and be sure not to disturb them before they have hardened as they are very fragile. They don't keep long, but a pile of these stripey sweets on a white dish or stemmed cake plate makes a pretty centrepiece to a spring luncheon party planned round a dish of poached trout, green and coloured salads, and the traditional Maytime dish of whipped cream on p. 115.

Berkshire was famous for its trout, according to the seventeenth-century divine Thomas Fuller, in *England's Worthies* (Elinor's father-in-law, Bessels Fettiplace, qualified as a Berkshire worthy solely on account of his name: 'Reader, I am confident an instance can hardly be produced of a surname made christian in England, save since the Reformation ...'). Thomas Baskerville saw them for sale in 1641 at Newbury market in Berkshire: 'It is well served on Thursdays and Fridays with sea fish because it lies in the road to Oxford, and for river fish it hath delicate trout, jack and excellent crawfish, with such other sort of fish as the river Kennet affords.' Lady Fettiplace's recipe for buttered crawfish is given on p. 157, and here is her poached trout:

TO BOYLE A CARPE OR TROUTE

Poached Carp or Trout

Take water and salte and let yt boyle a little then cut yor Carpe on the backe as you doe a troute put him in yor boyleinge lickoure when yt boyles a good pace put in a bowle of ale and some wine vineger a little parsly, marierome, and time, when hee is boyled enough lay him in a dish on sippetts w^{t}h some buter, wine vinegere, sliced ginger and a little suger and so serve yt

Carp (generally unobtainable in my experience, at any rate at an ordinary fishmonger) is a large freshwater fish, bony and bland, said to be virtually tasteless and no doubt much improved by copious quantities of strong sharp sauce. The English taste for livening up a dull fish with vinegar evidently goes back to the middle ages, when sweet vinegary sauces were served with both fish and meat. But, even with a fine, white wine vinegar rather than the fierce, brown, chip-shop malt, a bowl of ale tends to overwhelm the delicate flavour of trout, so I use a glass of white wine (also commonly recommended by cooks of the period) instead. Sliced ginger means fresh green ginger root, readily available in Asian grocers shops, sometimes even in supermarkets, which gives a delicious fragrance and flavour quite unlike the dry, snuff-coloured, powdered variety. The fish is to be served in a little, aromatic, sweet-and-sour sauce, very like the classic Chinese way of braising a fish in water with sherry or wine and vinegar, sugar, butter, soya sauce and sliced ginger root.

Gut the trout if it hasn't been done already. Score the fish or, if it is very large, fillet it by sliding a sharp knife along the backbone close to the rib bones, all of which can then be removed along with the head and tail. Lay the whole fish or fillets carefully side by side in a pan that just fits, containing a little boiling salted water (say half a cupful for a couple of medium-sized trout), no more than enough to lap round the edges. When the water shows signs of bubbling again, lower the temperature—a nice practical period tip—by adding the glassful of wine, and a dessertspoonful of chopped, fresh herbs. Cover the pan and poach gently, ten to twelve minutes for small trout, fifteen or so for bigger ones ('boil' in Lady Fettiplace's usage seems to mean something more like simmer) on top of the stove or in the oven.

Now strain off the juices, if you are serving the fish in the pan in which it was cooked, or transfer it to a serving dish, and keep it warm while you make the sauce. Add a scant tablespoonful of white wine vinegar to the cooking liquor, and reduce it if necessary by fast boiling to a small cupful. Add a teaspoonful of sugar, two or three slices of peeled ginger root (I generally add this at an earlier stage, with the herbs, and remove it with them at the end), with a knob of butter stirred in last to thicken the sauce a little and correct any sharpness. This makes a runny, well-flavoured reduction to pour over the fish. The Chinese would thicken it with cornflour; modern French, or for that matter English, practice would probably be to stir in two or three tablespoons of cream (which is very good). Lady Fettiplace left her sauce a good deal more liquid, and thickened it with sippets, but I find them too sloppy in texture for soft fish, so prefer to serve this excellent dish with a bowl of anachronistic new potatoes, boiled, buttered and sprinkled with more parsley, marjoram and thyme.

Besselsleigh Turnips

Root vegetables are nowhere specifically mentioned by name in Lady Fettiplace's book, although carrots and parsnips were common, and Besselsleigh (which belonged to the Fettiplace family) was famous for its turnips, judging by one of the shopping list jingles collected by Baskerville on his travels round the district:

Scotch collops
Studely carrots by Calne
Besselsleigh turnips by Abingdon
Saffron at Saffron Walden
Nottingham and Pomfret [Pontefract] for liquorice
Arundel mullet as they hear
Is the best in England for good cheer
But at 6d a pound 'tis pretty dear.

Home produce on its way from garden to table was seldom worth noting unless it required special treatment, generally pickling, which must have begun with the year's first tender vegetable crops round about now. May is the month for gathering the young, succulent, blue-green sprigs of samphire, which grows on rocky shingle round the south and west coasts, and on the eastern sea marshes, where it is traditionally served with marsh mutton and still sometimes sold at the fishmongers (Elizabeth David points out that it is occasionally stocked elsewhere by Greek shopkeepers, who call it *glysterda*). It should be boiled or steamed, like asparagus, which it somewhat resembles in taste, and eaten with plenty of melted butter. Lady Fettiplace must have got hers from an inland market—Norfolk samphire can be bought to this day at Sidney Street market in London—and in sufficient quantities to pot up for salads out of season:

THE BEST WAY TO PICKELL SAMPHIRE

Pickled Samphire

First picke and wash yt very cleane, then take water and salte which when yt boyles put in yor Samphire let yt boyle 2. or 3. walmes, then take yt out and lay it abroade on a cloath, then take whight wine vinegere and salte, make yt boyle, at wch time yor samphire beinge through cold put yt into yor wine vineger and salte in wch let yt boyle untill yt bee as greene as at first, then take yt upp and lay yt abrode till yt bee cold, then put yt in a glass fill upp yor glass with fresh whight wine vinegere stoppe yt very close and preserve yt to yor use

Proportions for the brine are 2 oz. salt to 1 pint water: 'let yt boyle 2 or 3 walmes' (or warms) means bring it to the boil two or three times to scald and blanch the samphire. Rinse it in cold water before laying it to dry on a cloth. Take enough white wine vinegar to cover the sprigs of samphire, bring it to the boil with 1 teaspoon of salt, simmer the blanched sprigs for 7 to 10 minutes, and leave to get quite cold before potting up.

This is the simplest and most basic pickling technique, in regular use in country households before canning factories, freezer plants and flying turned home-preserved vegetables from a necessity into a luxury. Not that you could very easily buy samphire nowadays, fresh or pickled, let alone broom buds and purslane, both popular delicacies in Lady Fettiplace's day. Broombuds—small, shield-shaped, and pure chrome yellow—were highly prized at court feasts, both for their beauty and on account of their ancient connection with the house of Plantagenet (*planta genista* is the broom's Latin name). They make a nice, plump, slightly bitter morsel, tasting something like a very mild caper:

TO KEEPE BROOME BUDDS

Pickled Broom Buds

you must putt yor Broome buddes as soone as you have gathered them in water and some sharpe vergis, then lett them boyle 2 or 3 walmes then take them from the fire & putt a little salte to them powre them liccoure and all into a milcke panne, When they are through cowld strayne the liccoure from them and putt them into sharpe vergis and salte and soe keepe them all the yeare, this way you may preserve Samphire, Purslane, or any other greene herbe

Purslane is a fleshy-stemmed garden plant with dark green leaves, not unlike an inland samphire: it was once widely cultivated for salads, and is nice either boiled or raw with oil and vinegar. It should be washed and dried before pickling. Broom buds need no preparation, except that the calyx holding each bud should be nipped off, or it will discolour the deep-lemon-coloured petals with what look like tea stains. Simmer them for two or three minutes in salted water with a spoonful of white wine vinegar (a more effective alternative, already beginning to replace vergis or verjuice in a great many Fettiplace pickles). Leave them to get thoroughly cold before potting them up in more vinegar in small sealed jars. Lady Fettiplace's recipes for pickled cucumbers, artichokes and green walnuts are given on pp. 143–5, pickled mushrooms on p. 173. Considering the fierce, corrosive bite, and dark, floor-stain colour of modern commercial pickles, perhaps her milder methods might be worth reviving.

Precious Oils and Ointments

For apothecaries and dispensing chemists—and anyone running a fair-sized country household in those days had to some extent to be both—this month and the next saw probably the year's busiest harvest. Lady Fettiplace has 'A Comfortable Oyntment for ye stomach or any Ache w^t^ever, which is to be made in May or June, w^n^ Herbs are in their strength'. She gives any number of herbal oils, and medicinal salts made from dried herbs burnt to ashes, moistened with water, filtered and evaporated by boiling. Stillroom windowsills, ledges, leads and porch roofs filled up from May onwards with stoppered glasses, containing crushed herbs topped up with olive oil and set to steep in the sun, sometimes for weeks or months on end. Oil of roses took almost a full twelve months, 'oyle of Hipericon' (*Hypericum perforatum* or St John's wort)—'a most pretious balm'—was made by the gallon, and improved with keeping: 'it easeth and alayeth marveilouslie the passion of the stomack, & pains of the bladder, & lower parts of the bellie, & thighes ... This dissolveth all bruses, healeth all wounds, without any scarres ... it avayleth against poyson, and it cureth all kinds of crude rotten Agues ...'

May Butter

May Butter was another ancient remedy, rich in vitamin D, for rickets and pains in the joints. Lady Fettiplace made hers by mixing the butter with plantain water and leaving it to bleach in the sun 'until the Dogge Days' (which begin with the rising of Sirius, the dog star, round about July 3). Fresh butter rinsed in May dew was pounded with cloves and cowslip petals to make an ointment for cuts and wounds. May dew itself was considered to have special healing properties, soothing, refreshing and good for the complexion: Lady Fettiplace made a lotion for sore eyes from 'may deaw gathered of the barley'. More than half a century later, Samuel Pepys' wife rose at three in the morning on May 26, 1669, and set out in the coach with her maid to collect May dew for a facewash, leaving Pepys fast asleep in bed. Compared to this charming, frivolous, thoroughly urban excursion, Lady Fettiplace's book gives on almost every page a strong sense of a practical, working, rural economy that supplied its own wants, and serviced virtually all its own needs.

Dew came from the barley field, cream from the cows milked by her maids night and morning, butter from her own dairy. Her book is full of churns, cheese vats and cream pots, brass skillets for warming the milk and the flat earthen milk pans in which it was left to cool on the flagged stone dairy floor. She made her own Angelett Cheese in the vat, as well as a much simpler cream or 'rush' cheese that anyone could still make at home:

TO MAKE FINE CHEESE

A Cream or Rush Cheese

To every gallon of the mornings milk take a quart of sweet creame, & with hot water make it as hot as it comes from the Cow, & so ren it, when the Cheese is a week ould lay it in Rushes.

Warming the milk by adding hot water—alternatively, cooling it with water straight from the well—was common practice in the seventeenth century.* Set the mixed milk and cream (two pints of milk to half a pint of single cream is a more manageable quantity) with rennet according to the directions given on p. 101, and drain the cheese thoroughly before laying it up in rush baskets. It is nice strewn with sugar and cinnamon like the clotted creams described below, but it will not keep long and, like all these creams and cheeses, should be made and stored only in scrupulously clean utensils.

Wash your Pails and cleanse your Dairies,
Sluts are loathsome to the Fairies,

wrote Robert Herrick, whose experience of life in the Devonshire countryside in Lady Fettiplace's day taught him a good deal not only about rural sluttishness and brutality, but about the tremendous labour of organisation behind the great communal festivals marking off the year, like Shrovetide and May Day. 'Cakes and Cream' were the traditional offerings laid out for the returning villagers, who had spent most of the night in the woods, pairing off with much scuffling and giggling, in his 'Corinna going a-Maying'. Lady

*I am grateful to Elizabeth David for this information.

Fettiplace gives many recipes for both: her yeast-baked fruit cake is on p. 137, but the usual accompaniment to a bowl of cream was one of the Bisket Breads (ancestors of our sponge fingers) given at the end of this chapter. She also gives three sets of instructions for rich, thick, clotted cream, made from the top of the morning's milk alternately cooled, heated, 'dripped' with cold fresh cream, heated again and left to stand overnight. One 'clouted creame' was flavoured with cinnamon and mace, heated very slowly on a trivet over small embers—'keep it in a seath [seeth] nere uppon all the day, let it not boile at all'—then cooled as slowly on rushes or flags, sliced and served with a little raw cream in the bottom of the dish. Another is layered to make what later ages called a Cabbage Cream:

Clotted Creams

TO MAKE A CREAME

Tak clotted creame, & laie it in a collender, a laying of creame, & then sprinkle it with rosewater, then lay another laying & so betwixt everie laying of creame you must sprinkle rosewater, & so let it stand all daie, then put sugar to it, & so serve it, & it will be like butter.

Names, or rather the lack of them, at such an early stage in the evolution of English cooking, make all this dairy work extremely confusing. One Fine Cheese is a firm white cheese, another is the sweet dish cream given in the last chapter; A Creame may be cooked, clotted, curdled or raw, or it may in fact be an egg custard made from almond milk (see p. 158). Lady Fettiplace's Creame Called a Foole is what we should now call a trifle, just as this next one comes near to what was already in her day commonly known as a syllabub:

TO MAKE A CREAME

A Whipped Cream or Egg-white Syllabub

Take a pinte of thick Creame, & a quartar of a pinte of white wyne, & some rose water & sugar, & some Cynamon beaten, & the whites of three eggs, put all these in a pottle pot, & shake it, still keeping the pot close, as the froth riseth take it up, & so dish it & serve it.

This mass of sweet fragrant semi-liquid foam, poured into a bowl or individual cups and eaten at once, is still closely related to the first primitive syllabubs which were made by milking a cow straight into a bowl of sweet, spiced cider or ale, and drunk on the spot. Tudor and Jacobean syllabubs were meant to separate, so that whoever ate one first spooned up the froth, then drank the winey liquor left in the bottom of the bowl. Cow milk spurting from a height naturally whipped up a light spongy foam: pouring milk or cream at arm's length into a sack posset produces the same effect, and so does the method described in this recipe of shaking up a pint of cream in a pottle pot, which holds four times that much.

The pint is a U.S. pint, or 16 fluid ounces of cream, mixed with 4 fluid ounces white wine, 1 tablespoonful each of rosewater and sugar, cinnamon and 3 egg whites. Beat the egg whites first separately to make the cream lighter still. Indeed, you may find yourself obliged to beat the whole thing with an anachronistic whisk in a bowl if you haven't got an authentic, tightly stoppered, two-quart-capacity pottle pot. Syllabub may be eaten right away or left to stand till the curd thickens on top over wine and whey in the bottom. Here is a way of using up the leftover egg yolks:

TO MAKE A CUSTARDE

Custard and Custard Tart

Take thicke creame put some nuttmegge and suger into yt and boyle yt well on the fire, then beate the yelkes of vi egges very well and take some of yor boyled creame and stirr yt w^{t}h yor egges then put yt to the rest of your Creame and boyle yt apace on walme, then put yt in a dish and let yt stand untill yt bee cold, if you make a baked custarde put yor egges yor spice and suger to yor Creame as soone as you have scumed yt and beate yt well together, then straine yt through a strainer of cushion canvase, and so bake yt, yor spice must bee nuttmegge and Ginger

Quantities are probably round about a pint of single cream and six egg yolks, depending on the size of your eggs and on how thick you want your custard, if not nowadays on the time of year, which mattered considerably in the days when watery winter milk was a quite different article from the rich, creamy, grass-fed yield later in the year ('if it be in the Summer, when the Cream is thick and best, take but two or three yolks of Eggs,' wrote Sir Kenelm Digby, thickening two quarts of cream for a posset. 'But in the Winter when it is thin and hungry, take six or seven; but never no whites ...'). One rounded tablespoonful of sugar should be plenty. Heat the custard gently, noting the careful instruction to add a little hot cream to the beaten eggs in their bowl first for fear of curdling. Season it with powdered ginger and nutmeg, and stir it till it coats the back of the wooden spoon: if you 'boyle it apace on walme' (a walme being not so much a warming-through as a boiling-up) you may well end up with something more like scrambled eggs. Though Lady Fettiplace does not say so, the baked version of this dish was almost certainly a custard tart, the custard being poured into a pre-cooked pastry case or 'coffin', which was normal practice for baking anything in the days before metal or pottery ovenware. Bake it for 30 to 40 minutes in a slow oven (Mark 3, 163°C, 325°F).

It is good hot or cold, best of all warm, but none of these custards or creams should ever be chilled more than very briefly in the fridge. An old-fashioned larder with slate shelves, a stone floor and thick insulating walls is a convenience we have long since forgotten, like the slow, gradual, permeating heat of wood embers which can keep an earthenware pan 'in a seathe nere uppon all the day', or for that matter having a cow on hand to provide thick, yellow, untreated cream. Dorothy Hartley describes the ordinary farmer's wife grading her temperatures with a delicacy that would be impossible in a modern kitchen: 'Creams, blancmanges and jellies were always set stone-cold being kept on the stone floor of the cold underground cellar till served; custards were only ordinarily cold; milk dishes, fermenties, junkets etc. were only dairy-cold. This was a subtle distinction, and flavoured for accordingly, as freezing tends to subdue flavour and destroy aroma completely.'

Sponge Biscuits

Lady Fettiplace's crisp, light, sweet biscuits go well with these creams, custards and curds. The word originally meant hard, dry, durable army or starvation rations, twice-cooked—*biscoctum* in Latin—so as to defeat even the jaws of a weevil. They were stored in biscuit bags and doled out in time of hardship or war. This is the point of Jacques' compliment, in *As You Like It*, when he says that the fool's brain is 'as drie as the remainder biscuit After a voyage'. But Lady Fettiplace's elegant, fragile, twice-cooked finger biscuits have moved on already a long way from their jaw-cracking, tooth-splitting origins. She gives half a dozen bisket breads, nearly all based on the same rich foamy batter of sugar and eggs mixed with flour in what afterwards became the classic proportions for sponge cake or sponge fingers.

Terminology is again thoroughly confusing at a point before proper names had yet been assigned to different sorts of biscuits. The basic formula made what was called in France *biscuit de roy* or *biscuit de Savoye*, and remained the standard basis for sweet cakes right up to the time of the French Revolution. On this side of the Channel, it developed on the one hand into the traditional English sponge cake, on the other into every kind of plain and fancy biscuit, jumbles, sugar snaps, ladies' fingers and lemon thins. According to Barbara Ketcham Wheaton in *Savouring the Past*, there are two dozen varieties of biscuit-batter-based cakes in François Massialot's *Nouvelle*

Instruction pour les confitures, les liqueurs et les fruits (1692), as well as one of the first recipes for meringue, 'a little sugar-work, very pretty and very easy ... can be made in a moment'. Nearly a hundred years earlier, Lady Fettiplace gives six different biscuits, one of which—French Bisket Bread—is a classic almond macaroon, while another—White Bisket Bread—is a meringue.

It is notoriously unwise to base any theory solely on the date at which a recipe first made its way into print. But it seems safe to say that in 1604, English home-baking, in a fairly modest country house like the Fettiplaces', was well up with the best professional French pastry cooks' techniques. Massialot's book was not translated into English until 1702 (and the Oxford English Dictionary gives the first appearance of the word 'meringue' in the language four years later). Elizabeth David cites a recipe for *biscuits de sucre en neige*—a sort of syrup-based Italian meringue—from La Varenne's *Le Patissier françois* published in 1653. Clearly Lady Fettiplace did not invent ordinary meringues (nor for that matter did Massialot), but she indisputably made and ate them well before they are generally thought to have been invented at all.

TO MAKE WHITE BISKET BREAD

White Biscuit Bread or Aniseed Meringues

Take a pound & a half of sugar, & an handfull of fine white flower, the whites of twelve eggs, beaten verie finelie, and a little annisseed brused, temper all this together, till it bee no thicker than pap, make coffins with paper, and put it into the oven, after the manchet is drawen.

Quarter quantities—easier to manage unless you are catering for a party, in which case the meringues would have to be made in batches—are 2 egg whites to 4 ounces of sugar. A teaspoonful of flour is barely noticeable in the final result, unless perhaps it improves the texture; and the crushed aniseed flavouring is, in my view, a decided improvement on the insipid sweetness of ordinary meringue. Try one level teaspoonful, but you may need more if, as often happens, your aniseed is sold stale. Tempering all this together till it be no thicker than pap means beating till it reaches the consistency of a spoon dish, like bread-and-milk or baked apples, in other words till it is stiff enough to form peaks. Don't forget to beat the egg whites first, before you put in the sugar. The paper coffins, or cases, must be oiled: sheets of Bakewell paper are very effective. Drop the mixture on it in small spoonfuls. The oven should be low (Mark 1, 135°C, 275°F), in which case they may safely be left for an hour or more.

Manchet is fine white bread, baked at a moderate heat (Mark 4, 177°C, 350°F) and put into the brick oven when it had cooled a little from the fiercer temperatures needed for coarse household bread. White Bisket Bread went in as the manchet loaves were withdrawn, and would have dried very slowly so that it hardly took colour. If it browns at all on the outside, it is cooking too fast. A variety of other sweetmeats—fruit 'cakes', marmalades and candies, apples or pears to be dried—also went into the bread oven at this stage, but don't put anything in with meringues that is likely to give off steam, or they will be irretrievably spoilt.

The other bisket breads given here are all variations on what we should now call a sponge mixture, recorded at the precise moment when it split off from what afterwards turned into meringue. Both sponge cakes and meringues evolved from a thick foamy batter made with essentially the same ingredients, except that egg yolks are included in the sponge version and the amount of flour substantially increased.

TO MAKE BISKET BREAD

Biscuit Bread or Sponge Fingers

Take one pound of flower, & one pound of sugar, one ounce of annisseeds, half an ounce of coriander seed, mingle these together, take viii eggs beat them verie well, then put in your stuff, then beat it alltogether very well, then take dishes & annoynt them with butter & put the stuf into them, Let the oven be as hot as it is for manchet, when it is browne at top turne it, & set it in againe, if you will have it light put the yolks of viii eggs more to it, & beat the sugar with the eggs, before the flower bee put in.

A bread oven would easily have held the several dozen biscuits envisaged in this recipe, but again quarter or half quantities are more appropriate to the capacity of a modern oven. For 4 oz. flour, 4 oz. sugar and 2 eggs, you will need about 1 level teaspoon of crushed aniseed and ½ teaspoon of coriander (the orangey flavour of coriander is the best of all these ancient, traditional biscuit flavourings, I think: don't use ready-powdered coriander, buy it whole and grind a few seeds in a mortar or with the back of a spoon).

Don't forget the afterthought: beat the sugar with the eggs *before* adding the flour (which should be sifted, and sliced in with a metal spoon). Another, almost identical but in some places fuller recipe—'To make biskett Cakes'—directs that the eggs are to be beaten first 'verie well' by themselves, then beaten again with the sugar 'till it be melted' (that is, until the two separate ingredients have coalesced into a thick, light, foamy mass). Then you put in the flour with three spoonsful of rosewater, '& beat it well the space of an hower'. Karen Hess gives an even more exacting contemporary instruction: 'beat y^{m} 2 houres before you strow in ye floure & then beat y^{m} 2 houres longer'. Modern balloon or electric whisks are, admittedly, a good deal quicker than a wooden rod or bat. Even so, the process still takes time and energy, but hardly more than you need for making a mayonnaise, and you get the same sort of satisfaction from watching the yellow grainy liquid gradually growing paler in colour, fusing and firming in texture, as you beat in the air. It should be stiff enough by the end to hold the tracks of the whisk when you withdraw it.

The batter is now to be dropped in teaspoonfuls, or piped in finger lengths, onto greased plates or baking sheets. Bake them in a preheated, medium oven (Mark 4, 177°C, 350°F), for 10 to 15 minutes, or until they are beginning to brown round the edges. You must watch them carefully, for they go too far in a moment. As soon as they are ready, slip the biscuits off with a knife or fish-slice, and return them to the oven upside down to harden off for a few more minutes. I like them still pale and very slightly chewy in the middle, like *langues de chat*, with the same neat, orangey-brown rim or edging.

This bisket bread is made to the same basic formula as Gervase Markham's Fine Bread of 1615, Robert May's Bisquite du Roy in 1660, and Elizabeth Raffald's Common Biscuits in 1769 (May uses two fewer eggs, Mrs Raffald substitutes grated lemon peel for the traditional flavouring of seeds). All were intended to produce the kind of biscuit that may conveniently be stored between layers of paper in an airtight box. But the difference between this biscuit mixture and a sponge cake is purely one of technique. The first person to bake his or her bisket bread in larger quantities in a tin, or any sort of greased dish with a raised rim, would have invented the true sponge (as opposed to the Victoria sponge, which contains butter and was not thought of till the nineteenth century, when it eventually put paid entirely to the yeast-raised cakes of Lady Fettiplace's day). Mrs Raffald does indeed give the same sponge mixture, only slightly decreasing the flour, under the title a Cake Without Butter. Lady Fettiplace's mixture, baked in half quantities in two seven-inch sandwich tins for fifteen to twenty minutes, and filled with one of her apple and orange marmalades (specially good with coriander), makes an excellent sponge cake.

Sponge Cakes

Here is a variation on the standard formula which leaves out a number of egg whites (convenient for anyone proposing to make White Bisket Bread) and replaces the coriander flavouring with caraway seeds:

TO MAKE LIGHT BISKET BREADE

Light Biscuit Bread or Seed Biscuits

Take a pound of flower & a pounde of sugar, & some caraway seeds & annis seeds, searce your sugare very small, take to every pound of sugar the yokes of xvi egges & the whites of fowre, & beat them verie well, then put in your flower & sugar & seeds, beating it all well together, then annoynt yo[r] dishes with buttar & poure in yo[r] batter, & so set it in the oven till it bee baked, the oven must not be so hot, as for manchet.

This must be the ancestor of nineteenth-century seed cake, commonly kept in the sideboard with a bottle of Madeira for serving to anyone who might drop in, much as Justice Shallow invited Sir John Falstaff (in *Henry IV*, *Part II*) into his orchard 'to eat a last year's pippin of my own grafting with a dish of caraways and so forth'. Perhaps Elinor Fettiplace's father, Sir Henry Poole—High Sheriff of Gloucestershire where Shallow served as J.P.—observed the same hospitable custom in his orchard at Sapperton, which had a strategically placed 'banqueting house', or garden pavilion, where guests might sample a bowl of cream or some home-grown pippins with a dish of these fine caraway biscuits.*

The last of Lady Fettiplace's bisket breads is, as its name implies, the closest to its ship's biscuit ancestors. Coarser and more durable than any of the others, or indeed than any modern manufactured biscuit I know of, it packs and keeps well, and makes excellent iron rations for children camping or swimming, or indeed for anyone on a serious expedition. In the days of long journeys on horseback, or in unsprung coaches over bumpy cart tracks, it would have been a wise traveller that set out with a handful of these in his pocket.

TO MAKE BISKET BREAD STIF

Stiff Biscuit Bread

Put to a pound of flower half a pound of sugar, nyne whites and six yelks of eggs, finelie beaten, mould it together, & make it up in a roule to bake it, when it is baked slice it & drie it, in the oven on a gredyron, you must put in some anniseeds, & coriander in the moulding.

*The model for Shakespeare's Shallow is popularly supposed to have been Sir Thomas Lucy, J.P. of Charlecote, Stratford-on-Avon, whose granddaughter, Joyce Lucy, married Sir Henry Poole's 'beloved cousin', Sir William Cooke of Highnam in Gloucestershire. The first person to identify Shallow with Lucy in print was a seventeenth-century rector of Sapperton, Archdeacon Richard Davies.

There is no need to beat the sugar and eggs to a froth for a dough stiff enough to roll. Mix the flour and sugar, be generous with the spices, and moisten it with the lightly whisked eggs. I find six yolks and nine whites makes the mixture far too runny for moulding. Perhaps this is evidence for the theory, canvassed by some, that seventeenth-century eggs were smaller than ours, although I haven't noticed any sign of it elsewhere. At all events, you may very well find you have to leave out a couple of eggs, or alternatively increase the flour and sugar in proportion, say half as much of each again, before you can make the dough up in a roll. Mould it with your fingers on a floured board into two sausage shapes, short and chunky if you want a fair-sized biscuit (which will be the shape and size of the cross-section). Bake them on a greased baking sheet in a moderate oven (Mark 4, 177°C, 350°F) for 30 to 40 minutes, or until they are firm and pale fawn on the outside.

They may be sliced, thick or thin, as soon as they are cool enough, ready for the final drying out on a wire rack, or on the bars of the oven shelves, at the lowest possible temperature. Karen Hess gives a similar, though very much plainer, seventeenth-century recipe for French Bisket, which was also to be baked in a long roll: '& when it is a day old, pare it & slyce it, & sugar it with powder sugar [icing sugar gives a fine professional confectioners' finish], then bake it again for an hour.' The biscuits, when cold, were to be rubbed with sugar again, 'then box them up & they will keep 2 or 3 years'.

6
JUNE

The very best rain water was bottled at this time of year ('Take rayne water in June, strayne it into a glass and preserve it to yor use, and when yor eyes are sore wash them therew^{t}h, this water will remayne sweete all the yeare'). So was the first soft fruit. Strawberries and cream were a special treat at a time when there was no fruit at all for more than half the year, except for imported sour oranges and lemons, or last year's dried apple rings, leathery pears, and sweet preserves. Lady Fettiplace gives well over two dozen recipes for preserved cherries, peaches, apricots, strawberries, raspberries, barberries, gooseberries and grapes. She must have grown a fair proportion of them at home in the kind of orchard described, in *The Country Housewifes Garden*, by Lady Hoby's friend William Lawson, who edged his orchard paths with roses and soft fruit: 'Your borders on every side hanging and dropping with Feberries, Raspberries, Barberries, Currans, and the Roots of your trees poudred with Strawberries, Red, White, and Green, what a pleasure this is!'

Lawson meant the little wild, or 'voluntary' native woodland strawberry, a favourite for underplanting in Elizabethan gardens before it was superseded by the great scarlet strawberry arriving from Virginia later in the seventeenth century. Lady Fettiplace cooked the fruit to make strawberry sweetmeats or 'cakes', distilled the juice as a remedy for the stone (a use for which it is still recommended in Grieve's *Modern Herbal*), and gathered the astringent leaves for a great many other healing preparations. Some of her raspberry preserves are given later in this chapter, and her barberry jelly is on p. 209. Feberry or feaberry was a country word for gooseberry, much liked in tarts and puddings, useful also as a zest, like sorrel, to sharpen a savoury sauce or bring out other flavours. Gooseberries made a sauce for pork, lamb, veal and roast duck as well as for mackerel, and were so popular as a stuffing for green geese that Karen Hess suggests this may have been how they got their name.

Anyone who bilks at these traditional sour purées may care to try Lady Fettiplace's pleasant, piquant sauce for chicken, in which the tartness of gooseberries supplies an essential but not at all dominating element. I have tried it at other times of the year with tinned or bottled gooseberries but these are no substitute for the small hard green fruit that comes at the start of the season, and gives a delicate lemony tang almost impossible to identify unless you know what it comes from, and particularly good with a dry meat like chicken.

TO BOILE CHICKINS

Chicken with Herb and Gooseberry Sauce

Take a good handfull of parselie, pick it small, & a good handfull of gooseberries, & a pretie quantitie of tyme, mince it small, & three large mace, & put these all together in a dish, & a little pepper, & salt, & half a pinte of white wine, & some broth that the chicken were boiled in, & a piece of sweet butter, & let it boile halfe an hower, & when the chickins are boiled inough, put that broth to them, & serve them; put some suger into it.

The quantities given are about right for a medium-sized bird, weighing between three and four pounds, which will feed four to six people. Put it in a large pan with salt, pepper and a few vegetables or potherbs (say a carrot, onion, stick of celery, more parsley and thyme). Cover it with cold water, bring the water to the boil, scum it and simmer very gently with the lid on, probably for an hour or so if it is a roasting fowl, about twice as long for a boiler; but be careful not to overcook it.

Half an hour before the bird is due to be done, start the sauce. Top and tail the gooseberries (I reckon a handful at four to six ounces), chop them finely with the herbs by hand or in an electric mixer, and put them in a small thick pan with the wine (cut the amount to a glassful if half a pint seems too extravagant), seasonings and a generous cupful of the chicken broth. Twenty to thirty minutes' slow simmering will produce a well-reduced, well-flavoured sauce which is slightly thickened and disproportionately improved in flavour by the addition of a large knob of butter at the end. Or you could stir in a cup of cream, which produces a nice compromise between Jacobean piquancy and the thicker consistency generally required of a modern sauce. Lady Fettiplace would probably have added a good deal more broth so as to make a sauce sufficiently liquid to moisten the sippets on which the chickens were served: you will get a rather similar effect if you carve the bird before it comes to table, and arrange the slices on a bed of rice with a runnier version of this sauce (use at least a pint of broth) poured over. The berries and herbs will by this time have lost most of their colour, and yielded their flavour to the sauce which can be blended or sieved at this stage for smoothness' sake, but I rather like the greeny, grainy original texture. Either way, the dish is improved by a snipping of fresh bright green parsley at the last minute.

Like the egg-and-lemon sauce for stewed mutton given in Chapter Four, this sauce is especially good with a roast bird. Baste the chicken liberally with butter and proceed more or less as above, stewing the gooseberries and herbs in white wine with a cup of chicken stock, and finishing off by adding the buttery juices from the roasting pan. It is also excellent cold, if you substitute cream for butter and thicken the sauce with a couple of egg yolks. The chicken is nice, hot or cold, with new potatoes and a green salad.

Gooseberries, Verjuice, Wine Vinegar and Lemons

The gooseberries in this sauce work as an astringent in place of the dash of lemon juice which serves the same purpose in modern cooking, or the vinegar and its gentler alternative, verjuice, always cropping up in sixteenth- and seventeenth-century sauces: 'then to the Broth put a good lump of Butter ... and if it be in Summer, so many Gooseberries as will give it a sharp taste; but in the Winter, as much Wine Vinegar,' wrote Gervase Markham in a recipe for jugged hare or duck. Sharpeners not only bring out the flavour of a soup or stew, they are also an essential corrective to fatty meats like mutton—hence the Seville orange sauce given on p. 41—just as they counteract the oiliness of a salad dressing. 'By English cooks this point is not and never has been sufficiently appreciated,' wrote Elizabeth David in *An Omelette and a Glass of Wine*, describing the dullness and difficulty of cooking in the aftermath of the second world war without lemons to enliven elderly boiling fowls, stringy ewe mutton, pancakes, pulses and fish.

By the 1940s it had, of course, long been forgotten that verjuice—made in the autumn from crushed and fermented crab apples—was the original native substitute for expensive or unobtainable imported lemons. It is still often said that the verjuice and vinegar, as well as the spices central to old English cookery, produced violently flavoured sauces intended to disguise tainted meat. But in fact, with a discriminating cook, the opposite is more likely to be true: any of these sharpeners should be used delicately, a little at a time, to correct and accentuate flavours, not drown them out. 'If you find the taste [of Mutton Hotch Pot] not quick enough, put into it the juice of the half Limon, you reserved,' wrote Sir Kenelm Digby. 'Take white wine as much as will cover . . . & add thereto as much vergis as will season yt,' wrote Lady Fettiplace, nearly half a century earlier, giving directions 'To boyle Neats ffeate'. To accuse cooks like these of over-flavouring involves the assumption, not borne out so far as I can see by internal evidence, that their palates were cruder and coarser than ours.

A dish like the next one would surely tend to point to the opposite conclusion. Buttered gooseberries are an ancient delicacy, peculiarly English like summer pudding (with which this recipe has points in common), smoother than gooseberry tart and only less rich than gooseberry fool.

TO BUTTER GOOSBERRIES

Buttered Gooseberries

Take your goosberries before they are ripe, & put them in a dish with a good piece of sweet butter, cover them close & let them boyle till they begin to break, then stirre them till they bee all broken, then put in some sugar to them & rosewater & the yelks of two eggs beaten, so stirre it alltogether, & serve it upon sippets.

Take a pound of gooseberries, topped and tailed, and cook them gently in an ounce of butter until they are soft enough to mash or beat to a pulp. Sweeten them—you will need a good deal of sugar—flavour with a couple of tablespoons of rosewater, and add the two beaten egg yolks, a little at a time, stirring with a wooden spoon over a gentle heat until the purée thickens slightly. Now take a china bowl—what Lady Fettiplace calls 'a faire purcelan dish'—and line the bottom with sippets, or very thinly cut slices of slightly stale, crustless white bread. Pour in the gooseberry mixture, which should still be fairly runny, and leave it till cold and set, overnight if possible so that the thickening of breadcrumbs becomes thoroughly soaked and taken up by the fruit.

This sounds like an ancestor, or at least a collateral relation of late nineteenth-century summer pudding, made from ripe soft fruit freshly picked in country-house kitchen gardens. Summer pudding must be ranked among the glories of what used to be called good plain cooking, spectacular to look at, exquisite eating on account of its simplicity, freshness and rich bouquet of flavours, each fruit distinct like the separate flowers in a nosegay. Its secrets are, first, to cook the fruit as above scarcely at all, only just enough for the juices to run (and these must be copious: a properly made, well turned-out summer pudding should be a deep even crimson, with no streak or fleck of white showing); second, to oil the mould before lining it with bread; third, to include a handful of gooseberries, which provide an essential if unorthodox ingredient in my favourite recipe (the others, all optional, are red and white currants, strawberries, raspberries, black and white cherries), passed on by a friend who rightly said that, though the taste must not predominate, the balance of a summer pudding is quite spoilt without the acid action of gooseberries.

Buttered gooseberries turn out a pale lime green, if you use early fruit. Later in the season, they will deepen to a rich winey red as you cook them. Colour was extremely important to Tudor and Jacobean cooks, who preserved the same fruit in different shades of green, white or red—'reds' ranging all the way from soft orangey pink to purple-black—depending on the technique employed. Roughly speaking, the more protracted the cooking process, the darker the fruit will be: any green apples will turn plum-red if stewed long and slowly enough in a covered pan. For a green gooseberry preserve, Lady Fettiplace specifies immature berries ('take them some three weeks before they bee ripe') which were to be seeded, sometimes skinned as well or scalded in boiling water to fix the colour, then cooked as briefly as possible. Clarity was second only to colour, which was why gooseberries had to be laboriously seeded or, if cooked whole, removed with a slotted spoon ('as they looke cleare take them out') from the syrup, which was to be strained, then poured over the berries packed into glass jars or stone gallipots. Tudor and Stuart cooks were as touchy about dull colouring or any hint of cloudiness in their preserves as the houseproud Yorkshirewomen of the nineteenth and even twentieth centuries, who reckoned to divide a pastry tart case into up to a dozen diamond-shaped sections and fill each with a different shade or variety of jam.

But looks were no more important than taste. For a Jacobean gooseberry marmalade made with sack or sherry, turn to the instructions To Preserve Pippins on p. 182. Here is another recipe which makes the best-flavoured whole fruit jam I have ever tasted:

TO PRESERVE PLUMS OR GOOSEBERRIES

Plum or Gooseberry Preserve

Take to every pound of plums a pound of suger, then beat it smal, & put so much water to it as will wet it, then boyle it till it bee sugar againe, then put in the plums, & let them boile very softlie, till they be doone, then when they bee cold put them up, if they begin to grow then set them where fire is in a cupboord; you may doe respis this way & gooseberries, but you must boyle them verie soft, & not put them up till they bee cold, & likewise may Cherries bee doone as your gooseberries & respis.

Respis are raspberries (rasps was the old country name). This is a favourite seventeenth-century technique, never mentioned so far as I know in modern cookery books, for minimising the cooling time so as to preserve the colour, shape and fresh taste of soft fruit. Moisten the sugar with as little water as possible, say a quarter to half a pint per pound, put it in a large thick-bottomed pan, and stir over the gentlest possible heat without boiling until it is all dissolved. 'Boyle it till it bee sugar againe' means boil the syrup hard till it reaches what cooks of the period call 'candie height' (240°F, 115°C, on the sugar thermometer), when it will crystallise if you beat it. Anyone who has ever made the mistake of stirring boiling syrup at this stage will know that it is apt to solidify, leaving a pan of hot, hard sugar candy which is to be liquefied again, according to Lady Fettiplace's directions, by the addition of cold, raw fruit.

Fresh Fruit Preserves

This may sound alarming but it works. In fact the method is foolproof, now as then, for anyone without a sugar thermometer. Simply tip in the clean dry fruit (plums should have been picked over, stalked and stoned, gooseberries topped and tailed), and leave it over the merest whisper of heat until the sugar has melted for the second time. You may stir it from time to time, prodding and chipping away at the layer of solid candy in the bottom of the pan, but so long as the pan is thick enough and the fire low enough, the mixture can safely be left to look after itself. The whole process may take as long as an hour by which time you will probably find, if you test a drop on a cold saucer, that the preserve sets of its own accord without ever being brought to the boil. This strikes me as a marked improvement on what we think of as conventional jam-making technique, keeping far more of the fruit's fragrance and flavour, at the same time abolishing the strain on nerves and temper involved in dealing with pots of dangerously bubbling, spitting, boiling hot fruit pulp.*

Leave it to cool a little, then ladle it into clean, dry, warm glass jam jars or stone pots and seal them with clingfilm or with the waxed paper circles and transparent tops sold by stationers for jam-making. These should be put on when the jam is either boiling hot or stone cold as Lady Fettiplace directs, so as to prevent moisture forming in the space between the jam and the lid on the jar. Seventeenth-century cooks sealed their pots with rounds of hand-made writing paper dipped in brandy, and tied them down with pieces of clean dried bladder (still used down to this century) or three more layers of paper, one white and two brown. Even so, the contents were liable to go mouldy on top if damp or air got at them: hence Lady Fettiplace's warning, 'if they begin to grow then set them where fire is in a cupboard'. Stillroom cupboards with slatted shelves and charcoal heaters inside must have been fumy but necessary, if summer fruit was to be preserved through the winter in the damp, draughty, stone-floored, otherwise unheated back parts of the house.

Gooseberries set easily and well with no trouble at all, but raspberries are another matter. They make the finest-flavoured preserve which is also the easiest to spoil by over-cooking, since they contain very little acid or the setting agent known as pectin. In several recipes, Lady Fettiplace prudently advises cooking the fruit in three or four tablespoons of extra raspberry juice with no added water at all. Here is one of them, not unlike those eighteenth- and nineteenth-century recipes for an uncooked raspberry preserve made from fruit gathered in the middle of a hot day, mixed directly with sugar and cooked simply in the warmth of the sun. Lady Fettiplace's lightly boiled version yields a delicious, runny preserve, less apt to spoil or ferment, but still fresh-tasting and brilliantly coloured, as she says. Use it to fill puff paste tartlets—especially pretty if you fill half with red raspberry and half with grass-green gooseberry preserve—or as a sauce with white creams and

*I am grateful to C. Anne Wilson of the Brotherton Library, University of Leeds, for a succinct account of the theory behind Lady Fettiplace's practice: 'the explanation lies in the interaction of temperatures. Fruit-pectin is released not at boiling point, but at 70°C or 158°F. Fruit brought to that temperature will set as jam, provided the acid balance is just right, and there is no surplus water present, either added or due to watery fruit-juice in a poor summer. As the very hot candied sugar is beaten into the uncooked fruit, the temperature of the mixture is raised enough to release the pectin and produce a set without the fruit ever being brought to the boil. Hence the excellent flavour and colour of the preserve.'

blancmanges, poured over fresh peeled peaches or, later in the season, with a plain apple tart.

TO PRESERVE RESPIS WHOLE

Raspberry Preserve

Take the fairest grossest respis, you can get, way them with your sugar, being verie finelie beaten, first straw a little of your sugar into the pan, then cast in your Respis *& the rest of your sugar upon it, take to a pound of respis the iuice of half a quarter of a pound of other* Respis, *then straine the rest upon your sugar & respis, then set them over the fire being moderate untill the sugar bee a little dissolved in the bottome, & somtime shake your pan for burning in the bottome, this doone, let them boile up faster, as your scum ariseth take it of cleane, let them boile thus hardly half a quarter of an hower, then take them up, & let them lie betweene two silver dishes for an hower, then set them over the fire againe, & quicklie give them one walme or two more, & no more; This way will make them both look of a good culler, & very red.*

Gross, in this context, means large and luxuriant. Other parallel recipes make it clear that the fruit is to be weighed, pound for pound, with an equal quantity of white sugar, and that the process is much easier to manage if you deal in comparatively small amounts: 'preserve but on pound at a time' is Lady Fettiplace's warning at the end of another, almost identical raspberry recipe.

Take your time over the preliminary heating, stirring and shaking, and don't let the mixture boil until the sugar is all melted. The fruit will partly disintegrate in seven minutes' fast boiling but it does retain colour and flavour, and quite a few whole berries. Take off the scum with a metal spoon for clarity's sake. Cooling and re-heating helps excess moisture evaporate ('quicklie give them one walme or two more' means bring to the boil again once or twice). Silver dishes were called for because a pewter or iron container is apt to discolour red fruit: aluminium is better, and a copper pan best of all. Stir with a wooden spoon for the same reason.

Here is a sparkling red jelly, elegant but tricky:

TO MAKE IELLIE OF RESPIS

Raspberry Jelly

Take Respis *& set them on the fire, with some sugar, let them boile till they bee broken, then straine them, but doe not squise them, then put a good deale of water to it, & as much sugar as will make it sweet, & boyle it till it bee iellie, when you make iellie of any other thing, put some water into it, when you set it on the fire.*

The fruit should be warmed very gently—*not* boiled in the modern sense—till the juices run, then dripped through a jelly bag, an item in constant use in the Fettiplace stillroom: if you disobey instructions out of impatience and squeeze the bag, the jelly will be cloudy not clear. Quantities normally given in modern cookery books are 1 lb. sugar to 1 pint fruit juice, but it might be a wise precaution to follow Lady Fettiplace's advice, in a recipe for preserved cherries, and top up each $\frac{3}{4}$ pint of juice with '3 or 4 spoonfuls'—just under $\frac{1}{4}$ pint—of redcurrant juice (which is a far more reliable setter). I don't understand the need to include sugar with the berries during the initial softening, but whatever you add should presumably be deducted from the final amount.

The jelly should be boiled to a stiff set, then put up in small, straight-sided, glass or stone pots, ready to be turned out when wanted in winter: 'Thin round slices of this jelly, laid at the bottom of round cups, and filled in with cool ivory creams, turned out in clusters on a silver dish, and garnished with green angelica leaves, were characteristic "pretty" side dishes till the eighteenth century,' wrote Dorothy Hartley in *Food in England*. These side dishes were traditionally set, four by four, in a symmetrical arrangement round the centrepiece and main dishes: in Mrs Raffald's engraving of the second course for a January dinner party—twenty-five dishes in all—the sweet side dishes were Snow Balls, Moonshine (a moon and stars made of almond flummery, or blancmange, set in a lemon cream sky), Burnt cream, Rocky Island, Floating Island, Pistacha Cream, Fish Pond (ten flummery fish swimming, over and under one another, in a deep bowl of clear calves' foot jelly) and '5 Globes of gold web with Mottoes in them'.

In summer many of the side dishes for the banqueting course or dessert would have been fresh fruit: plain or gilded willow baskets of tiny scarlet strawberries, cherries, apricots, peaches, figs and grapes. The marked emphasis on preservation in Tudor and Stuart cookery books seems to me to reflect not so much a preference for cooked fruit over raw, as an insatiable demand for fruit all the year round. Our own perennial harvest of frozen, tinned and imported fruit has only comparatively lately removed the housewife's ancient, traditional obligation to spend the sunniest days of the year sweltering over soft fruit on a stove, like Sir Ralph Verney's friend, Lady Gardiner, who sent apologies for not writing herself, 'being almost melted with the double heat of the weather and her hotter employment, because the fruit is suddenly ripe & she is so busie preserving ...' Hulling strawberries, stripping currants, stringing beans and shelling peas for the freezer are light work compared to the imperatives of jam-making in seasonable or unseasonable weather. 'I praye tell youre mother I will doe oup her sugar if she hath currants a nowe,' wrote Sir Ralph's aunt, Mrs Isham, on June 22, 1639, 'for this late wind hath bin so bige that most of them was blode of the treeses.'

Lady Fettiplace gives no currant preserves, though there is a currant wine at the end of this chapter, and she did add currant juice to preserved cherries. Here is another receipt which uses raspberry juice with pleasant results:

TO PRESERVE CHERIES

Cherry and Raspberry Preserve

Take suger and Cheries a like Quantity put as much water to yo[r] suger as will wet yt, and boyle yt till yt allmost come to suger againe, then stone yo[r] Cheries and put them in, and two every pound of them put in 3 sponfulls of the Juice of Red Respice *wth them let them boyle so fast that the sirop may boyle upp above the Cheries till they are boyled enough, sciminge of yt as the scum ariseth, as soone as you take them of the fier put them presently into a dish either of silver or earth there let them stand untill they bee allmost cold then put them upp. if you will preserve them duble you must put two Cheries on a stalke and tye 3 or 4 of the stalkes together untill they are preserved*

Carnation cherries (carnation meant flesh-coloured, presumably a variety of white cherry), or the dark, bitter, well-flavoured morellos, are specified as best for preserving in a splendid, late seventeenth- or perhaps even eighteenth-century recipe added at the back of Lady Fettiplace's book. The syrup is to be boiled till it thickens a little, and will draw out to a short thread if you dip in your thumb and forefinger (240°F, 115°C, on the sugar thermometer). Scumming is very important to produce the desired effect of cherries, single or double, suspended in translucent syrup. The later recipe advises you to clarify the syrup by sprinkling in a little extra sugar, removing the cherries as soon as they look clear, packing them into jars and covering them with the syrup (which should turn to jelly as it cools) strained through a piece of fine lawn.

Lady Fettiplace herself made boxes of dried and crystallised cherries (her recipe for the latter is emended in her own hand at the end, 'and drey them oupe'), highly prized right down to Mrs Beeton's day as a delicacy for dessert at dinner. Her cherry marmalade is simple to make, keeps well and may be eaten neat with a teaspoon from a saucer, as the French still sometimes serve jam, or used as an elegant filling for a winter tart of pâté sucré. It comes out thick, dark and syrupy, the sort of thing sold in fancy jars by old-fashioned grocers at Christmas, with nothing rough about it at all except the title.

TO MAKE RUF MARMALAD

Take a pound of cherries & pull out the stones, then way to everie pound of cherries a pound of sugar, put it on the fire, & stir it together, then take out some of the licor from them, & boyle it till it will cut; this way you may doe grapes & respis.

Cherry Marmalade

'Boyle it till it will cut' means boiling the fruit until it forms a soft mass thick enough to cut with a knife, or at least to hold the knife's track on the bottom of the pan. In practice, it is often wise to stop cooking before this point is reached as the mixture will continue to thicken as it cools. Leave it fairly runny for what Lady Fettiplace calls 'tartstuff', stiffer if you mean to slice it or set it in moulds. In my experience, it solidifies quite quickly and there is usually no need to remove any of the liquor (but this will depend on the type and ripeness of the cherries). The first time I made Ruf Marmalad it set so fast that I didn't realise what was happening, and had to wet it again by 'dripping' with cold water, a practice sanctioned elsewhere by Lady Fettiplace, and also by the professional confectioner, John Nott, whose *Cooks Dictionary* contains comforting advice about not panicking if your sugar begins to crack and turn to caramel before you can stop it: 'But in Respect to the other well condition'd Boilings, if after you have preserv'd any Sweet-Meats, some Sugar be left that is *crack'd*, or greatly *feather'd*, and is of no further Use in that Condition, you need only to put in as much Water as will boil it over again, & then you may bring it to what Degree or Quality you please, and mix it with any other sort of Sugar or Syrup ...'

Points to watch with Ruf Marmalad are, first, the initial tricky stage when sugar and fruit must be heated together very slowly, with constant stirring, until the sugar is all dissolved; and, second, when setting point has been reached by fast boiling, the final, much trickier stage when you must take up your wooden spoon and stir ceaselessly, or the mixture will burn on the bottom of the pan with horrible results. Pot it in jars or, for a stiff sweetmeat, let it boil a little longer, then leave it to set on an oiled tin, cut it when cold and thoroughly dry in strips and squares, and box it, arranged on white paper or lace paper doilies, in one of those lidded wooden cartons made for holding cigars or crystallised fruit.

The wines Lady Fettiplace calls for in cooking are imported clarets, malagas and malmseys, sack, canary and Rhenish wine (except for a single pint of raspberry wine recommended as an improvement to a strengthening broth—a whole sucking pig seethed in goat's milk—'for a consumption'). So presumably were the wines drunk in the Fettiplace manors at Appleton and Besselsleigh. But at the back of her book someone has added, in good black ink and scratchy, hen's-track writing, instructions for making the kind of light summer wines that can still be produced at home with very little trouble from garden fruit or the produce of a pick-your-own fruit farm. These fruit wines come immediately after the main body of the manuscript, only four pages after Lady Fettiplace's own last scribbled instruction at the foot of a sauce for roast mutton. Perhaps the hand that wrote them belonged to her daughter-in-law, Margaret Fettiplace, or to her niece Ann Horner in the manor house at Mells, or possibly to one of the three Horner daughters. Whoever it was evidently had considerable experience of home wine-making, and was anxious to pass it down in the family.

TO MAKE GOOSBERIE WINE

Gooseberry Wine

Take for every 3 pound of fruit a pound of sugar, & a quart of fair water, topp and taile ye fruit, bruise ye fruit & steep it 24 howers in yͤ water then let yͤ clere liquor run off through a hair sive to wch add yͤ sugar & stir it til ye sugar be disolved, then put it into a earthen stove or barrel close covered a fortnight or 3 weekes & draw it into bottels well corked, and bound down with a lump of sugar at 3 monthes it will be readie to drinke, during yͤ 24 howers, it must be serverall times stirred.

Currant, Raspberry and Cherry Wines

In yͤ same maner wee make corrain or Rasberie, but ye Cherrie wine differs, for wee doe not bruise yͤ cherries, but stone them and put yͤ water & sugar togeather & give it a warm over the fier, then put in yͤ fruit, & let it stew with a gentle fier halfe a qr of an hower, then let yͤ liquor run without pressing, & use it as yͤ other, yͤ best for yͤ use, are yͤ moraw, morellae, yͤ black flanders, or John tradeskin cherrye,
All these wines may be put into a runlett to worke, but must have sum small vent, till yͤ workin be over.

The kinds of cherry mentioned here are all black or deep red ('moraw' was probably a form—not mentioned in the Oxford

Dictionary—of murrey, meaning mulberry-coloured; morellos are the bitter cherries still sold for jam-making; 'black Flanders' were presumably an imported variety; John Tradescant's cherry was one of many fruit and vegetable varieties popularised by that celebrated gardener, importer and collector, who worked successively for Robert Cecil at Hatfield, the Duke of Buckingham and Queen Henrietta Maria). The proportion of fruit proposed is a good deal higher than is generally recommended in modern recipes, but otherwise the technique has hardly changed since the seventeenth century. Modern practice favours much sterilising of equipment and the addition of commercial wine yeast, but there are still home wine-makers who prefer to work without yeast, relying (as everyone was obliged to do before Pasteur) on the wild yeasts present on the skins of unsprayed fruit freshly picked and set to steep at once.

Use a glass fermentation jar with an airlock if you haven't a suitable earthenware pot or barrel (a runlett was a cask of variable size), and leave the wine in it until it has stopped fermenting. The sugar lump, placed between the cork and the bladder tying it down, sounds like a precaution to prevent corks popping out. According to Dorothy Wise, in her immensely popular booklet on *Home Made Country Wines*, first put out in 1955 by the *Farmers Weekly*, both gooseberry and redcurrant wines improve with keeping: the former, in particular, should be kept if possible till the gooseberry bushes are in bloom again the following summer. Here is an apricot wine from the same page in the same rough spiky hand:

TO MAKE APRICOCKE WINE

Apricot Wine

Take 3 pound of sugar, & 3 quarts of water, let them boile togeather & take off ye scum when it ariseth, put in 6 pounds of Apricocks pared & stoned let them boil till they be tender then take them up, & when ye liquor is cold bottel it, you may if you please let ye liquor have one warm, with a sprigg or two of flowered clary when ye Apricocks are taken up; it gives it a flavour, ye Apricocks make a good service for yor tables for present spending

Quantities and method in this recipe are very much as specified by the *Farmers Weekly*, which includes yeast and slightly less fruit, and leaves out the optional flavouring. Clary is a relation of common or garden sage with strong blue, or white and purple, aromatic flower spikes, much used in the seventeenth century in Rhenish wines and muscatel (hence its German name, *Muskateller Salbei*). The leftover apricots are good in pies or tarts, or eaten just as they are with whipped cream: I suspect that whoever wrote this recipe meant them to be dried out a little in the bread oven, as in Lady Fettiplace's many versions of dried and lightly crystallised fruit, before being served up 'for present spending'.

Other apricot recipes are given in Chapter Eight, together with Rattafia and Morella Brandy, but I included this one here for the sake of a last line that chimes with the clown's song in *Twelfth Night*—'What is love? 'Tis not hereafter/Present mirth hath present laughter'—and because it seemed a suitable table companion for the even more Shakespearian recipe that follows. This is for a fruit cake, raised with yeast rather than eggs as cakes invariably were in the sixteenth and early seventeenth centuries, before mediaeval notions of cake-baking evolved into what we mean today by a fruit or plum cake (for the very different 'plum cakes' of the period, see p. 176.)

Lady Fettiplace's cake, big enough to cut into well over a hundred slices, would have been made for a wedding, a festival like Twelfth Night, or one of the great celebratory feasts that punctuated the rural calendar at times like harvest, hay-making and sheep-shearing in June. Perdita's shopping list in *The Winter's Tale* suggests that she was proposing to make just such a cake for the sheep-shearing feast at the end of that play. Her brother is despatched to market to buy her five pounds of currants, four pounds each of prunes and 'raisins o' the sun' (this was also Lady Fettiplace's term for ordinary raisins, from French *raisins*, or grapes, dried in the sun), with mace, seven nutmegs, a race (or root) or two of ginger and three pounds of sugar. Thirteen pounds of dried fruit to three pounds of sugar and seven nutmegs were correct proportions for a great cake, heavily spiced and so stuffed with fruit that it scarcely needed any further sweetening. Lady Fettiplace's recipe calls for four pounds of currants with no more than a seasoning of sugar, and the same spices (plus cinnamon and cloves), to be made up with everyday ingredients—flour, butter, barm, ale and milk—none of which would have had to be bought specially. The result is what we should call a currant loaf or fruit bread: moist without being heavy, rich but not over-sweet and, as Elizabeth David points out in *English Bread and Yeast Cookery*, much better for you than our own fat and sugary modern cakes.

TO MAKE A CAKE

A Great Cake or Fruit Loaf

Take a peck of flower, and fower pound of currance, one ounce of Cinamon, half an ounce of ginger, two nutmegs, of cloves and mace two peniworth, of butter one pound, mingle your spice and flowre & fruit together, put as much barme as will make it light, then take good Ale, & put your butter in it, all saving a little, which you must put in the milk, & let the milk boyle with the butter, then make a posset with it, & temper the Cake with the posset drink, & curd & all together, & put some sugar in & so bake it.

A peck is the fourth part of a bushel, or twelve and a half pounds of flour, so, unless you are catering for serious numbers, reduce these quantities by eight. Mix 1 lb. 10 oz. plain flour with ½ lb. currants, 2 level teaspoons of cinnamon and 1 of ginger, a generous grating of nutmeg and 4 ground cloves. Make your posset by warming a glass each of milk and brown ale—about three quarters of a pint in all—with 2 oz. butter and 1 rounded teaspoon sugar. Dissolve 1 oz. fresh yeast (or ½ oz. dried) in a cupful of the posset, add this to the first mixture and knead your dough till it turns into a springy and cohesive mass. Leave it in its bowl with a cloth over the top in a warm, draught-free place to rise for an hour or so.

When it has doubled in bulk, knock the dough down, knead it again, and fill two greased loaf tins (Lady Fettiplace would probably have cast her dough without hoop or tin in a huge round cake on the floor of her bread oven). Leave the dough for another 40 minutes or so to rise again, and bake it in a hot oven (Mark 6, 200°C, 400°F) for 25 to 30 minutes. Glaze the top if you like, as it comes from the oven, with the icing of rosewater and sugar for the marchpane given on p. 228.

A second set of instructions, To Make Cakes, produces a rich little bun, made in very much smaller quantities—two quarts, or four pounds, of flour to one pound of butter and half a pound of currants—enough for only about eight dozen buns. Here is a third recipe for spiced saffron buns:

TO MAKE CAKES

Saffron or Fruit Buns

Take flower & sugar & nutmeg & cloves, & mace, & sweet butter, & sack, & a little ale barme, beat your spice, & put in your butter, & your sack, cold, then work it well all together, & make it in little cakes, & so bake them, if you will you may put in some saffron into them or fruit.

For two dozen buns or cakes, quantities are 1 lb. flour, 2 oz. sugar, a generous pinch each of freshly ground nutmeg, powdered cloves and mace, 4 oz. butter, about ½ pint sack (use sherry well diluted in water), and 1 oz. yeast. The buns will be rather dull unless you include either 4 oz. currants or about ½ teaspoonful of saffron filaments (generally sold in something like this quantity in a tiny sealed paper envelope).

First put the saffron to steep in a little of the warmed sack, while you prepare the dough. Whatever the recipe may say, modern fresh or dried yeast prefers its liquid warmed, so melt the butter in the rest of the sack and, as soon as it has cooled to blood heat, dissolve the yeast in some of it. Mix together the flour, sugar and spices, work in both the saffron and yeast mixtures, and add as much more sack as you need to make a light, firm, elastic dough. Leave it to rise, shape it into buns, range them on baking sheets and leave them to prove again in a warm place. Bake 20 minutes in a hot oven (Mark 6, 200°C, 400°F).

These are closely related to modern hot cross buns, and to the Almond Cakes on p. 85, all three being the sort of cakes commonly served with ale on high days and holidays to revellers like Sir Toby Belch in *Twelfth Night*. The shepherd's wife in *The Winter's Tale* served hers with a nip of something stronger and, though the shepherd's household was a relatively humble one, his fond description gives a vivid glimpse of a contemporary of Lady Fettiplace's hosting a party in June:

when my old wife lived, upon
This day she was both pantler, butler, cook;
Both dame and servant; welcom'd all; serv'd all;
Would sing her song and dance turn; now here
At upper end o' the table, now i' the middle;
On his shoulder and his; her face o' fire
With labour, and the thing she took to quench it.
She would to each one sip . . .

7
JULY

On July 25, 1607, a gentleman named William Bush who was crossing the Berkshire Downs broke down near Childrey, where he was forced to abandon his vehicle and take refuge in a lodge belonging to Lady Fettiplace's kinsman, Sir Edmund Fettiplace of Swinbrook. Bush was travelling in a home-made contraption—part tricycle, part rowing boat, part flying machine—an amphibious pinnace, or warship, billed to be able to pass by air, land and water: he had begun his journey five days earlier by firing off his twelve ship's cannon before attempting, with the aid of twenty men and a winch, the ascent of Lambourn church tower, parts of which fell off in the process. Journeys like this one were all the rage at the time, following publicity stunts like Will Kemp's famous jig in 1600, and the scandalous romp round Berkshire organised the year after by Elinor Fettiplace's cousin, Mary Wroughton. Thunder, lightning, howling gales and an estimated forty gallons of rainwater in the hold of his pinnace obliged Bush to spend July 26, which was Sunday, sheltering with the Fettiplaces before pushing on towards London (he eventually got there on August 19), accompanied by hordes of inquisitive and sometimes unruly onlookers who 'caused such sustenance to be brought unto him, as either that place or their store or provision could afford him ...'

The journey was written up at the time in a pamphlet by Anthony Nixon, who does not specify the nature of the Fettiplaces' hospitality, nor the light refreshments—bought and home-made—so copiously supplied by spectators along the route. No doubt there were cakes and ale, perhaps cold rabbit pie and hard tack in the form of Bisket Bread Stif, with luck something more warming like this dish of veal which makes a nice hot dinner for a rainy day in July:

TO BOILE A BREAST OF VEALE

Breast of Veal with Piquant Sauce

First boile the veale, in water with a bundle of good herbs, untill it bee very tender, then take some of that broth, & some tyme & parselie, & marierome & spinage, & a little winter saverie, & the yelks of three hard eggs, chop the herbs & the eggs together, & put it into the broth with some whole mace, let the broth bee very thick with herbs, let it boile all together, till it bee boyled inough, then when you dish up the veale, you must take some vineger & butter & sugar, & put it in the dishe wherein you serve it, & warme it, & so with the herbs upon the veale serve it, you must lay some capers in warme water, & lay them on the veale.

The only snag to this dish is the very great difficulty of buying breast of veal. It is one of those cheap cuts, like pigs' trotters, once considered a challenge to a cook's ingenuity, rejected nowadays by both butchers and their customers as too fiddly to bother with. I have managed to get breast of veal only from the sort of old-fashioned, generally rather expensive family butcher who still believes there is more to meat cookery than quick fry-ups, roasts and grills. If you buy meat for the freezer and have it cut up to your own specifications—a curious return to what must have been common practice in the days when each country house had its own stockyard—it is well worth saving breast of veal for this recipe with its pretty, summery, yellow-and-green sauce.

Persuade the butcher, if you can, to bone and roll the meat. It makes no difference to flavour but a great improvement in looks (especially if you stuff it as well with breadcrumbs, herbs, and seasonings mixed with an egg). Put it into a lidded pan that fits as closely as possible, with the bunch of herbs, salt (which should, so far as I can make out, nearly always be understood in dishes like this one), and enough water barely to cover. Bring it slowly to the boil, removing any scum that rises to the top, and simmer gently with the lid on for roughly twenty minutes per pound of meat, plus an extra quarter of an hour.

Wash some fresh herbs and strip off their stalks. You will need a generous cupful in all. Don't overdo the spinach: 8 to 10 leaves is enough with a small bunch of parsley, 3 or 4 sprigs of thyme and marjoram, 2 of winter savory (so called because it stays green all winter). Mince them finely by hand or in a blender, mash in three hardboiled egg yolks and moisten, as soon as the veal is cooked, with a cup of broth flavoured with mace. The vinegar, butter and sugar may be melted together in the bottom of a warm serving dish, as Lady Fettiplace directs, but I see no reason why they should not be amalgamated with the green sauce itself. Add a tablespoonful of white wine vinegar to the egg, herb and broth mixture, and reduce it a little by fast boiling. Now stir in a generous knob of butter, with a scant seasoning of sugar, just enough to correct over-sharpness. Pour it over the meat, sliced in rounds in its dish, and decorated with the plumped-up capers.

This sauce is made from the same ingredients as a modern French *sauce piquante*, still served with hot boiled veal or tongue, or a *sauce gribiche* for cold meat. Lady Fettiplace's version is also excellent cold (boil the veal bones with the meat so that the stock jellies, and substitute olive oil for butter). The making of a *sauce verte*, or green sauce, must have been another technique too well-known to be worth writing down, though she mentions it in passing to illustrate how to pound mixed herbs—'All these must be bruis'd together in a morter, as you beat green Sawce'—for a Comfortable Oyntment. Sorrel, crushed with vinegar and sugar exactly as we still make mint sauce, was so popular as a relish for meat that one of its ancient country names was green sauce. Hugh Buttes, author of *Dyets dry dinner* (1599) and afterwards vice-chancellor of Cambridge University, made his green sauce from a bouquet of sweet herbs pounded with rose vinegar, a clove or two, and garlic.

Green Sauce

Artichokes, which go well with veal as a starter, were a relatively recent import at the start of the seventeenth century, beginning to be grown in gardens up and down the country, and already something of a craze at court. People ate them boiled with oil and vinegar, then as now, or for special occasions dressed in this excellent sauce:

TO DRES ARTICHOCKS

Artichokes in Cream Sauce

Take thick creame, & sugar & nutmeg sliced & mace, & boile it together, when it is almost boiled, put in the bottoms of Artichocks, boyle them in it a little, then put in some butter, & so serve it: Boile the bottoms first till they bee tender in water.

Allow one artichoke per person; half a pint of thick cream will be plenty for six. Put the artichokes in a large pan of boiling salted water, acidulated with some lemon juice or a little vinegar, and cook them for about thirty minutes until they are tender (test a leaf). Take them out and leave them to drain upside down. When they are cold, strip off the leaves, scraping away the soft part at the base of each leaf, and discarding the rest. Remove the hairy chokes and keep the bottoms. For the sauce, simply heat the cream almost to boiling point with the nutmeg, mace and a scant level teaspoon of sugar; don't forget to add salt (a splash of lemon juice may be an improvement). Re-heat the artichoke bottoms in this sauce with a knob of butter stirred in at the end. Make a mound of the extra artichoke flesh in the middle of a warm serving dish, arrange the bottoms round it and pour the sauce over them.

With recipes like this one, no wonder Lady Fettiplace was anxious 'To keep hartichocks all the year'. Elizabethan sea voyages had stimulated a surge of invention and experiment on the part of cooks provisioning ships that might not see land for weeks or months on end. They potted shelled green peas in clarified butter or mutton fat, waxed eggs, dried beans, baked and bottled clotted cream. They preserved all kinds of vegetables—onions, cabbages, beans as well as fancier produce like samphire and artichokes—in verjuice, vinegar, brine or a combination of all three. Lady Fettiplace's artichokes, stored in brine in great stoppered stone jars, needed only to be rinsed ('and when you spend them, wash them in hot water before you boyle them') as needed for winter salads, pies and hot vegetable dishes.

Artichokes done this way—blanched but not cooked and very lightly pickled—retain more bite and flavour than the tasteless tinned variety. They might be worth trying if your greengrocer can supply a whole boxful or, in a good year, if you grow your own like Lady Fettiplace, who sowed hers in March for harvesting the year after: 'Plant Artichocks in the new of the moone about our Ladie day in Lent [March 25], & cut them close to the ground, & at winter open the earth about the root, & lay some dung therein, & in frostie weather cover the root over with dung.' The taste could be improved, according to Charles Estienne in *The Countrey Farme*, by soaking the seeds for three days before planting 'in the iuce of Roses or Lillies, or oyle of Bay, or of Lavander'; and the plants must be protected from predators as well as from frost ('Two sorts of beast doe annoy the roots of Artichocks, Mice & Moules'). Lady Fettiplace grew cucumbers in the same way; and again, if you mean to make your own cucumber pickles to eat with pâté or cold meat, you may have to grow them yourself as the neat little early pickling cucumbers, so easy to buy fresh or bottled in France, are hard to come by in the shops over here. This recipe is no trouble at all, and will do for either artichokes or cucumbers:

To Grow Artichokes

TO KEEP HARTICHOCKS ALL THE YEARE

Pickled Artichokes and Cucumbers

first take a gallon of faire water, & another of the strongest veriuice, & a good handfull of salt, put them together on the fire & boile them, & scum them cleane, take half an handfull of fennell, & half a handfull of hyssope cleane washed, & put into the brine & boile it altogether, & when it is throwly boiled to a good sharp brine, then throw in the artichocks & scald them, & pluck them out againe, then let the artichocks & the brine bee throwe cold before you put them up, then put the bottoms downwards & the herbs on the top, & let brine alwayes cover them. Even so I use the Cowcumbers.

Cider vinegar is probably the nearest available equivalent here to verjuice, though for cucumbers white wine vinegar might be preferable since it has less effect on colour. A second artichoke recipe suggests colouring the liquor, after the vegetables have been removed, with two handfuls of nettles (fresh, tart, soft green in spring, rather like spinach juice), boiled for a few minutes, then strained out. Use sea salt, if possible, as the chemical additives in ordinary cooking salt may spoil or cloud the pickle, and avoid metal utensils which will also discolour it: use an enamel pan, a wooden spoon and glass or stone jars.

Two gallons of brine will probably cover between ten and sixteen pounds of vegetables, but they are more easily done in half or quarter or even an eighth of this quantity. Two pounds of cucumbers, one pint of water, one pint of verjuice or vinegar, and a level tablespoonful of salt will fill four ordinary, screw-topped one pound jam jars or honey pots. Artichokes will need larger, broader, wide-necked pots. Discard any damaged vegetables, wash and wipe the rest well. Tiny artichokes may be left whole, bigger ones should be neatly trimmed with the stalks and tough outside leaves thrown away. Use only immature cucumbers, no more than two to four inches long, if you can get them, or the hump-backed, furrowed, uneven ridge cucumbers sold later in the season (trim and slice them if necessary), not the bumper-sized, glossy green commercial ones with waxed skins. Boil the brine for five minutes or so, add the vegetables in batches, and bring the liquor back to the boil before removing them with a slotted spoon. Pack them tightly in sterilised jars, pour over the cold brine, close the lids and store in a cool dry place.

Here is another recipe, very similar in technique to French pickled *cornichons* and Jewish dill pickles:

TO KEEP COWCUMBERS ALL THE YEARE

Pickled Cucumbers

Take to fourtie Cowcumbers a quarter of a pound of burnt allum, & as much veriuice as will cover them, then let it boyle, when it boyles wash the Cowcumbers in water, & put them in, & let them boyle till they bee tender verie softly, then take them from the fire, when they be cold put them up in a close vessell, put some pepper to them & dillseed in the boyling.

Don't crush the peppercorns or dill seed, or they will spoil the look of this pickle. Powdered alum may be bought at chemists, and is still used in sour dill pickles to keep the cucumbers crisp. It is not easy to follow Lady Fettiplace's instructions as to quantity without knowing what size of cucumber she had in mind: forty medium-sized ridge cucumbers might weigh as much as ten to twelve pounds, while forty little picklers would come to something more like half that weight, requiring probably round about three pints of verjuice to cover them. Either way, it might be wise to reduce the four ounces of alum to one or two teaspoonfuls.

The next recipe on the same page, applying the same method to artichokes, calls for a quarter of a pound of alum, a quart of verjuice and an unspecified amount of water to fifty artichokes. They were to be brought to the boil four times ('let them boyle two walmes ... then let it boyle, two walmes more')—just long enough to soften and blanch the artichokes—which indicates an equally brief boiling for cucumbers. Paul Levy's recipe (in the Habitat *Cook's Diary* for 1980) for Ada Gail's Authentic Jewish Pickled Cucumbers calls for about two gallons of a very similar brine to be poured, boiling hot, over six pounds of scrubbed cucumbers, which are then to be left for two or three days until they start to ferment. The fermenting process may be encouraged, according to another of Lady Fettiplace's recipes, by adding 'some small wort', or malt infusion, readily available in any house that brewed its own beer. They will be ready to eat in three or four weeks, and should keep much longer.

Early July was also the time for making a characteristically pretty preserve of green walnuts, stuck with cloves and suspended in a rosewater syrup, good for the digestion, comforting to the stomach, nice as a sweetmeat after dinner or as a relish with ham, tongue, turkey or a cold game pie.

TO PRESERVE WALLNUTTS

Take yor wallnutts the first full moone after Midsumer put them into on end of a Bagge and a stone into the other end. to keepe them under water. you must have two kettles on the fier wth water. put yor Bagge wth wallnutts in the on kettle and let them boyle till you see the water change couler. then take them forth and put them into the other, doe this untill the bitterness bee gone. then make yor Seruppe redy with Suger and Rosewater and Clarifie yt, then take yor nutts out of the Bagge and pill of the uttermost skin boyle them in yor sirrope untill you thinke them throughly preserved. in each wallnutt you must stick a qter of a Clove when you put them into yor Sirope

Green Walnuts in Syrup

The first full moon after midsummer day (June 25) falls at the end of June or in early July, which would be later nowadays since the seventeenth-century calendar was a week and a half ahead of ours (eleven days—September 3–13 inclusive—having been subtracted in the year 1752). Hence presumably the refrain in that otherwise baffling nursery rhyme about gathering nuts in May, which might perhaps have applied to the very first green walnuts in a good year. They should be roughly the size of nutmegs, and soft enough to pierce with the blunt end of a darning needle ('Gather your wallnuts when you can thrust a pinn through them' is Lady Fettiplace's instruction in 'to make wallnut watter'). It was a typically ingenious cook that devised this time-saving method of blanching the nuts with a bag, a stone and two kettles of water. Lady Fettiplace gives no quantities, but a contemporary recipe, supplied by Karen Hess, specifies one and a quarter pounds of sugar (wet it with half a cupful of rosewater to make the syrup) to each pound of walnuts.

Virtue of Green Walnuts

Lady Fettiplace made soothing gargles and cough syrups from the juice of ground green walnuts, mixed with honey, or distilled with 'to every quart a shillings worth of the best venice triacle' (Venice treacle was the costliest of all the medicinal treacles considered a sovereign remedy since Roman times); and she applied powdered green nutshells externally 'For the Evila', which was the King's Evil or scrofula (Grieve's *Modern Herbal* supports her on both counts, recommending the identical gargle for an inflamed or ulcerated throat, and walnut oil as a treatment for eczema and leprous skin diseases). People in the seventeenth century still made no great distinction between health and beauty. A great many of Lady Fettiplace's recipes would be difficult to classify into medicinal, decorative or strictly culinary categories. A dish of violets with almond butter, a salad decorated with green walnuts in syrup, lemon-yellow broom buds or pickled gilliflowers (clove pink carnations), might be said to be good for you in more senses than one. 'For the Pashion of the Harte' Lady Fettiplace prescribed, among other remedies, 'Conserve of red Jilloflowers' mixed with ambergris and musk, and washed down with a good draught of spiced claret wine.

Gilliflowers, or clove July-flowers (named for their scent of cloves, also supposedly because they flower in July: July-flowers of the wall were what we mean by wallflowers) were much used 'in ornament, and comforting the spirits, by the sense of smelling', according to William Lawson in *The Country Housewifes Garden* (1617). 'I may well call them the King of flowers except the Rose ...' wrote Lawson, who grew them in nine or ten different colours, some as big as roses. The only authentic seventeenth-century variety vouched for today at the Royal Botanic Gardens in Kew is the old red clove carnation, with a deep carmine flower that is indeed the size of a rosebud. Any large modern pinks will do nicely (the colour was named from the flower in the eighteenth century, not the other way round), provided the colour is sufficiently strong. Lady Fettiplace's recipe for preserving them is so simple that any gardener who doesn't grow them already might find it worth planting a clump to ornament winter tables as much as summer borders.

TO MAKE SALLADS OF GILLOFLOWERS

Preserved Gilliflowers or Red Clove Carnations

Take Red gilloflowers and Cutt of all the whight from them soe lett them stand all night, then take stronge wine vineger and as much sugger as will make it sweete boyle it 2 or 3 walmes then take it from the fire and when it is through cowlde, put yor gilloflowers into it and soe keepe them for yor use this way you may doe any other fflowers

The white base of the petals should be nipped off because it is said to be bitter. Weigh the petals, which must be perfectly dry, measure out an equal weight of sugar and dissolve it in white wine vinegar (which should do no more than barely boil or it will set solid). Allow one fluid ounce of vinegar to each ounce of sugar. These are the proportions given by Hannah Woolley, in *The Gentlewomans Companion* (1673), who reckoned a pound of sugar per pound of gilliflowers, which would be enough to fill a plastic carrier bag or large basket. But the recipe is worth trying even with only one or two ounces of petals, packed well down in small stone or glass pots (the little, dark, screw-topped containers used for pills are ideal as they keep out the light). Pour the cold syrup over them and seal tightly. They will keep their bright colour so long as neither air nor light gets at them. A spoonful of crimson petals, stirred into a bowl of pale green lettuce leaves dressed with oil and lemon, adds not only colour but a delicate, sweet-and-sour flavour of flowers to a plain salad.

Roses

Gilliflowers and roses—kings of the garden—were the main crop to be processed in the stillroom this month. 'After I had praied, I was busie with Roses,' wrote Lady Hoby on July 22, 1600. 'Busie with Roses' might have meant distilling rosewater, or working on any one of a dozen preparations—syrups and conserves, rose powders, creams and lotions—included in Lady Fettiplace's book. She dried rose petals ('they cool, bind and are cordial,' wrote Culpeper) over a slow stove on a silver dish, and crumbled them into a pan of boiling sugar candy with lemon syrup to make little 'rose cakes', like lemon drops, for people with sore throats to suck.

Rose Remedies

Her Honie of Roses, made from a pound of damask rosebuds stirred into a quart of clarified honey, is virtually identical to the rose honey listed in the 1930s, according to Grieve's *Herbal*, in the official *U.S. Pharmacopoeia*. Roses, astringent, cooling and tonic, were the main ingredient in her tinctures for bathing and bandaging sore or 'bloudshotten' eyes.

They were also the traditional base of cold cream—Lady Fettiplace's Oyntment of Roses—much in demand at a time when a white skin was an essential requisite in a woman. Lady Fettiplace gives a fierce, smarting, brimstone and camphor based Water for Pimpells, and any number of remedies 'for a Red face', as well as gentler waters to purify and cleanse the skin, to make it white and smooth, to get rid of sunburn and freckles. She also includes vapour baths, and face masks made from pounded 'whight lillie roots' or home-made pomatum ('when you think fit doo it over your face in the morning, and weare a clean mask till you bee readie'). Then there are rose-based scents and 'perfuming waters', compounded with citrus peel and spices, ambergris, civet and musk: the sort of thing Ben Jonson had in mind in *Volpone*, when that prince of con-men sets out to seduce the reluctant Celia in terms of an upmarket cosmetics commercial:

Thy baths shall be the juice of July-flowers,
Spirit of roses and violets,
The milk of unicorns and panthers' breath
Gathered in bags, and mixed with Cretan wines.

Spirit of Roses

Lady Fettiplace distilled spirit of roses as a by-product of her precious, perfumed 'oile of Roses sweet', which was made from crushed petals steeped in cumin water for almost twelve months, then transferred to a glass still: 'first you shall have with a soft fire the spirit, & then the water & oile, the oile will swim like a thin fat, or greace on the top, wch you must continually take of ...' This sounds very much like the secret of attar of roses, said to have been discovered by chance round about the time Lady Fettiplace's book was written at a wedding feast in Persia (when the Moghul Emperor Djihanguyr, son of the great Akbar, floating with his bride on a canal filled with rosewater, noted a film of exquisitely perfumed oil separated and drawn to the water's surface by the heat of the sun), and manufactured in Shiraz from about 1612. Grieve's *Herbal* says that it takes thirty roses to produce one drop of oil, or ten thousand pounds of flowers for a single pound of oil. Lady Fettiplace made hers in an earthen pot of one or two gallons capacity, cramming the petals hard down, 'for the quantitie els wilbee very small'.

These quantities go well beyond anything available from even the grandest of twentieth-century rose gardens. Clearly Lady Fettiplace and her contemporaries had access to supplies on something approaching what we should think of today as a commercial scale: a single recipe for rose syrup, supplied by her kinswoman Mistress Mary Poole, calls altogether for eleven gallons of rose petals, which would probably mean stripping at least an acre of rose bushes. Possibly, at a time when the head gardener of a large estate like Hatfield thought nothing of ordering plants by the thousand, roses were grown like other fruit as an orchard crop rather than as part of the kitchen or flower garden. Or perhaps they were indeed supplied by commercial growers: Sir Hugh Plat, in *Delightes for Ladies*, gives a characteristically practical tip on snapping them up at bargain prices: 'This way you may distill Rosewater good cheap, if you buy store of Roses, when you find a glutte of them in the market, whereby they are sold for 7 pence or 8 pence the bushell, you then engrosse the flower [buy them up wholesale].'

No one today is likely to be able to lay hands on a whole bushel of roses—eight gallons—from flower shop, greengrocer or garden. But even a single basket or bowlful of petals, weighing perhaps half a pound, will yield three or four pots of Lady Fettiplace's exquisite rose petal jam:

TO MAKE CONSERVE OF ROSES

Rose Petal Conserve or Jam

Take Red Rose budds, Cut of the whights then boyle them in water untill they bee very tender, then wey tō every pound of Roses and water 3 poundes of suger and boyle yt together till yt bee thicke enough stirr yt still on the fire and untill yt bee colde then put yt in glasses and preserve yt to yo[r] *use*

Pick the roses early in the morning, well before midday and the full heat of the sun: they should be perfectly dry, not yet full blown but not so tightly furled that it is hard to pull off the petals, leaving the stems and stamens behind. Hold each rose firmly in one hand and pull the stem away with the other, then snip off the paler or whitish part at the base (said to spoil both colour and taste) with a pair of sharp scissors. Stew them in just enough water to cover, probably a pint per pound of petals. Sir Kenelm Digby says they need a good half hour or longer in a covered pan. They will give off a wonderful smell but turn a dreary, nondescript, thoroughly discouraging colour—'pale like linen' in Digby's phrase—which is rectified, becoming a beautiful deep claret red, as soon as the added sugar begins to dissolve.

Half a pound of petals, stewed till tender in half a pint of water, will weigh probably round about one pound, and need by Lady Fettiplace's reckoning three pounds of sugar. Add the sugar a pound at a time, stirring until it is all melted; then boil fast till it is as thick as cream and a drop poured out on a cold plate will form a skin if you push it. I find that, if you use the old-fashioned damask roses Lady Fettiplace had in mind, the conserve sets pretty well as soon as it reaches boiling point, and will almost certainly crystallise if cooked much longer. The proportion of sugar to roses is so high that it is quite likely to crystallise in any case; a little tartaric acid added to the syrup is said to prevent this, or you could reduce the amount of sugar (Digby used four pounds of sugar per pound of petals). Even if it crystallises rock hard in its jar, you can still melt it in hot water or a slow oven, and use it in any of the ways suggested below. Digby claims that the candied crust which forms on top of the pot if you leave it uncovered for a few days in a warm place will prevent mildew forming on the beautiful purply-red conserve underneath.

This conserve, a very good cordial to strengthen the heart and spirit according to Culpeper, is extremely sweet, rose-scented, faintly oriental (a virtually identical jam is still made in Greece and the Middle East). Put it up in small pots and, once a jar has been broached, keep the lid on, as with pot-pourri, so as to preserve and concentrate the fragrance. Try it in tarts and pastries, as a flavouring for plain apple jelly, or served neat, a teaspoonful at a time, with any of the white creams and cream cheeses given in Chapters Four and Five. It is unexpectedly good in brown bread sandwiches, or in a wholemeal pastry case which contrasts agreeably with the scent and texture of rose petals (the crunchiness of crystallised roses is a bonus in these two and the following recipe). But it is best of all stirred into whipped cream, with a little extra rosewater, and frozen to make Groves' Ice Cream, named after the friends who invented this delectable twentieth-century refinement on a seventeenth-century original. It is, as Flann O'Brien's third policeman said, almost too nice to mention.

Groves' Rose Ice Cream

Another even more concentrated and decidedly more complicated recipe calls for the flowers to be crushed and steeped—'put in so many as may almost drink up the licour'—in equal parts of red rose water and freshly squeezed rose juice. This mixture is brought to boiling point but not actually boiled, so as to preserve its fragrance and colour, then stirred into a pan of hot crystallised syrup made from three pounds of sugar to each pound of rose mixture. The roses liquefy the syrup to make a conserve without further boiling, rather runny but a brilliant red and wonderfully scented.

Lady Fettiplace used it to cheer and comfort the sick, and to disguise the taste of her herbal remedies. Anyone in need of refreshment on a hot day might try a Rose Petal Water Ice, made from half a pot—or three heaped tablespoonfuls—of either of these conserves mixed with boiling syrup (one pint of water, four ounces of sugar, the juice and rind of one or two lemons, simmered together for five minutes). Leave the mixture until it is thoroughly cold, then strain and freeze it, beating it well when half frozen by hand or preferably in an electric blender. The result is a particularly beautiful hot-pink ice. If you turn it into a sorbet, by beating in a stiffly whipped egg white half way through the freezing, it will come out what used to be called Shocking Pink (Schiaparelli's *Shocking* was packaged in it), a favourite colour of the swinging 'sixties and also with Lady Fettiplace's contemporaries. Try decorating this sorbet with other flowers of the Tudor period—a wreath of tiny purple heartsease or violets, a shredded bright orange nasturtium or a scattering of marigold petals.

Rose Petal Water Ice

Rose Sorbet

Here is a third conserve of roses, uncooked and so simple a child could make it by hand, simpler still in an electric blender:

TO MAKE CONSERVE OF ROSES

Take the buds of red roses & cut of the white, then beat them in a morter, till they bee verie fine, put to everie pound of roses, two pounds of sugar, put in your sugar when your roses be verie small beaten, then beat it all together, & put it up.

Fresh Rose Petal Conserve

This fragrant, dark, purply conserve of raw roses was commonly prescribed for coughs, colds and lung complaints (Lady Fettiplace mixed hers with raisins and oil of vitriol, 'as much as will make yt a little sowreish'), a treatment still recommended in modern herbal medicine for coughs and lung haemorrhage. It is perhaps a little too chewy to use neat in tarts or fillings, but it keeps well and is very good in autumn or winter for scenting and flavouring fruit jellies, syrups, or any plain apple pudding or purée (suspend a little muslin bag of the conserve in the hot apple mixture while it is cooking).

Its properties go well beyond the strictly medicinal, as with so many of Lady Fettiplace's preparations including the syrup below, clearly a popular medicine since she made it up in astonishing quantities and gives three separate recipes. It cooled the liver and comforted the heart, according to Culpeper, and may still do so in a long drink.

TO MAKE SEROP OF ROSES

Take damask roses buds six handfulls, & cut of the tops, and take a quart of faire running water, & put the roses theirin, & put them in a basin, & set them over the fire, that the water may be but warme one day & a night, then in the morning squise the roses hard between your hands out of the water, & then put in as many fresh, & let them stand still on the fire, this doe nine times, then take out your roses, cleane out of the water, & put in as much sugar as will make it sweet, and boyle it till it come to a serop; you must put to everie pinte a pound of sugar.

Red Rose Syrup

The rose petals should be pressed down and just covered with water, so if you are using only a couple of handfuls, allow two thirds of a pint. Put the petals in a covered basin or jug, or in the top half of an enamel double boiler, over warm but not boiling water, and in Sir Hugh Plat's words, 'in three quarters of an houre, or one whole houre at the most, you shall purchase the whole strength and tincture of the Rose ...'

Plat changed his petals seven times, Lady Fettiplace's recipes vary between nine and as little as three changes: the water must be reheated each time, and the rose liquor will evaporate a little, reducing in quantity as it improves in quality. Add the sugar at the end, dissolving it without ever allowing the syrup to boil, and remembering to reckon a pint at the old measure of 16 (*not* 20) fluid ounces. The more rose petals you can afford to use, and the darker they are, the stronger your syrup will be, but even half a pound of medium pink petals produces a small bottle of surprisingly dark, wine-red, rose-scented liquor, well worth keeping in the fridge for mixed drinks. Try it with white wine, or to give a new meaning to pink gin, or in the Cooleinge Julepp described towards the end of this chapter.

Although any scented red roses will do nicely in Lady Fettiplace's recipes, she herself always specifies the fragrant, light crimson damask roses, originally brought back from the East by the crusaders and used in perfumery ever since. Lady Hoby also grew musk roses which flowered twice, summer and autumn, in her Yorkshire garden. Anyone not already familiar with the delicate beauty and rich scent of old roses might try either, with perhaps the ancient Apothecary's Rose, *R. gallica officianalis*, brilliant crimson pink with gold stamens, virtually extinct by the 1930s according to Grieve's *Herbal* but readily available nowadays from specialist nurseries. It was probably the red rose of Lancaster, and may still be grown alongside the white rose of York—the great *Alba semi-plena*—together with their pink-and-white striped cousin, the sixteenth-century damask rose York and Lancaster. The Apothecary's Rose has a striped offspring, the exquisite *Rosa mundi*, also newly revived and so popular it can often be found in the more enterprising garden centres. Roses like these, grown with plain and pied gilliflowers—flecked, ringed, fringed or spotted like sops-in-wine—give some idea of our ancestors' pleasure in bright pure colours, clear contrasts, streaked and sharply stencilled patterns, splashes of gold, shapes more finely modelled than the double carnations and hefty hybrid teas favoured today. It is the same refined and fanciful taste that lies behind Lady Fettiplace's striped sugar plate, her printed jellies in Chapter Nine, her multicoloured tarts, milk-white creams and the array of jewelled fruit sweetmeats described in Chapter Twelve.

Haymaking and Picnics

July meant haymaking. When she wasn't busy with the rose harvest, Lady Hoby spent a good deal of time this month in the hay fields: 'After I had praied I went about the house and gott all out to the hay,' she wrote on July 11, 1600; and again on the last day of the month: 'I brak my fast and went abroad with the haymakers, and after I came home I praied and went to dinner.' All these haymakers had to be supplied with provisions as well as vast quantities of mildly alcoholic, cooling, thirst-quenching drinks, brewed specially at this time of year as they were at the festive season. The average consumption of small beer at Ingatestone Hall, probably round about a gallon per head on normal days, shot up at haymaking and harvest when a draught of 'sugar beer', with a slice of the sort of fruit cake described in the last chapter, remained the traditional labourers' elevenses right down to the early years of this century. The Lemmon-Mead made in April (see p. 105) should be ready to drink round about now, and makes a powerful restorative for people working all through the heat of the day, or for the sort of picnic got up by Lady Hoby and her friends on the evening of July 8, 1600: 'I was busie, wrought [sewed] & after took my Coch and went into the feeldes, and I did eat my supper with my mother and other freendes ...'

Dog Days

The best and strongest meads were said to be the ones made now and left to ferment in the full heat of the Dog Days, which fall this month and next, before, during and after the rising of Sirius the dog star. This was generally held in the seventeenth century to be not only the hottest but the most unwholesome period of the whole year, a time of malignant vapours when men wilted and dogs, being specially apt to run mad, had to be dosed against rabies. Lady Fettiplace gives three herbal remedies for the bite of a mad dog, including the curiously mild-sounding one (box leaves, pennyroyal and primroses in hot milk) inscribed by her secretary with a confident flourish on the penultimate page, 'By mee Anthony Bridges'; and a fourth—For a Mad Doggs Biting—that was to be administered hopefully to the rabid dog itself. Unhealthy influences at this time of year might be warded off with soothing juleps, a class of drink handed down by the Arabs and already beginning, like so much else in the culinary repertoire, to lose its medicinal connotations. This one makes a pleasant long drink served cold with ice cubes and a mint leaf or two, white wine, white rum, perhaps even Bourbon like its distant descendant, the modern American mint julep.

A COOLEINGE JULEPP:

A Cooling Julep

Take a quarte of ffrench barly water, and put therto of the sirrope of bleaw violets 2 ownces, Red rosewater 4 spoonefulls, the Juce of 2 limondes, sirop of the Juce of Cittrons 2 ownces, stirr all these together, and when you are dry or in yor burninge heate drinke 2 or 3 spoonffulls at a time, as ofte as you please

Lady Fettiplace gives instructions for preparing 'french barligh', which was ordinary, home-grown barley corn soaked, beaten 'with a beetle' in a sack, rubbed, winnowed and wetted—'I think five times beating will hull it cleane, if you take paines therein'—washed and dried off in the bread oven. A packet of bought pearl barley will probably have to do instead, though both taste and texture are different. Take three tablespoons of barley, wash it in several waters, and simmer it for ten minutes in a quart of fresh water which must then be strained and cooled. Citron syrup was made by boiling together equal parts of sugar and the squeezed juice of the citron or pomecitron, a larger and less acid relation of the lemon and lime, either of which will do instead. Syrup of blue violets and red rosewater (made, according to Sir Hugh Plat, by steeping a handful of 'crimson velvet coloured' rose petals in a stoppered glass of ordinary rosewater) would presumably produce a purple plum- or wine-coloured julep. Failing these, try ordinary rosewater with syrup of red roses or any of the coloured syrups given below. Mix the julep well in advance if you can, as it needs time to develop its full flowery flavour.

Lady Fettiplace gives another cooling julep flavoured with branches of rosemary, mace, grape juice, lemon syrup and rosewater. Experiment was clearly in order. Besides the red rose and violet syrups already quoted, she includes individual syrups of rosemary and purple clary flowers, as well as her cousin Mistress Gresham Thynne's Sirope of Red Cockle (otherwise known as field Nigel-weed), and this all-purpose receipt:

TO MAKE SIRROPE OF ANY HEARBE OR FLOWER

Herb and Flower Syrups

Fill an Earthen Jugge full of the herbes or flowers you will make sirroppe of, then ad to yt as much springe water as yor Jugge will receive, so let yt stand where yt may bee kept warme 2 howers, then straine yor licoure from the rest very hard, then to that licoure put more of the herbes or flowers, and let yt stand 2 howers as you did before, thus you must doe 3 times strayninge out the licoure and putinge in fresh herbes the last time ad to every pinte of licoure 2 pound of suger smale beaten, set yt in yor Jugge againe in a pott of warme water till yor suger bee disolved but cover yt not untill yt bee cold

Strawberry and Raspberry Syrups

If you will make sirrope of strawberies or Respice *or such smale fruite, put them hole into a Jugge and let them stand without any licoure,* Let *them stand warme 2 howers, then to each pinte ad 2 pound of suger, yt must then stand in a pott of warme water till yt bee disolved, then let ye clearest run through a Jely bagge which preserve to yor use*

Try making this with lemon balm or elderflowers, marvellously scented and blooming in every hedgerow at this time of year (Lady Fettiplace used them—dried, powdered and moistened with ale—to cure the stone). Follow the instructions for rose syrup given earlier in this chapter, and beware of insecticides if you use garden flowers. For a more concentrated syrup, leave the flowers to steep longer and change them more often: somebody—probably Elinor Fettiplace herself—has written in '2 howers', crossing out '24' three times in the manuscript, and substituting 'thus you must 3 times' for the original 'vi times'. Store these heavy syrups in corked jars or bottles in the fridge, and serve them with ice cubes, soda or barley water and alcohol if you like for long, cool drinks in the dog days.

8
AUGUST

August meant cutting the corn, harvest home, more hot work in the stillroom, more picnics and eating out of doors on a scale that must have required considerable organisation. Carts made their way to the fields at mid-day loaded with baskets, wallets, great cakes, casks and leather bottles: one hundred and twenty reapers working on three farms belonging to Ingatestone Hall (the Fettiplaces still owned at least as many in Elinor's day) consumed, in a single week in August 1552, half a steer (sent out ready carved from the kitchens), half an ox, four whole sheep and one hundred and sixty-two gallons of beer.

This sort of menu is barely touched on in Lady Fettiplace's book, presumably because basic roasting, baking and brewing techniques were too commonplace to be worth recording. Here is an altogether smaller and more delicate dish of buttered crayfish, which makes a nice start to a summer lunch or supper in the garden. These were the native crayfish Baskerville saw, fresh from the River Kennet, for sale in Newbury market. English rivers and streams used to be full of them and, though they are now almost wiped out by disease, you can still sometimes get them at this time of year from fish farms, or you could substitute Dublin Bay prawns. Crayfish look something like little lobsters, and turn scarlet like lobsters when cooked. This is the last culinary recipe in the book, clearly a favourite since it was copied out twice in the same wording on two consecutive pages by two different hands—one scratchy and cramped, the other large, round and neat—belonging perhaps to Lady Horner and one of her daughters, or whoever else last used Lady Fettiplace's manuscript as a working cookery book.

TO BUTTER CRAWFISH

Boyl the Crawfish and pick the fish out of the bodys tails and claws then take to an Hundred two or three spoonfulls of water and as much white wine a Blade of Mace or a little nutmeg a little salt and Lemmon peel let it simmer togather then put in the crawfish and shake e'm together and when they are through hot put in half a q^{r} of a pd of Butter keep e'm shaking till the butter be melted then put in a little juice of Lemon: you may if you please boyl the shells in the water you put in|

Buttered Crayfish

This is in essence a more elaborate version of the freshly caught shrimps of seaside holidays, boiled, peeled, buttered, sprinkled with lemon juice and eaten hot with bread and butter. Mrs Beeton's Potted Crayfish was still made, nearly three hundred years later, from the same ingredients in exactly the same quantities and proportions—one hundred crayfish mashed with mace, salt, pepper and two ounces of butter. Serve the crayfish in a watercress border with good brown bread, more white wine to drink and a green salad incorporating some of the sharp herbs and cresses, purslane, nasturtium, sorrel or any of the many other leaves that gave bite and variety to a seventeenth-century salad.

Lady Fettiplace's salad calendar included radishes—'Radish prove best that sowen a day after the full [moon] in August'—as well as successive plantings of lettuce ('All those seedes which you sow in the wane of the moon in Marche, will never runne to seede. And for those you will have run to seed the last quarter of the moon in Aprill is best to sow them in'). Summer was the time 'To make a Lettuse Pye' from 'the best leaved lettuse you can gett', boiled, quartered, buttered, mixed with three hardboiled egg yolks, raisins, currants, nutmeg, cinnamon, sugar and pepper, and finished off in the mediaeval manner: 'when the pye is baked make a sirrope of clarrette wine, suger, and vineger w^{t}h the yealke of an egg, beate it all together and put it into the pye and soe sarve him to the boarde'. This pie, which tastes as uncouth as it sounds, belongs to an antique tradition looking back to the Romans, and forward to the dried fruit and sugar seasoning still used to excellent effect in Italian vegetable cookery. Its adaptability may be seen in the rather good spinach tart given on p. 44. But this Lettuse Pye seems a throwback to an earlier age, and I mention it only because it serves in a sense to show up the unexpected modernity of so much else in Lady Fettiplace's repertoire.

Lettuce Pie

Continuity between her day and ours is the most obvious thing about a meal beginning with, say, a dish of buttered crayfish, going on to slices of the veal in piquant sauce described in the last chapter, and ending with the fool given below, which is in fact closer to what we should now call a trifle. The two words were interchangeable, according to John Florio's much-quoted dictionary definition of 1598—'a kind of clouted cream called a fool or a trifle in English'. This one is made from a rich egg custard poured over sippets soaked in sack or sherry: a little later in the century, fruit fools or creams were already being made, as they still are today, by mixing the custard with a purée of raspberries, red currants, gooseberries or quinces. A seventeenth-century fool was to cooking what an eighteenth-century folly was to architecture, a frivolous indulgence, strictly inessential to the serious business of food or shelter but nonetheless delightful for that.

TO MAKE A CREAME CALLED A FOOLE

A Fool or Trifle

Take thick creame and boile it with some sugar & a nutmeg sliced when it hath boiled a prettie while, put in the yelks of fower eggs well beaten, & stirre it about, & then take it from the fire, & put in two or three spoonfulls of rose water, then stirre it till it bee almost cold, then have sippets, cut in a dish and wet them through with sack, & then poure the creame to them, and when it is cold put some sugar & nutmeg smale sliced upon it, and so serve it.

For 4 egg yolks, you will need 1 pint of warm cream, sweetened and spiced (the sliced nutmegs often called for in cookery books of the period were perhaps a less desiccated version of the hard, dried nutmegs we know now). Two or 3 spoonfuls of rosewater would be about ½ a gill, or ⅛ of a pint, if you take a Jacobean spoon as holding roughly an ounce of liquid. Make the custard in a double boiler or bain marie, what Lady Fettiplace called *balneo Mariae* (a bath mild and gentle enough for the Virgin herself, according to the Oxford Dictionary). Her sensible precaution—'stirre it till it bee almost cold'—prevents curdling, and ensures a thick even cream to pour over your sherry-soaked sippets. These may be slices of crustless white bread, brioche, stale sponge cake, sponge fingers, or—best of all—the bisket bread on p. 119.

Almond Cream or Trifle

The last is quite possibly authentic, since instructions To Make a Creame on the next page call for an almond-milk custard thickened with layers of white wafers, which were another favourite and very old kind of crisp, brittle, thin biscuit. Like the fool above, this cream is more of a trifle, scented with rosewater and musk, and left to set in what sounds like individual bowls ('& so serve it in dishes when it is cold'). The secret of composite puddings like these two, or the Buttered Gooseberries on p. 126, is to leave them to stand overnight or longer until the sippets are thoroughly impregnated with the sherry and custard or fruit purée. If you make either the custard or the layer of sippets too thick, the result will be bready and solid rather than light and smooth to the palate as it should be. Serve these creams stone cold, or only very slightly chilled in the fridge. The simple strewing of sugar and spice could be replaced, as it often was on contemporary fools and trifles, with a more elaborate dressing of scarlet comfits, candied fruit and flowers, angelica, citrus peel, sliced dates, and 'fine carved sippets' or fancy biscuits. Fools like this were direct ancestors of the sumptuous Edwardian trifle, relegated today to children's parties, cafeteria-, hotel- and school-food only because of the substitution of commercial custard powder, synthetic whips, tinned fruit and packet sponges, for cream, eggs, fresh fruit and home-made bisket bread.

Here is a second fool concocted from the same ingredients, only put together slightly differently and baked in its dish to make something more like what we know as bread-and-butter pudding. This is another despised English dish degraded because nineteenth-century cooks economising on cream, eggs, dried fruit and sherry were too lavish with the bread in the bottom of the dish. Properly made, Lady Fettiplace's fool is nice hot in winter (see Chapter Eleven for The Lord of Devonshire his Pudding, and other variations on the same basic formula), but perhaps nicer still cold with a jug of thin cream in summer. If you bake it in a deep enamel dish or loaf tin, it makes good portable picnic food to be sliced and eaten in the fingers.

TO MAKE A FOOLE

A Fool or Baked Batter Pudding

Take the top of the mornings milk, boile it with some whole mace & nutmeg cut in quarters, when you take it from the fire put in a piece of butter into it, then have manchet cut thin, & poure the Creame hot upon it; so let it stand till it bee almost cold, then put to it the whites of two eggs, & the yelks of five & some sugar & rosewater, & two spoonfulls of seck, & a little salt, mingle it altogether & straine it, & put some currance into it, put it in a dish & bake it, & so serve it. You must make the stuf no thicker than batter.

Melt a good knob of butter in 2 pints of hot, spiced, 'top of the mornings milk' (use Channel Island milk, or half milk and half cream), and pour it over 4 or 5 thin slices of stale, crustless white bread. The preliminary soaking more or less dissolves the breadcrumbs, which are then to be beaten with 2 whole eggs and 3 yolks, previously whipped to a froth, 3 or 4 tablespoonfuls of sugar, 2 of rosewater, sack (2 Jacobean spoons held probably the equivalent of 4 modern tablespoons), and salt. Straining this bread mixture through a sieve would produce the smooth texture so much admired at this period, but the food tastes just as good unstrained. Add 4 oz. of currants, and bake in a greased dish for between 1¼ and 1½ hours in a moderate oven (Mark 4, 180°C, 350°F) until the pudding is firm, golden and slightly risen: Lady Fettiplace would have baked hers in the bread oven as soon as the bread had come out. This is a substantial pudding which will be plenty for six or eight of what Shakespeare called huge feeders, or for at least ten dainty ones.

This fool was copied out as part of a batch of sweet puddings, together with the White Pott below and the fine whipped Creame of Wealcruds on p. 102. White potts are common in seventeenth-century cookery books: John Nott collected eleven from various predecessors for his *Cooks and Confectioners Dictionary* in 1726. They are nearly always some sort of baked bread batter pudding (though two of Nott's are rich rice puddings, and one incorporates a layer of apple purée). The one below is good hot, better cold with cream and some sort of sharp fruit sauce made from gooseberries, red currants, damsons, or later in the season a big bowl of blackberries sprinkled with lemon juice and sugar.

TO MAKE A WHITE POTT

White Pott or Sour Cream Pudding

Take creame put to it as much flower as will make it as thick as batter that you make bisket bread with. then put in as many crums of bread as you can take up once in your hand, some mutton suet, small minced, & two eggs yolks & whites, & some salt, & some mace, & some sugar, two good spoonfulls of sowre creame out of the creame pot, temper all this together, then butter a dish & put it in, so bake it, & serve it.

The first direction is puzzling: presumably it means the sort of stiff light spongy batter that spreads if you drop it in spoonfuls on a baking tray. Nott is no great help since the consistency of his white potts varies considerably, ranging from four pints of cream, one dozen egg yolks and a whole penny loaf of bread, weighing probably about six ounces (or one pint cream, two egg yolks, one and a half ounces breadcrumbs) to two pints of cream, eight whole eggs and one and a half penny loaves. Devonshire White-Pott, using unspecified quantities of milk, eggs, flour and breadcrumbs, was to be 'about the thickness of Batter for Pan-cakes'.

I have made a nice, not-too-solid white pott from 1 pint thin cream or creamy milk, 4 oz. plain flour, 1 oz. fresh breadcrumbs (which is as much as I can take up once in my hand), 1 tablespoon of beef suet (failing mutton), 2 eggs, 2 tablespoonfuls sugar and 2 generous Jacobean spoonfuls—roughly $\frac{1}{2}$ gill, or $\frac{1}{8}$ pint—of sour cream. Mix the flour to a paste with a little of the cream, then gradually beat in the rest of the ingredients with a pinch of powdered mace or nutmeg. Butter the dish very well, and bake the pot for 40 to 50 minutes in a medium oven (Mark 4, 180°C, 350°F).

White Pott with Fruit

Turn the white pott out to eat cold with more dollops of sour cream on top. Or it makes a pleasant alternative to a pastry base for a fruit tart, if you bake it in a shallow round flan tin (it will probably take only half an hour to cook), and serve it with fresh soft fruit or a thick cooked fruit purée. It is specially good with the leftover apricots from the Apricocke Wine on p. 135, where the thrifty cook recommends bottling the liquor and using up the fruit in a pudding ('ye Apricocks make a good service for yor tables for present spending'); and also with the apricot preserve below.

TO PRESERVE APRICOCKS

Apricot Preserve

Take your fayrest apricocks pare them and stoone them, then take their waight in sugar and as you pare them lay them in the dry sugar on by another and cover them with sugar all over then cover them close with a dish, and let them stand till the next day, then boile them till they bee cleere and the syrrop thicke

This is a simple, foolproof jam, finely flavoured and 'of a good culler', which sets easily after a quarter of an hour or so, twenty minutes at most. There is no need, so far as I can see, to skin the fruit unless on grounds of strict authenticity (Elizabethan and Jacobean cooks were fastidious about removing skins, de-seeding gooseberries, straining out pips, so as to produce a perfectly smooth texture whereas we, in an age of bland machine homogenisation, tend to prefer a rougher finish). The overnight soaking in sugar will release the fruit juices, but don't forget to weigh the apricots *after* stoning them, and don't on any account let them boil before all the sugar has melted.

This is one of three different methods of preserving apricots, any one of which will work for plums ('but they must not be pared') or peaches as well. Lady Fettiplace used what is still the standard technique for jam-making, in which the fruit is stewed gently to soften it and extract the pectin or setting agent, then boiled fast with sugar until it will set. Alternatively, she dropped the raw peeled apricots into a thick hot syrup which was then left to stand, before the final boiling, till the fruit was tender and the syrup stone cold. This method, like the one given above, has the advantage of cooking the fruit with sugar only and no additional water. Here it is applied to peaches:

TO PRESERVE PEACHES

Peach Preserve

Take the peaches & scald them in faire water till they will skin, then pill them & wey to every pound a pound of sugar, put so much water to it as will wet the sugar, then boile it & scum it, & when it is almost could put in the peaches & boile them softlie till they bee doone, if you will make Cakes of them, pare them raw, & put them in a stone pot, & stue them in water as you doo plums, & when they are stewed make it up as you doo plums Cakes.

For how to make Plum Cakes, or sweetmeats, see p. 176. This recipe is for whole peaches (use small, finely flavoured, home-grown ones if possible) in clear syrup. Dissolve the sugar slowly in very little water—say half a cupful per pound—and boil the syrup for five minutes to thicken it a little before adding the peeled fruit. It will probably not need much skimming with modern refined sugar. The preserve is to be boiled until the syrup reaches whatever consistency you prefer: fairly stiff for spreading or jam, runnier for tart fillings or for use in trifles, fools and ice creams.

Lady Fettiplace's Marmalad of Apricocks, given below, was to be cooked till it was thick enough to cut with a knife, or at least hold the tracks of the blade, before being poured out to set in storage boxes for what her contemporaries called winter spending. If kept long enough in its box, it will turn into what country people used to call apricot leather. Alternatively, if you stop cooking at an earlier stage, you will have one of the very best breakfast marmalades.

TO MAKE MARMALAD OF APRICOCKS

Apricot Marmalade

Take to a pounde of Apricockes a pounde of suger wantinge 3 ownces wet yor suger in water & boyle yt untill yt come to candy then pare the plumes and cut them in quarters so put them into yor suger let them boyle till they will cut still stiringe and breakeinge them as fast as they boyle, when yt is enough put yt in boxes but cover yt not untill yt bee cold

This is the same method as for the gooseberry preserve on p. 128. Take a quarter of a pint of water per pound of sugar, make it into a syrup and boil hard till it reaches the soft ball stage (240°F, 115°C), and crystallises. Have the raw apricots (or 'plumes') ready peeled, stoned and chopped, add them to the pan of candied sugar and leave the marmalade to dissolve slowly over a very low heat before boiling it hard and vigilantly—'still stiringe and breakeinge them as fast as they boyle'—to a thick paste. Be especially careful in the final stages just before the marmalade begins to candy at the edges and leave the sides of the pan. Pour or spoon it out before it thickens too much. Chip boxes or the thin wooden cartons still made in France and Spain for biscuits and sweetmeats make a substitute for authentic marmalade boxes. Alternatively use an oiled metal baking tin or tray, turn the marmalade out as soon as it has hardened and store it in layers between foil or greaseproof paper in a cake tin.

Crystallised apricots and sugar plums, delicious and decorative, were another popular item on winter banqueting tables, judging by the number of recipes like this one.

TO DRIE APRICOCKS, PEACHES, PIPPINS OR PEARPLUMS

Crystallised Fruit

Take your apricocks or pearplums, & let them boile one walme in as much clarified sugar as will cover them, so let them lie infused in an earthen pan three dayes, then take out your fruits, & boile your syrupe againe, when you have thus used them three times then put half a pound of drie sugar into your syrupe, & so let it boile till it come to a verie thick syrup, wherein let your fruits boile leysurelie 3 or 4 walmes, then take them foorth of the syrup, then plant them on a lettice of rods or wyer, & so put them into yor stewe, & every second day turne them & when they bee through dry you may box them & keep them all the yeare; before you set them to drying you must wash them in a little warme water, when they are half drie you must dust a little sugar upon them throw a fine Lawne.

(by the Lady tracy)

The Lady Tracy was Anne Shirley, sister to the playwright Henry Shirley and wife to Elinor Fettiplace's kinsman Sir John Tracy of Toddington in Gloucestershire. Like the Verneys of Claydon, the Tracys of Toddington clearly had special stillroom equipment for this sort of work: the 'stewe' was a drying stove heated by a charcoal burner, perhaps fitted with slatted shelves or slots to hold a 'lettice', or lattice, of rods or wire. Use a cake rack or toasting grid, and dry the fruit out in any warm place—a plate warmer, airing cupboard, perhaps even in hot weather a gas oven with no more than the pilot light turned on.

Pearplums were a kind of long plum shaped like a pear or an electric light bulb. The fruit is to be laid in a thick-bottomed pan between layers of sugar which is then warmed very gently indeed until it has all melted to syrup. Do this as carefully as possible, stirring every now and then and scraping the sugar from the sides of the pan. As soon as the syrup is thoroughly dissolved, bring it to the boil once, remove the pan from the heat and leave it to stand for three days with a plate on top to submerge the fruit (there is no need to transfer it to an earthen pan if you used an enamelled pan in the first place). Repeat this boiling, cooling and soaking process three times. Now boil the syrup down hard with the fresh sugar till it thickens perceptibly and darkens a little in colour before returning the fruit to it: '3 or 4 walmes', or warms, means three or four boilings-up, say three or four minutes gentle boiling in all.

The last two directions give a professional finish to the crystallised fruit (which makes nice presents, boxed in little silver or frilly white paper cases). This sort of detail, clearly coming from an experienced practical cook, is not perhaps what you might expect at first glance from a Tracy of Toddington. The family were as old and illustrious as the Fettiplaces (William de Tracy—'a gentleman of high birth, state and stomach' according to Fuller—was one of the four knights who murdered Thomas à Becket, hence the Gloucestershire proverb: 'The Tracys have always the wind in their faces'). They were still a family to be reckoned with in the West country, powerful reformists in the sixteenth century, royalists in the seventeenth, heavily fined like both Fettiplaces and Pooles after the civil war, when Elinor Fettiplace's nephew, Sir William Poole, married Meriel Tracy, grand-daughter of the Lady Tracy from whom this recipe came.

Banqueting Stuff

Skill in cookery—at any rate in sauces, salads and sweetmeats, the kind of refined and civilised cookery described in Lady Fettiplace's book—far from being a sign of impoverishment or decay was an accomplishment practised by the highest in the land. The great Lady Anne Clifford, daughter to the Earl of Cumberland, wife to the Earls of Dorset and Pembroke successively, recorded in her diary making rosemary cakes in the castle at Knole, and a great deal of quince marmalade. 'I was busie about presarving sweetmeats,' wrote Lady Hoby on August 6, 1600: admittedly she was a puritan, hard-working, devout and unostentatious, but she was also an heiress, a woman of considerable property in her own right, and daughter-in-law to Lady Anne Clifford's aunt, Lady Russell, who specialised in organising state occasions, processions and feasts, including the party at which the Queen knighted Richard Fettiplace in 1600. A contemporary account of another splendid party three years later, given this time for the new King James stopping off on his progress from Scotland to visit Sir Anthony Mildmay at Apethorpe in Northamptonshire, illustrates the importance attached to prowess in the kitchen: 'The tables were newly covered with costly banquets wherein everything that was most delicious for taste proved more delicate by the Arte that made it seeme beauteous to the eye: the Ladye of the house being one of the most excellent confectioners in England, though I confesse many honourable women very expert.'

Lady Fettiplace herself must have been one of these honourable experts, judging by the amount of space given to fruit preserves and confectionery in her book. Lady Mildmay, born Grace Sherrington of Lacock Abbey in Wiltshire, was another West country heiress, and remained so proud of her art that, when she sat for her portrait at the age of sixty-two in 1613, she had a couple of stills and her household receipt book displayed in the background like the trophies of learning or war. Sir Hugh Plat, writing in 1602, fourteen years after the Spanish Armada, draws the parallel between the culinary and martial arts quite explicitly:

Empaling now adieu: tush, marchpane wals,
Are strong enough and best befits our age:
Let pearcing bullets turn to sugar bals,
The Spanish feare is husht and all their rage.
Of marmelade and paste of Genua,
Of musked sugar I intend to wrighte,
Of Leach, of Sucket, and Quidinea,
Affording to each Ladie, her delight ...

Lady Fettiplace's Quidinea, or Quince Paste, may be found on p. 201, her Leach on p. 81, Orange Marmalades on pp. 66–8, and Marchpane on p. 228. The crystallised fruit given earlier in this chapter are dry suckets, and so are the Plum Cakes on p. 176. Here is something nearer to a modern jam:

TO PRESERVE GREENE GRAPES

Green Grape Preserve

Take a pound of sugar, & a pound of white grapes, before they be through ripe, then take your grapes & scald them in a water, so long untill you may pull of a thinne skinne, then slit them on the side, then put as much water to the sugar as will wet it, then boyle your syrop first, then put in your grapes, & so let them boyle; not verie fast, untill they bee throughlie doone; This way you may doe pearplums or gooseberries. when they bee scalded you must boyle them in water, till they look greene, then put them in the syrope.

Scalding the fruit in hot water and peeling it was a way of intensifying the colour of green preserves, but this one will taste just as good if you leave out the preliminary stages. Slitting the grapes presumably released the pips which will float to the surface in any case during boiling, and should be removed with a slotted spoon. The preserve will be 'throughlie doone' as soon as the syrup shows signs of jelling.

In a cold English summer when grapes fail to ripen, this is a useful recipe for anyone with a vine like Sir Ralph Verney, who grew 'goode Eateing grapes of severall sorts' in his garden at Claydon before the civil war. But for a Jacobean housewife with her banqueting tables in mind, the greenness of a grape preserve was quite as important as its delicious taste. Paintings like the Unton panel in the National Portrait Gallery, commissioned by Elinor Fettiplace's cousin Dorothy, show diners seated on either side of a long table symmetrically set all down its length with big and small dishes in bright contrasting colours. Banquets put on for a special occasion—a wedding, a birthday, a royal entry or progress—were as much part of the art of spectacle as the accompanying pageants, tourneys, masques and festivals. Lady Mildmay's array of confectionery for the King in 1603 would have been dazzling to look at, brilliantly coloured, intricately patterned, formal, hierarchical, quite possibly allegorical as well.

Culinary skill, then as now, gave scope for the ambitious and competitive spirit. Anyone prepared to set aside a little time over the next two or three months to make sweetmeats from each fruit in turn—apricots, plums, apples, quinces, rosehips—may get some inkling of the satisfaction women like Grace Mildmay and Elinor Fettiplace must have given and got from their displays of sweetmeats, glowing, jewelled and embossed as elaborately as the interiors of the period. Suckets could hardly be simpler to make, or the results more impressive, but it is important to start round about now with

Green Fruit

the green or unripe fruit which provides the sharp end of the palette, essential to balance the autumnal reds, oranges and purples that come later in the year. Lady Fettiplace gives half a dozen recipes for green fruit, together with a note on timing that has somehow got shuffled and copied out by her secretary in the middle of a recipe for face lotion: 'Doo green apples at St. Jamestide, greene peare plums in the middle of August, greene white plums in the middle of June'. St James' Day is July 25; Michaelmas (mentioned in the next recipe) is September 29. Theoretically, eleven days should be added to each of these dates to accommodate the calendar changes of 1752, but there are so many modern varieties of plum and apple cropping at staggered intervals that in practice the easiest rule is to pick them four or five weeks before they are due to ripen, according to Lady Fettiplace's instructions below. You will need only a small amount: housewives of the period normally worked with a single pound of fruit at a time, which will produce two or three small pots of fruit preserve, or something like two dozen pretty little green suckets.

TO PRESERVE GREENE FRUIT ANOTHER WAY

Green Apple Cakes or Sweetmeats

Take the apples before they bee ripe, I take it you gather your apples about Michaelmas, & let this bee some moneth or five weeks before, then heat some faire water & let it boyle, then take it of & let it stand till it bee somwhat colder, so put in your apples to scald, & cover them with some little dish or pieplate, that may fall in upon them to keep them under the water, & have another skillet full of water ready heat against that bee cold, they wilbee a great while a scalding, & at last will hardlie peele but with takeing up the skin with the point of a knife, when they are peeled set over the fire one of the skilletts of water; but in any wise, let it be the same water they were scalded in, & not fresh water, & when it boyles put in your apples, & let them boile till they turne greene, wch wilbee quickly, then take the weight of them in sugar, & put as much water to it as you shall think good, but not over much, for the lesser the better, so there bee inough to boile them throughly, so put them into it cold, & set them over the fire, & let them boyle a pretty fastnes, till you think they bee well; you must not make your syrup first of any of the greene fruit, but put the sugar & the fruit on the fire together.

Skinning small sour green apples is fiddly work (though a great deal less so than skinning sweet chestnuts, or knobbly Jerusalem artichokes), but effective. The preserve will be a true apple green, quite unlike the nondescript, yellowish or browny tinge of ordinary stewed apple pap. It sets well (pectin being always most abundant in unripe fruit), and tastes particularly good, not over-sweet, stronger and more appley than a purée of ripe fruit (which tends to insipidity without some sort of sharpener like lemon peel, ginger or spices).

The trick of the initial scalding and skinning is to shift the apples from one pan of water as soon as it cools to the second, which should have been reheated meanwhile. After three or four changes of water, the skin will peel off even the hardest fruit quite easily in strips and swathes with the help of a small pointed knife. Remove only the colourless, paper-thin outer skin, leaving the green apple peel. Keep the apples submerged in water as hot as your fingers can bear, as you do when peeling chestnuts. Reheat one of the pans of water as soon as the apples are all done, and simmer them in it. Another recipe—To make Cakes of Greene Plums—stipulates that the pan must be covered throughout this process, which will take a quarter of an hour, and that the plum pulp must then be strained through canvas. Apples are more of a problem. They will disintegrate during the final boiling, so, unless the pips are to be left in (which is possible but improbable, given such an extremely fastidious cook), the fruit must either be cored first or strained afterwards. The second alternative is perhaps the more likely, and quite easy to do at the end with a coarse nylon or hair (not metal) sieve.

The whole process is a great deal simpler than unfamiliarity makes it sound. Take a pound of green apples. Scald and skin them according to the directions above. Simmer them in the water in which they were soaked for fifteen minutes in a lidded pan. Now put them with a pound of sugar and a cupful of their water into a thick-bottomed pan over a gentle heat until the sugar has all dissolved. Boil hard, stirring constantly towards the end as the mixture thickens. It will be done as soon as it takes on a slightly shiny, gelatinous look and begins to pull away from the sides of the pan. Sieve it, and pour it out while it is still warm.

It can be made up either as sweetmeats, or as green marmalade. For sweetmeats, spoon the mixture out into oiled, patterned, patty-pan trays, or any similar small oiled moulds, and leave it till it is thoroughly dry, which will probably take several days even in warm weather. For marmalade, the mixture should be put straight into a foil-lined marmalade box (see p. 52), or spread on an oiled tin to set, before being sliced and boxed. A charming conceit, in a recipe for Dried Greene Plums, is to shape the thick sweet purée, or 'plumstuf', as soon as it has cooled a little, into round sweetmeats each with a dried plum kernel in the middle: the recipe ends, 'This way you may make Cakes of any other fruit', to which Lady Fettiplace has added a last word in her own handwriting: 'or of plumes grene or marmalad'.

Green Plum Cakes

The final apple preserve is a firm, shiny fruit butter of a fine texture, good flavour and pure soft green colour, quite unlike Lady Fettiplace's translucent, colourless White Pippins (done with oranges, see p. 67), or the rich, claret-coloured Red Pippins on p. 181. This green is the complement of a true red, which is why the two go so well together in the raspberry and gooseberry tartlets suggested earlier, or in a patterned array of winter sweetmeats: try some of these apple suckets arranged on a plate with rosehip or coral-coloured quince suckets to make a pattern in what we still think of as traditional Christmassy colours. The only snag is that, though green apple sweetmeats keep well, the colour deteriorates with time.

This particular recipe for green fruit is part of a batch of notably detailed and well thought out preserves: it comes after iellie of oringes, and is followed by a preserve of red wardens or pears, conserves of roses and rosehips, and the raspberry preserve on p. 130. Whoever supplied them evidently had a whole repertoire of different greens in mind to go with her various reds, for the recipe is followed by a note at the foot of the page—'turne the leaf'—and further instructions on the next page:

AN ADDITION TO THE GREEN FRUIT

Green Plums, Gooseberries and Grapes

Greene plums are to bee doone in the same sort, being taken a good while before they bee ripe, & you must bee more carefull in scalding of them for feare of breaking; white wheaten plums must bee peeled, but white peare plums if you take them a prettie while before they bee ripe wilbee greene without peeling, but they must bee scalded & boyled as the other bee. Likewise gooseberries & grapes being peeled must bee doone even as the plums are.

Lastly, for anyone whose teeth are set on edge by so much sweet stuff, here are two fruit cordials that seem to belong not so much to the early seventeenth-century banqueting board as to the more intimate Restoration tea table. At the end of Lady Fettiplace's book, on almost the last blank pages before the index, someone with a pretty, flowing hand and a fine nib has copied out a dozen receipts, including the Lemmon-Mead given on p. 105, another mead, cherry brandy and at least three more of the 'filthy strong waters' (orange water, cinnamon water and ratafia) Mirabell expressly forbade on his wife's tea table in Congreve's *The Way of the World.* Here is a cherry brandy set down probably round about the time Lady Wishfort first helped herself to a bottle of it in the middle of her toilet, hoping to put a little colour in her cheeks, when she found the maid had locked the make-up cupboard and gone out taking the key with her:

TO MAKE MORELLA BRANDY

Cherry Brandy

Ten p^d^ of Morella Cherrys stript off ye stalks to 2 Gallons of Brandy; crack all ye stones & infuse y^m^ by themselves. Let ye cherrys stand in ye Brandy a full fortnight well broke & mixt. put a p^d^ of fine sugar, then squeeze your cherrys very well & mix both this & your infus'd Brandy together. Sweeten it to your Taste & philter it

The labour required to stone ten pounds of cherries by hand, let alone cracking *all* the stones, would be as prohibitive nowadays as the price of two gallons of brandy, but it might be worth experimenting with smaller quantities: 1 lb. bitter morello cherries to a bottle of brandy and just over 1½ oz. sugar. Proportions are much the same in modern recipes for cherry brandy which is normally made, like sloe gin, by the easier method of pricking the fruit and leaving it to soak in spirits for anything up to six months. Presumably the squeezed cherry juice would produce something altogether fruitier. Here is another of Lady Wishfort's regular standbys:

TO MAKE RATTAFIA

Ratafia or Apricot Brandy

Take a Gallon of Brandy, put it into a wide-mouth'd Glass; then take 4 dozen of Apricocks, pare y^m^ & cut y^m^ into quarters, & put y^m^ to ye Brandy. Then take ye Kernels out of ye stones & bruise y^m^ a little & put y^m^ to ye Brandy; Blader down ye Glass & set it in ye sun for 14 days or 3 weeks according to ye heat of ye weather. Then strain it of & put it into Bottles for use.

9
SEPTEMBER

Ben Jonson, inviting a friend to supper and promising not to spoil the occasion by reciting verses, apologised for the plainness of the food:

It is the fair acceptance, sir, creates
The entertainment perfect, not the cates.
Yet you shall have, to rectify your palate,
An olive, capers, or some better salad
Ushering the mutton ...

He offered also a chicken with lemons and wine for sauce, a rabbit, perhaps some larks or a game bird if any could be had for ready money, and he proposed sending out for something decent to drink:

Digestive cheese, and fruit, there sure will be;
But that, which most doth take my Muse and me,
Is a pure cup of rich Canary wine,
Which is the Mermaid's now, but shall be mine.

This sounds a simple but satisfactory menu of the sort laid on in London cookshops or lodging houses by hard-up poets, playwrights and literary types from that day to this. It is essentially a scaled-down version of the three-course meals served in a much larger contemporary establishment like the Fettiplaces'. Elinor's lemon-and-white-wine sauce for meat is on p. 91, her baked rabbit on p. 56, and here is her version of mutton with capers:

TO BOYLE A BREAST OF MUTTON

Breast of Mutton with Piquant Sauce

First boyle him in water and salte, then take halfe a pinte of whight wine vineger, and as much of the broth yor muton was boyled in, large mace, and some suger a handfull of parsley, time, and sweete marierom, the yelkes of fower hard egges and a little of the rine of an oringe, yor herbes egges and oringe rinde must bee chopped smale and boyled in your broath, when yt is well boyled lay yor muten on sippetts in a dish, and put a good peece of sweete Buter into yor broath and so powre yt on yor muton, On the topp lay sliced Limondes and capers but yor Capers must bee layed in warme water the space of a quarter of an hower ere you lay them on yor meate

Breast of mutton (lamb will do instead) is a humble cut, much improved in both looks and flavour by this decorative green-and-yellow sauce with its garnish of capers and lemon wheels. A single, good-sized breast of lamb, weighting 1½ to 2 lb., will be enough for three or four. Chop it into sections, removing as much fat as possible, and simmer it in enough salted water to cover—probably not much more than a pint—in a lidded pan for 1 to 1½ hours. Remove the meat to a very hot serving dish and keep it warm. Add a tablespoon of white wine vinegar to the liquor, and reduce it if necessary by fast boiling to about half a pint (equal parts of vinegar and broth is decidedly too fierce for modern taste: perhaps Lady Fettiplace's breast of mutton was larger, her vinegar milder, or her broth already greatly reduced). Simmer this mixture for a few minutes.

Have ready a handful of chopped parsley, thyme and marjoram, pounded with the yolks of four hardboiled eggs (use one or two of the chopped whites, if you like, to strew on top at the end). Stir in the broth with a seasoning of sugar, mace (or nutmeg), the grated rind of half an orange (add a squeeze of lemon juice, if you are using an ordinary sweet orange), and more salt if necessary. Reheat the sauce, which will be quite thick, with a knob of butter and pour it over the meat. Don't forget the capers previously plumped in hot water. Serve it with a dish of green beans or glazed carrots or simply with a green salad.

This is a concentrated, modern version of what would originally have been a more copious and much runnier sauce, intended to be sopped up by sippets. It is clearly an ancestor of plain English caper sauce, also of the classic French *sauce gribiche*: a *pot-au-feu* is still served in France with something very like this garnish, except for the orange peel—a touch well worth reviving, especially in winter when you can get Seville oranges.

A chapter on storage in *The Countrey Farme*, which Lady Fettiplace possessed, recommends keeping oranges and lemons out of season in a cool, underground cellar, or alternatively salting them down in barrels like olives: Lady Fettiplace certainly used the juice and rind of Seville oranges to flavour the sweet potatoes (see the next chapter) harvested at the end of the summer. She stored raw quinces to keep 'all the yeare' in barrels, packed down in a liquor made from leftover stewed peel and cores ('Take the cores & parings of all the quinces you spend ...'). By the month of September her store-rooms must have been beginning to fill up with barrels and stone jars of pickled artichokes, cucumbers, samphire and perhaps mushrooms. Here is a late seventeenth-century recipe, added near the end of her manuscript in the same handwriting as Lemmon-Mead on p. 105 and the fruit liqueurs at the end of the last chapter. It is a light, fresh-tasting pickle, as far removed as possible from the fierce, tangy, concentrated catsups so popular as a relish in the nineteenth century. These marinaded mushrooms, aromatic and lightly spiced with green ginger in white wine, may be kept for enlivening winter salads (hardly necessary now that mushrooms are readily available all the year round), or eaten right away, in which case they make a nice change from mushrooms *à la Grecque* to start a meal.

TO PICKLE MUSHROOMS

Pickled or Marinaded Mushrooms

Take your Buttons, clean y^{m} with a spunge & put y^{m} in cold water as you clean y^{m}, then put y^{m} dry in a stewpan & shake a handfull of salt over y^{m}, y^{n} stew y^{m} in their own liquor till they are a little tender; then strain y^{m} from ye liquor & put y^{m} upon a cloath to dry till they are quite cold. Make your Pickle before you do your Mushrooms, y^{t} it may be quite cold before you put y^{m} in. The Pickle must be made with White-Wine, White-Pepper, quarter'd Nutmeg, a Blade of Mace, & a Race of ginger.

'Buttons' were the round, tight knobs of young field mushrooms (this recipe pre-dates by a century or so the Oxford Dictionary's first recorded instance of button mushrooms in 1743), often cultivated for home consumption on the larger estates in the seventeenth century. Modern commercial button mushrooms will do very well instead. Make the marinade or pickling liquor first. For 1 lb. mushrooms, you will need about $\frac{1}{3}$ pint of white wine, 6 white peppercorns, half a nutmeg, a blade of mace and a 1 inch piece of fresh ginger root, peeled and sliced. Put them all into a small saucepan and simmer, covered, with the lid on, for ten minutes (add a few spoonfuls of water if the liquid shows signs of evaporating). Leave to cool.

Wipe the mushrooms clean. Put them, whole, in a large, thick-bottomed saucepan with a heaped teaspoonful of salt, and heat them gently, shaking and stirring with a wooden spoon from time to time, especially at first before the juices begin to flow. Keep the lid on between stirs. Gradually the mushrooms will plump up, squeaking and giving off a wonderful smell, as they begin first to sweat lightly, then to stew in their own juice. This is an excellent way of cooking them, concentrating their flavour, keeping their shape, and wasting none of their liquor. It will not take long till they are tender, ten minutes at the outside. Watch them constantly, and if you catch them at exactly the right moment, there will be little or no liquor to strain off.

Pot them when cold in sterilised and tightly sealed jars if they are for pickling; or, if they are for present spending, pour the marinade straight on to the mushrooms in their pan as soon as they are done, tender, moist, and absorbent but not yet oozing juice. Decant them into a bowl or dish and leave them, covered, for a few hours to develop their flavour. Serve them with chopped parsley, and plenty of fresh bread—or sippets—to mop up the juices. Alternatively, you could simply pour a little hot thick cream over the cooked mushrooms and eat them at once by themselves, on toast, with scrambled eggs, or as a stuffing for Lady Fettiplace's version of a two-egg omelette:

TO MAKE A LIGHT FRAYSE

A Light Fraise or Savoury Omelette

Take wheten flower and cold water if you make 4 frayses put in eight egges whights and yelkes you must beate yt very well together and make yt no thicker then thicke Creame put nuttmegge salte and ginger therein, then let yor butter bee scaldinge hott in yor pan and powre in yor Batter, as yt doth begin to bake stirr yt wth a knife untill yt will frye w^{t}hout stickinge, then turne yt in a dish and fry the other side untill yt bee enough

This seventeenth-century quick snack, midway between a substantial pancake and a reinforced omelette, goes back a long way. Dr Johnson defined a fraise as a pancake with bacon in it. The Oxford Dictionary quotes from John Gower's *Confessio Amantis* in 1390:

He routeth with a sleepy noise
And brustleth as a monkes froise
Whan it is throwe into the panne.

Clearly fourteenth-century monks fried their fraises in sizzling hot butter exactly as Lady Fettiplace describes, according to what remains classic omelette technique today. I find that half an ounce, or a level tablespoonful, of flour per egg, mixed with a little water to the consistency of double cream, produces a thick pancake which is indeed good with lightly fried, chopped bacon. Cook it in plenty of butter, be generous with the spices, and serve it with more melted butter, more spices to strew on at table and a green salad, or with some sort of sauce. The mushrooms given above go very well. So does the boyled spinage on p. 43. Nutmeg and ginger are unexpectedly good with either, or for that matter with a sweetened apple purée, which is the traditional filling for the pudding still called Friar's Omelette.

Lady Fettiplace's frayse is also good cold, wrapped or rolled round a filling, easy to pack for picnics and to eat in the fingers. In pre-industrial days these solid pancakes were made in huge quantities, perhaps fifty or a hundred at a time, and carried in baskets down to the harvest field to be eaten with wedges of cheese or cold meat and washed down with small beer or mead. The combination would still make an admirable picnic.

The last of the corn harvest in September coincided with the first of the ripe orchard crops, gathered presumably on the same large scale as the rose harvest. Lady Fettiplace gives altogether four dozen recipes for plums, apples, pears, quinces, rosehips and barberries, all of which had to be sorted, stored, strung up to dry, packed in straw, or processed, potted and boxed over the next couple of months. Here is a simple classic plum jam:

TO PRESERVE PLUMS WHOLE

Plum Preserve

Take to everie pound of plums one pound & a quarter of sugar, beat the sugar, & put as much water to it as will wet it, then boyle it & scum it, then take it from the fire, & when it is almost cold put in your plums, & turne them up & downe in the syrupe, then set them on the fire, & let them boile verie softlie till they bee all broken, then take them of, and let them stand two howers, then set them on the fire againe, & boile them quite up to all sorts of plums or gellies of plums, you must take more then their weight of sugar.

'Plums whole' in this context seems to mean that the fruit is not stoned first (the stones will float to the top and can be removed with a slotted spoon), rather than that the preserve contains whole fruit. The result is what we think of nowadays as conventional jam, what the French call *confiture*, to be eaten with a teaspoon, spread on bread or cakes, used for filling tarts and pastries.

Next is an all-purpose recipe for the fruit cakes and marmalades so popular in the seventeenth century. It sets out very clearly the difference between the two, which was purely a matter of the drying-out method used at the end, not of ingredients, proportions or basic technique. Both were made from the same thick fruit purée, what we should nowadays call a fruit cheese. For plum marmalade, it was poured out and left to cool like a slab of toffee, then cut up into squares for eating only after it had thoroughly dried out in its box. Plum cakes were small individual sweetmeats, cut, stamped, or moulded, and dried out separately before being packed in boxes for storage.

Recipes for damson cheese still linger on in modern cookery books: ideally, it should be made from the small, hard, spicy, old-fashioned damsons, black-skinned and green-fleshed, which produce a cheese of incomparable flavour, fine squidgy texture and rich colour, 'almost black, cutting a deep purple' in Dorothy Hartley's phrase. By the nineteenth century, plum cheeses were generally potted up in oiled, straight-sided, wide-mouthed jars, kept for six months (they improve with keeping up to two years, after which the cheese begins to shrink from the sides of its jar, crusting over with sugar and growing steadily darker and chewier), then eased out and sliced in rounds. Among the Victorian dinner-party desserts described by Miss Hartley, a damson cheese was one of the handsomest, turned out whole and stuck with white almonds, 'crimson in a pool of port wine on a gold-washed dish'. Here is Lady Fettiplace's recipe for this prince of old English sweets.

TO MAKE PLUM CAKES

Plum Cheese and Marmalade

Take plums & pare them, then set them on the fire, in a dish, & let them stand till they bee broken, then take their stones from them, & prick them small, then way to every pound a pound of sugar, & wet the sugar with water & set it on the fire, let it boile till it bee sugar againe, then have your plums hot on the fire, & put it to the sugar & stir it well together but let it not boile, so poure it out & set it wher fier is to dry: This way you may make Cakes of Respis, *strawberries, barbaries, peches or any other fruit, but you must straine out the stones and the skins of the smale fruits; If you will make marmalad of any of this, then when it is hot poure it into boxes, & set it in a cupboord wher fire is, to dry, till it will cut. That which you will have for Cakes poure on a pieplate & when it is dry on the one side, cut it & turne the other side to dry, & let that dry also.*

Cakes of Raspberry, Strawberry, Barberry or Peach

Instead of laboriously skinning the plums, then stoning and pricking (or mashing) them, it is probably simpler to strain the cooked pulp, whatever the fruit you are using. Pushing the purée, skins and all, though a hair sieve till you are left with only the bare stones is hard work, but worth it for concentrated richness of colour and flavour. The preliminary slow softening of the fruit, which Lady Fettiplace did 'in a dish' over some sort of charcoal burner, can be done nowadays in a covered pot in a slow oven. Weigh equal amounts of sugar and strained fruit pulp. Wet the sugar with half a cupful of water per pound and dissolve it slowly, boil hard till it candies, then melt the sugar again by the addition of the hot fruit pulp (see the instructions To Preserve Plums or Gooseberries on p. 128 for how to do this). The mixture should now be ready for drying out without further boiling (if the plumstuff still seems too runny, simply boil it on gently, *stirring all the time*, till it begins to thicken a little and cohere), which is why Lady Fettiplace's preserves are often so much better flavoured than a modern jam or cheese where the fruit may need as much as thirty minutes' hard boiling before it will set.

Now you must decide how to dry it out. If you want separate plum cakes, pour it onto plates to dry, then cut or stamp it out (for more elaborate decorative effect, turn to the instructions for Printed Gellie on pp. 184–5). For marmalade, put it straight into a lined box, or pour it out onto an oiled baking tin in a layer three quarters of an inch or so thick, leave it to dry for a few days, then roll it out thin with a rolling pin on a sugared board, cut it into rounds or squares, and store them in boxes between layers of greaseproof paper. Miss Hartley describes how plum cheeses were made and stored in country farmhouses right up to the beginning of this century according to a method that sounds very like Lady Fettiplace's three hundred years earlier: 'The cheeses were sometimes poured out into deep old dinner plates and after some days in a dry store cupboard, were turned out and stacked one atop the other with spice and bay leaves between, and the whole pile covered over from dust and kept in the warm dry cupboard till shrunk and crusty with candied sugar. Such an old damson cheese was a foot high, a foot across, and quite hard.'

Here is an alternative method of keeping plums, the Jacobean equivalent of freezing fruit straight from the tree:

TO DRY PLUMS

Crystallised Plums

When your plums bee ripe, gather them in boughes & hang them upon a line in some open place, where the Sun & the wind dooth come, so let them hang till they bee readie to drop from the boughes, then make a sweet syrup with hony & water, when it hath boyled & scummed, put the plums into it, then they will sink to the bottome, let them stand on the fire till they come to the top of the water, then take them out, & dry them in the oven, after the bread is drawne, so put them in boxes & keep them.

Other recipes direct that the plums be dried out in the oven '2 or 3 times', that is over two or three daily bread bakings, the fruit being left to grow cold in the intervals so that the alternate heating and cooling might help the sugar to penetrate the plums without breaking them up. They are to be regularly turned, either on pie plates or on the same footed board pierced with holes on which Lady Fettiplace dried out her pears.

Dried Plums, Grapes, Pomegranates and Pears

The Frenchman Charles Estienne explains in *The Countrey Farme* how to pack damask plums for keeping in boxes between layers of strawberry or vine leaves. Sir Hugh Plat advises drying them in the sun (or, on sunless days, in a slow oven), which must have produced some sort of prune. He also buried hazel nuts underground in earthenware pots, pegged out grapes on lines stretched across a closed press or cupboard to last till Easter, and kept his pomegranates even longer in the Elizabethan equivalent of a centrally heated bedroom ('lap them over thinly with wax, hang them upon nails where they may touch nothing, in some cupboard or closet in your bedchâber, where you keep a continuall fire ... This way Pomegranates have been kept fresh till Whitsontide'). Estienne strung up his grapes over the mantelshelf to dry in the warmth of the chimney, and hung pears by their tails previously dipped in pitch: perhaps these were the French pears Parolles was so scathing about in *All's Well That Ends Well*—'And your virginity, your old virginity, is like one of our French withered pears; it looks ill, it eats drily; marry, 'tis a withered pear ...' Lady Fettiplace gives three different ways of drying pears, which were in each case to be peeled and cooked first, with or without sugar (once in the 'strong wort' used for brewing beer), before being hardened off in the bread oven: a trick Shakespeare liked no better than the French method, judging by Falstaff's description of himself at a low ebb in his fortunes as 'crestfallen as a dried pear'.

Shakespeare, always so painfully fastidious about ill-cooked or badly-served food, makes no bones about the dreariness of dried fruit in winter—leathery old pears, rotten apples, musty nuts—in the days before the comparatively new art of preserving brought the colours and flavours of summer to the dinner table all the year round. The first sugar refineries opened in London in the 1540s, still just about within living memory when Lady Fettiplace was compiling her book. Even so, only a fairly substantial household could have afforded to preserve fruit in anything like the splendour and fantastic variety she describes. Her fruit recipes, perhaps more than any other particular category, tend to come in batches, each apparently collected from the same source, which suggests that her contributors included quite a few confectioners as knowledgeable and enthusiastic as she was herself. The largest of these batches includes more than a dozen recipes, beginning on page 113 with Candie Flowers, moving on via candied eringo roots (eringo, or sea holly, a noted aphrodisiac, remained a popular speciality in seaside gift shops for the next two centuries*), various sorts of crystallised fruit, white pippins, white quinces, rose and quince cakes, to end on page 120 with the violet balls and Syrupe of Blue Violets quoted in Chapter Four. A helpful note in the middle, immediately after instructions To Preserve Peaches, runs: 'You must preserve peares if you will have them red, as you doo red quinces, and doo them white as you doo white quinces, if you will drie them after, you must take them out of the syrup, & put them in scalding water, then take them out & dry them, & so candie them.'

Red and White Pears

Red and white quinces are described in the next chapter, together with the many-coloured tarts on which a seventeenth-century hostess like Lady Mildmay might build a whole reputation. Here is a single recipe, which applies equally well to warden pears (wardens were hard, green, well-flavoured cooking pears, going right back to the middle ages), and produces a wonderful syrupy confection of a lustrous ruby red:

*The roots were to be washed, scalded, peeled, the pith removed, then dried, plaited and candied in syrup: these were the lusty and restorative eringoes raining out of the sky, with sweet potato comfits, in *The Merry Wives of Windsor*. By the eighteenth century, their function had dwindled to cough candy. Anyone wishing to experiment today should bear in mind that only roots growing six foot or more beneath the surface are sufficiently succulent to be worth candying (See Sri R. Baba, 'Candied Eryngo', *Herbal Review*, Spring 1978, vol. 3, no. 2.).

TO PRESERVE QUINCES RED, OR WARDENS

Red Quince or Pear Preserve

Take to every pound of quinces, a pound & somewhat better of sugar, beat it & put it into a deep silver basin or pewter, to every pound of sugar & quinces take half a pinte of faire water, so boyle your syrup first, then pare & core your quinces as fast as you can, so put them in rawe into your syrope & two or three of the cores loose, then lay a pie-plate in upon them, so let them boyle verie softlie, & never take out your quinces, but let them boyle as long as the syrup, when the syrop comes to bee iellie, then they are doone.

If you are using small, hard cooking pears, there is no need to core them. Simply peel them and put them whole into the syrup, after it has boiled for a few minutes. Weighing them down with a pie plate to submerge the fruit ensures that it will be evenly coloured. The plate should just fit inside the covered stone jar or earthenware pot in which they are to be left to stew very slowly in the lowest possible oven, a process which may take as long as ten or twelve hours: 'It wilbee a great while before they will turne redd, & they must bee boyled very leisurely' runs another useful note by the contributor who supplied the recipe for green fruit quoted on p. 167.

Two pounds fruit to 2¼ lb. sugar and 1 pint of water (16 fluid ounces by the old English measure, not the modern imperial pint) should yield three pots of this exceedingly rich preserve, which keeps admirably and tastes unlike anything else I know. Use it in small quantities to fill a plain omelette or tart case, eat it with unsweetened cream cheese, or on the plain blanchmane described on p. 82. For a compote to be eaten right away, try doubling the amount of pears, and serve them well chilled. Like the rose conserve on p. 149, or any of these sweet, sticky preserves, Quinces Red or Wardens may be chopped and mixed with whipped cream and lemon juice or rosewater to make a memorable ice.

Quince or Pear Ice Cream

Perdita ordered saffron 'to colour the warden pies' for the sheep-shearing feast in *The Winter's Tale*. Shakespeare was describing the already somewhat countrified and old-fashioned, originally mediaeval practice of dyeing all sorts of food—both sweet and savoury—deep yellow with saffron, purple with turnesol or heliotrope, red with powdered sandalwood for a special occasion. Lady Fettiplace, always bang up-to-date in the kitchen, avoided these artificial colourings in favour of different cooking methods to produce her contrasting reds, whites, greens and ambers. Here is a companion to her Quinces Red made from apples, which come out a softer, more translucent, rose-scented red. This makes a very oriental pudding, as Cecil Beaton said of an almost identical Greek recipe which he contributed to *The Alice B. Toklas Cook Book* in 1954.

FOR RED PIPPINS

Take the pippins and pare them then way to everie pound a pound of sugar, then take half the sugar & put it to the pippins, then put a quarterne of a pinte of rose water, then cover them close, & put them in with the bread, when the bread is drawne take them & turne them & put the rest of the sugar to them, & put them in againe till they bee done.

Red Pippin Preserve

Pippins are fine sweet eating apples. Again the fruit is to be peeled and left whole (unless you are using large modern cooking apples, in which case they will need to be cored and sliced, and may well disintegrate), and 'boyled very leisurely'. Cook the apples, covered, with the rosewater and half the sugar in a moderate oven (Mark 4, 180°C, 350°F) for forty minutes, stir them and add the rest of the sugar. Finish cooking at the lowest possible temperature for a good many hours until they turn something like the deep, pinky colour of pomegranates. It is easiest to complete the final stage, when the syrup begins to thicken and coalesce, on top of the stove, stirring with a wooden spoon to prevent burning as the last of the juice evaporates.

Pot the apples in glass jars for keeping, or serve them as soon as they are thoroughly cold and set in decorative little china bowls or glasses. Beaton poured his Iced Apples into a mould and served them next day, turned out, decorated with candied fruit and surrounded with an egg-custard sauce, which may or may not be the custom in modern Greece but was certainly authentic seventeenth-century practice in England.

But, however charming to look at, the food in Lady Fettiplace's book was clearly meant to please the palate as much as the eye. Apples, though an excellent medium for other flavours, tend to be dull on their own, hence the many ingenious suggestions for accentuating their flavour. Using sharp unripe fruit was one, another was to add Seville orange peel (see the instructions for Green Fruit on p. 167, and White Pippins on p. 67). The rosewater added to the Red Pippins above was a third, a fourth was the sack in the Preserved Pippins below. This recipe also very clearly explains the distinction between a preserve and a seventeenth-century marmalade: a preserve consists of small whole fruit or pieces of fruit in a loosely jellied syrup (what we should generally call jam), while a marmalade was the same mixture in which the fruit had been allowed to disintegrate, and boiled longer, till it achieved a much firmer set.

TO PRESERVE PIPPINS

Pippin or Gooseberry Preserve and Marmalade

When you preserve pippins, put half sack & half water to them, & if you will make marmalad of them, when they are preserved break them to pieces, & let them boile two or three walmes after, & so keep them; yf you will make marmalad of gooseberries take them when they bee green, & pick out the stones, & chop them smal, then weigh their weight in sugar, & wet it with some sack, & put the gooseberries to it, & boile it together, till it bee doone, when it is almost boyled take out some of the syrupe, & boile the rest till it come to marmalad, when you preserve goosberries, take them some three weeks before they bee ripe, slit them & pull out all their stones, then take their weight in sugar, & set them in, then put two or three spoonfulls of water, & boile them apace till they bee doone.

The quantity of alcohol involved here is very small: say, ½ gill each of sherry and water, ¼ pint in all, per pound of apples. I have made gooseberry marmalade by this method, moistening the sugar and fruit (no need to chop or stone it, unless you insist on a green marmalade) with neat sherry, which gave off delectable fumes while cooking, but all the alcohol vaporised, leaving no discernible trace in the finished product. The same thing happened when they tried cooking oranges with whisky at the Elsenham marmalade factory (the experiment is described in C. Anne Wilson's *Book of Marmalade*). The problem was solved at Elsenham in the early 1960s by marinading the oranges in whisky, brandy or rum, so perhaps it might be worth soaking these gooseberries in sherry and sugar for a day or two, to absorb the flavour, before making them up into marmalade.

Quantities, for a pound of sugar and a pound of fruit, are round about 4 fluid ounces of liquid, which may be sack- or sherry-and-water for an apple preserve, neat sherry for gooseberry marmalade, plain water for a gooseberry preserve (Lady Fettiplace, testing this recipe herself, was dissatisfied with the 'two or three spoonfulls of water' specified in the last sentence, and corrected it tersely to '4. EF'). Warm all three ingredients very gently together, stirring until the sugar has all dissolved, then boil fast until the syrup reaches setting point. Pot it in jars, like jam, for an apple or gooseberry preserve. For a solid marmalade, you must boil the mixture on a little longer—mashing and breaking up the fruit, if it is apples, removing half a cup of the liquor, if it is gooseberries—until it begins to thicken into a stiffish mass.

The same distinction applies to fruit jelly which may be put up in glass jars as soon as it begins to set, or boiled on to a much stiffer consistency, poured into boxes to dry, and served cut up in squares as a sweetmeat. Lady Fettiplace's recipe, though primarily intended for plums, works particularly well with blackberries (ignored in this and other Stuart cookery books in favour of the now virtually extinct wild barberry), and with apples—either windfalls or crabs—which are vastly improved if the jelly is scented, coloured and flavoured by a little of the Conserve of Roses on p. 151.

TO MAKE JELLIE OF ANY FRUITE

Fruit Jellies

Take your fruit, & put it into an earthen pot, & set it in a pot of boyling water, & as they stewe poure out the clearest of the syrupe, wey to every pound theirof a pound of Sugar, put so much water to the Sugar as will wet it, & let it boile till it almost come to Sugar againe, then poure in the Jellie of your plums, w[ch] *must be kept hot on the fire all the while your sugar is boyling. then let the Sugar & that boile togither two or three walmes, & then put it out in Boxes, & set it a drying.* (*ef you well have hole freut ly in the gely you most presarve et with out stones and when the gely es redy to be dryed put et in and so drey et*)

This gentle method of softening the fruit by itself in a covered pot without boiling until the juices flow still produces the clearest and best-flavoured jelly: do it in the primitive but effective bain-marie described here, or (as Lady Fettiplace suggests elsewhere) in a low oven. The fruit should be washed first, and any bad parts removed, but there is no need to peel, stone or core it (or even to cut it up unless you are using large fruit like apples or quinces, which should be roughly chopped and will need to be moistened with water). Pour off the juice every so often, as it comes from the fruit, which may be strained at the end through a jelly bag (another ancient piece of equipment in regular demand in this manuscript). Modern practice would be to boil the sugar and fruit juice together till it jells. Lady Fettiplace boiled her sugar separately with a very little water to candy height—240°F, 115°C—before adding the fruit juice, which required a much shorter boiling time, and so retained more

Whole Plums in Plum Jelly

of its flavour. The note printed in brackets at the end of this recipe is an addition in her own handwriting, and means, I think, that if you want whole plums suspended in clear jelly, some of them should be carefully stoned, stewed very briefly by themselves, then set aside (the stewing liquor to be strained and boiled, presumably, with the rest of the plum juice) and added to the jelly only at the last minute.

A similar note about jelly, added at the foot of the next recipe in the same black hand and inimitable spelling, confirms that Elinor was herself one of those skilled confectioners of whom Lady Mildmay was the most celebrated. The decorative qualities of jelly have been largely forgotten in an age when fruit jellies come out of packets, garishly coloured, artificially flavoured, oversweet and strictly for children. The best we can normally do nowadays is scarlet redcurrant jelly with mutton, blue-black bramble jelly or cornelian-coloured crab apple jelly in a glass dish on the tea table. But for a seventeenth-century hostess interested in mounting a serious banqueting display, jellies which catch and reflect the light mattered as much as water in a formal garden design. The green apple suckets, raspberry, strawberry, rose and plum cakes, apricot and gooseberry marmalades given in this and earlier chapters all make dense, opaque blobs of colour. The translucent red and white 'printed gellie', described in such particularly clear and picturesque language below, could hardly be simpler to make; and it is plain, from Lady Fettiplace's scribbled addition (in brackets) at the end, that she set considerable store by clarity and colour:

TO MAKE PRINTED GELLIE

Printed Red and White Apple Jelly

Take pippins & pare them, & quarter them, then have water ready to boile, & put the apples in the water, then cover it close, & make them boile a pace, till the apples all sinke to the bottome of the water, then straine out the cleerest of it, & way to everie pound thereof half a pound of sugar, put the sugar into the licour, & boile it till it wamble up like sope suds, & that when you wipe it of the spoone, it will come cleane of without sticking, then wet your moulds in cold water, & if they bee woodden moulds dry them with a cloth, & if they bee of Tynne dry them not, but put your stuf in them, & when it is almost cold loosen it, with a wet knife, from the side of the moulds, & upon a wet trencher, slip it out of the moulds, & from the trenchers into your boxes: if you will have your gellie look red, you must boile it close covered: (ef whit thene uncovard: the best way to have et very clear es to byle your apeles un pared; But weshe them very clene:)

Allow just enough water to cover the apples, and follow the directions exactly. When you strain the juice, don't squeeze it or the jelly will be cloudy. It will indeed 'wamble up like sope suds' when you boil it with sugar, and take on the cohesive, gelatinous quality described above when it is ready to set. One pound of apples, unpeeled and cooked uncovered as Lady Fettiplace directs, yields half a pint of absolutely colourless juice. Peeled and cooked with a lid on, they may seem to take forever—perhaps as long as eight or ten hours—before turning a clear red. Either way, they set easily, almost as soon as you pour them out, where other fruit pastes, which have been sieved or pounded rather than strained, may take days to dry out.

Fancy Moulds for Banqueting Stuff

Carved wooden moulds, or patterned tin ones, were part of any Jacobean stillroom's equipment: wooden ones should be soaked for three or four hours before being wiped dry, tin ones are perhaps best lightly oiled, so long as you use a tasteless corn or almond oil. The nearest modern equivalent is probably the little tin chocolate moulds, available from specialised kitchen shops in stylised flower shapes, diamonds, lozenges and minute fluted triangles. Or you can use fancy jelly moulds: the popular fish-shaped variety, sold in shops everywhere for blancmange or fish mousse, is almost identical to a professional confectioner's hinged fish mould reproduced in B. K. Wheaton's *Savouring the Past* from a supplement to Diderot's eighteenth-century *Encyclopédie*.

I have used one of these jelly moulds for all sorts of coloured fruit pastes, most spectacularly for the Red Pippins on p. 181 (slice the apples first, but don't sieve them, if they are to be set in a mould), which turns out a glistening, sea-wet fish with finely flecked and speckled scales. Scallop shells make good and possibly authentic moulds; so do fluted or shell-shaped patty-pan tins. Alternatively, you can leave any of the stiffer fruit pastes to dry out in sheets or slabs, like toffee, then stamp them out with fancy pastry cutters into stars or hearts (one of the traditional French confectioner's stamps or cutters, pictured in Diderot's encyclopaedia, was in the shape of a minute heart), diamonds, clubs and spades. Box them as soon as they are dry, and have lost any trace of stickiness, between layers of greaseproof paper. All these sweetmeats, including the jellies, will keep their glossy sheen, glowing colour and fine flavour at least until the first fresh fruit takes their place at table next summer.

Storing Apples

Apples for storage, rather than for preserves, went into the apple close or loft. A John apple—so-called because it was not ripe till St John's Day—was said to keep two years, and taste best when thoroughly shrivelled. Certainly Lady Fettiplace reckoned to be able to cook her White Pippins in Lent. Charles Estienne gives half a dozen methods of storing apples, ranging from sealing them in waxed containers to hanging them up in a pierced earthenware pot from the branch of a tree all winter: 'But the ordinarie and safest manner of keeping apples is, after they are got and pickt, and the bruised ones put from the rest, to spread straw verie thin, or lay mats upon a boarded floor (for the earth floor is too moist, and the plaster floor too cold) and then spread your apples upon the same, so as they may lye close by one another, but not upon one another.' They were to be 'spread upon their eyes, not upon their tailes', and protected with mats in frosty weather: 'and thus shall you keepe apples all the yeare safe, both from rotting, withering, or wrinkling of their skinnes'.

This month and next were also the time for harvesting the tobacco which grew all over the West country in Lady Fettiplace's day. There were said to be six thousand plantations in the south of England in the seventeenth century, before they were stamped out by the government in a move to safeguard its huge revenues from imported tobacco. The weed was popularised 'in our part of North Wilts', according to Aubrey, by Sir Walter Long who married Elinor Fettiplace's cousin Catherine (daughter to Sir John Thynne of Longleat, and sister to the Gresham Thynne who contributed several recipes to this book). Long was a friend of both Walter Raleigh and his brother Carew, who established the first English tobacco plantations on their Devonshire estates. Here is Raleigh's tobacco syrup, a strong, sweet infusion something like the better known Cavendish Tobacco (named for another Elizabethan pirate, Thomas Cavendish, the second Englishman to circumnavigate the globe, who had first sailed to America on Raleigh's ill-fated Virginian expedition of 1585). Sir Walter was imprisoned in the Tower of London in 1604 when Lady Fettiplace, niece by marriage to Carew Raleigh, wrote his name in her own handwriting at the side of this recipe:

TO MAKE SEROP OF TOBACCHO. (*S*^{r} *W rallygh*)

Syrup of Tobacco

Take a quart of water & three ounces of tobaccho, put the tobaccho in the water, & let it lie a night & a day close covered, then boile it from a quart to a pinte, then straine it, & put to everie pinte a pound of sugar, then put in the whites of three or fowre eggs finelie beaten, then set it on the fire, & when it boiles scum it, then cover it close, & let it boile, till it bee serop.

I haven't tried this syrup but Charles Estienne, whose book Lady Fettiplace possessed, prescribes it in soothing juleps for lung trouble, curing an old cough and loosening phlegm. Tobacco, disinfectant as well as narcotic and sedative, was used to deaden pain, suppress toothache, kill worms and heal wounds. Lady Fettiplace put it in antiseptic herbal ointments (one, made from bonemeal, valerian and hyssop, has an after-thought in her own handwriting: 'put in som gren tobaccho').

Raleigh's second tobacco recipe (again the attribution is in Lady Fettiplace's writing) is for a potent alcoholic cordial, like Imperial or Cinnamon Water; perhaps this one had Indian origins, since he stipulates a pound of the better-quality, imported rather than home-grown tobacco. Like the Spanish Marmalad made with gold leaf and seed pearls (see p. 51), it must have been a costly preparation at a time when, by Aubrey's account, tobacco was sold for its weight in silver in West country markets:

TO MAKE TOBACCA WATER. (*by: S*^{r} *W:* R.)

Tobacco Water

Take twoe gallons of muscadell, a pound of bought leaf Tobacco, but not english, a pound of annisseeds, shread the Tobacco small, & pound the annisseed very small, then lay them all to stiep theirin, then distill it with a soft fire, & when you distill it, put in some reasins of the Sun, & so drink it.

The most famous local tobacco plantations were at Winchcombe in the Cotswolds near Sudeley Castle, home of Lady Fettiplace's brother-in-law, Lord Chandos. Twenty-five years after her death, Thomas Baskerville rode past the ruins of Sudeley, destroyed in the civil war by government troops (who had also recently been sent in to lay waste the tobacco plantations), and saw old Winchcombe wives still smoking their pipes of tobacco as they sat knitting. Aubrey describes the gentry in Lady Fettiplace's day smoking tobacco from silver pipes, while the common people made do with a walnut shell and a straw; and there is something undeniably familiar about Estienne's account of seventeenth-century addicts: 'They put fire to the end of this pipe, receiving and drawing in with their mouth wide open, so much of this fume as possibly they can, and affirm thereupon that they find their hunger and thirst satisfied, their strength recovered, their spirits rejoyced, and their brain drencht with a delightsome drunkennesse ...'

10
OCTOBER

The spice trade had dominated European cookery from the time of the Crusades, and Arab influence lingers on even now in the spices, dried fruit, almonds, sugar and citrus peel that still form the basis of preparations for a traditional English Christmas. In mediaeval and Tudor times, all these went into savoury pottages, soups, sweet-and-sour stews and hashed meat dishes, and most of them were consumed in staggering quantities. A single box of household stores, dispatched by Lord Lisle's London agent in May 1535, contained 91 lb. of fine sugar, 10 lb. of pepper, 2 lb. each of cinnamon and ginger, 1 lb. each of cloves and mace. The annual accounts at Ingatestone Hall seven years later listed 114 lb. dried fruit, 60 lb. sugar, 6 lb. pepper, between 2 and 3 lb. of cinnamon, cloves, mace, nutmeg and ginger (the first three cost round about five shillings a pound, perhaps double what a farm labourer could hope to earn in a week).

Moderation had set in by the time of Lady Fettiplace, who used dried fruit and spices mostly in the plum puddings, baked bread puddings, mince pies and fruit cakes that are still part of the repertoire today. She stands already firmly on our side of the line between mediaeval and modern cookery. But here is her recipe for chicken with a spinach sauce containing almost all the ingredients of Christmas cake. It is thickened according to the latest French fashion of the 1980s with egg yolks and puréed greens; but it is flavoured in the mediaeval manner, with ingredients so blended together that individual elements are almost impossible for a modern palate to decipher. Milder than a chutney, richer and more exotic than the purées of the *nouvelle cuisine*, this excellent sauce has more in common with the current fashion for food from the Levant than with conventional, strictly short-term notions of traditional English cooking:

TO BOYLE A CAPON

Chicken with Spinach Sauce

Take water & spinage, & whole mace, some parselie, & currance & reasins of the Sunne, & boile it till the water bee almost boyled away, then put in some sack & marrowe & dates, & whole pepper & ginger grated, & some prunes, & sugar, & boile it all together, when it is boiled inough put a little butter into it, & put it all to the Capon & serve it, put the yelks of two eggs beaten, into it.

For a good-sized bird, which will feed 4 to 6 people, take ¾ lb. of spinach (well washed and picked over), a small handful of chopped parsley, a blade or two or mace, a tablespoonful of currants and another of stoned raisins. Simmer them gently together in a very little water. As soon as the spinach is tender, remove the mace, add half a pint of sack (a glass of sherry diluted with water will do instead), 4 finely chopped dates, 3 prunes (previously soaked and chopped), and a spoonful of beef marrow if you can get it. Heat these together, seasoning with salt, freshly ground black pepper, a little grated green ginger root and a scant teaspoonful of sugar (adjust all these quantities to suit your taste). Whizz the sauce briefly in a liquidiser, or put it through the Mouli-légumes, unless you prefer it lumpy.

The sauce may be prepared beforehand up to this point, if it suits you better, and left to finish off later. When you are ready to serve the bird, re-heat the spinach mixture and add a couple of beaten egg yolks, little by little for fear of curdling. Warm the sauce very gently, stirring all the time until it thickens. Add a nut of butter, taste for seasoning and pour the sauce over the chicken which should be ready waiting, drained and sitting on a sippet, or slice of hot toast, in its serving dish. If you prefer a roast bird, simply leave out the butter, pour the juices from the roasting pan into the sauce and hand it separately in a gravy boat. Gervase Markham suggests 'thick sippets with the juyce of sorrel and sugar' as a rather similar, simpler and sharper relish for roast chicken.

More Sauces for Chicken

This is one of half a dozen sauces to go with boiled chicken: one is an almost identical spinach purée, another (given on p. 94) substitutes lettuce, a third calls for 'a good deale of spinage' to be added to the broth at the last minute, boiled briefly, then fished out and served alongside the bird as a vegetable, with a little sauce made from a ladleful of broth boiled down with sugar and an equal quantity of white wine. There is also a marrow sauce, thickened with boiled rice, and the piquant gooseberry sauce given on p. 124. All use white wine or sack, sometimes a splash of verjuice as well, added at the end as a sharpener. Several include dried fruit to give body, sweetness and flavour. The old, mediaeval tradition of meat pottage, cooked with spices, greens and dried fruit, survived right up to this century in a few Welsh, Scottish and English regional dishes like cockie-leekie, and that strange and stately centrepiece to a Lancashire high tea which consists of a cold chicken stuffed with prunes and coated in a thick, lemon-flavoured, white sauce, the white meat contrasting in a decidedly Jacobean manner with its black stuffing. Both dishes were originally designed to produce something succulent, and indeed, sumptuous, out of a tough, old, boiling fowl or a lean, scraggy cock. Their secret lies in cooking the bird very slowly indeed for a very long time over a peat or wood fire, leaving the pot in place as the banked-up fire dies down overnight, and re-heating it next day to serve in the evening for supper.

Nourishing Broths

Excellent broth was the point of cockie-leekie, which began as a meal in itself to be supped from a bowl with pieces of leek, prunes and meat floating in it. Lady Fettiplace gives a good many of these rich, concentrated broths made from chicken or mutton stewed as gently as possible, 'warme upon embers all night', or suspended in a sealed earthen pot in a cauldron of simmering water. A cock is to be seethed slowly in copious quantities of claret with herbs, mace, prunes, raisins and currants. 'A restoring Brothe' is made from a chicken boiled with herbs—parsley, fennel and succory or wild chicory roots, thyme and rosemary—and a handful of raisins in three pints of barley water previously flavoured with china root (*Smilax china*, a much-prized Arab remedy). 'A sovereigne iellie for a Consumption' is chicken consommé, made from a bird cooked in wine 'till the flesh fall from the bones', then pounded in a mortar and strained through a jelly bag to give the sort of nutritious, easily digestible 'invalid's jelly' so popular in Victorian sickrooms. A breast of mutton seethed in 'cow hot milk' (cow-hot means straight from the cow) was another delicate dish designed to tempt a poor appetite.

This is prescribed 'For the Back': most of the broths in Lady Fettiplace's book were for people suffering from back pain or kidney trouble, or for consumptives, all patients reckoned to need feeding up to restore and sustain their strength. There were, of course, more specific medicines, generally based on clary, comfrey and knotgrass (the first is still prescribed in herbal medicine for kidney complaints, the other two in cases of internal bleeding), administered in potions, powders or pills, supplemented with extras like a boneshard ointment or a clary omelette. But any patient would surely feel better for being dosed night and morning with a bowl of one of these nourishing soups, flavoured with herbs and a blade of mace or a scrap of bruised cinnamon bark, enriched with red wine, thickened with ground almonds, a spoonful of barley or pounded, hardboiled egg yolks. They taste quite unlike our own light chicken soups made, if not from a commercial stock cube, from boiling only the carcass and giblets for stock.

It would no doubt be absurd to subject a comparatively tasteless, plump, modern, battery-raised roaster to a technique designed for dealing with stringy, well-flavoured, farmyard birds. But if you can ever get hold of an inexpensive, elderly boiling fowl with a scrag-end of mutton (another cheap cut not always easy to come by nowadays), here is a simple almond soup 'For a weake Back' which is well worth trying, and not only by back-sufferers:

Rich Almond Soup

Take a rack of mutton & a chicken & boile it in water, with a handfull of reasins of the Sun, the stones pulled out, & an handfull of prunes the stones pulled out, & a handfull of the roots & leaves of the ditch ferne, & boile all this together, till the meat be very tender, then straine out the broth & crush the substance of the meat into it, then thicken it with almonds, & eat in the morning fasting twelve spoonfulls, & so much more an hower before supper.

Substitute a bouquet of sweet herbs—parsley, thyme, marjoram, perhaps a bay leaf—for the ditch fern (perhaps the royal fern, strongly recommended by Culpeper for 'both inward and outward griefs'), unless you are making the soup for strictly medicinal purposes. Just cover the meat with cold water, add salt, herbs and dried fruit, bring to the boil and scum, then cook in a covered pot in the lowest possible oven (Mark ¼ or ½, 100°C, 200°F) for at least six or eight hours, or overnight, until the meat has almost dissolved: 'boyle all this to the substance of broth' is Lady Fettiplace's instruction in one of her many other recipes.

Strain the broth, which will be a rich, fragrant, dark brown, and sort the meat as soon as it is cool enough, picking it from the bones and crushing out the surplus liquid through a sieve. Any leftover meat debris, pounded, seasoned if necessary, and mixed with clarified butter, makes a nice potted meat paste: alternatively, you could remove the chicken and mutton as soon as they are tender, after a much shorter cooking time, to serve as a separate meat course, in which case the broth will be paler and less powerfully

Potted Meat or Boiled Meat in Broth

concentrated, more like an ordinary modern chicken stock. In either case, let it grow cold so that you can skim off the fat which will rise to the top. Finish the soup off next day by simmering it for half an hour with some ground almonds (3 oz. to 1½ to 2 pints), then pouring it again through a fine sieve. Whizz the almonds briefly with a little liquid in an electric mixer so as to extract all their oil, and sieve once more. Serve the soup with a few more split almonds, lightly fried at the last moment in butter.

If almond soup goes back to mediaeval times, the buttered potato roots given below were still, in the late sixteenth and early seventeenth centuries, a brand new vegetable from the New World. Columbus had brought sweet potatoes back from America (our ordinary modern potato did not reach English markets until the 1640s), and by Lady Fettiplace's day they had become a regular autumn import from Spain, highly popular on account of supposed aphrodisiac properties. Sweet potatoes are harvested in September and October, the first Seville oranges not until November, so Lady Fettiplace, who combines the two in this recipe, must either have used oranges preserved from the year before, or stored her sweet potatoes in a root-chamber or barn until the beginning of winter. Failing Seville oranges, an ordinary sweet China orange sharpened with a little lemon juice will do instead.

TO BUTTER POTATO ROOTS

Buttered Sweet Potatoes

Take the roots & boile them in water, till they bee verie soft, then peele them & slice them, then put some rosewater to them & sugar & the pill of an orenge, & some of the iuice of the orenge, so let them boile a good while, then put some butter to them, & when the butter is melted serve them. This way you may bake them, but put them unboiled into the paste.

Choose sweet potatoes all of a size, if you can, and scrub them carefully as the skin breaks more easily than with ordinary potatoes. For 2 lb. sweet potatoes, boiled till tender, then peeled and sliced, take 2 tablespoons of rosewater, 2 rounded tablespoons of brown sugar, the grated rind and juice of 1 large orange (add lemon juice and reduce the sugar a little if this is a sweet orange). Either lay your sliced potatoes in a shallow buttered dish and pour over them a syrup made from the other ingredients, or mash them with the rosewater, orange and sugar. The first is the way Americans still serve glazed sweet potatoes at Thanksgiving, but I prefer the second method, both for looks—sweet potatoes are apt to develop a greyish tinge if you aren't careful—and because of the way the flavours penetrate the purée. Either way, bake the dish in a moderate oven (Mark 4, 180°C, 350°F), for 20 to 30 minutes, with the meat if you are cooking a roast joint, and don't forget a generous topping of melted butter.

Sweet Potato Pudding

Buttered sweet potatoes, or potato apples, go well with chicken, turkey, ham or pork, together with a dish of plain boiled spinach. Alternatively, step up the sugar and eat them, hot or cold, with cream for a pudding. Modern American cookbooks often contain recipes, presumably handed down from the first English settlers, for an exceedingly rich sweet pudding made from the identical ingredients. Here is a recipe for candying them to make a sweetmeat: try it in small quantities as a sweet relish for cold meat, like pickled pears or mango chutney.

TO PRESERVE POTATOES

Candied Sweet Potatoes in Syrup

Boile your roots in faire water untill they bee somewhat tender then pill of the skinne, then make your syrupe, weying to every pound of roots a pound of sugar and a quarter of a pinte of faire water, & as much of rose water, & the iuice of three or fowre orenges, then boile the syrupe & scum it, then cut your roots in the middle & put them into the syrup, & boile them till they bee throughlie soaked in the syrupe, before you take it from the fire, put in a little musk and amber greece.

This is the fuller and more precise of two separate recipes given by Lady Fettiplace. Musk and ambergris are missing from the second of these, which ends with directions to boil your potatoes in syrup 'till it look cleare, then when they are cold put them up in a glas and so keep them'.

Here is something altogether more familiar, a relation of Bakewell tart, which has the same rich custard filling made from egg yolks and butter, often with ground almonds and sometimes with a layer of jam or dried fruit spread on the bottom of the pastry as well. But I don't think any of these are necessary additions to Lady Fettiplace's fine, light Tart of Eggs which is creamy in texture, delicately flavoured and buttercup-yellow in colour.

TO MAKE A TART OF EGGS

Tart of Eggs

Take the yelks of 24 eggs, and half a pound of fresh butter, then beat them well together, then straine it into a dish, then season it with sugar & mace very smale beaten, & three spoonfulls of rosewater, let the paste bee hardened in the oven before you put in your stuf.

This must have made a very substantial tart indeed: quarter quantities will fill a moderate-sized, 9 inch tart shell or two small ones baked in 7-inch tins. Take 6 egg yolks, beat them till they are thick and fluffy, and stir in 2 oz. melted butter. Add 4 oz. sugar, a pinch of powdered mace or nutmeg, and 3 tablespoons rosewater (this is reckoning a Jacobean spoonful at four times the size of a modern one, which may be too much but, in my experience, any less rosewater leaves the tart far too dry). Pour the filling into a pre-cooked pastry case, and bake it in a moderate oven (Mark 4, 180°C, 350°F) for 30–40 minutes, or 20–30 for two small ones, until the filling has risen and set.

Coloured Tarts

A bright yellow tart like this one would often have been accompanied by a white tart, made from the leftover egg whites beaten and cooked with cream: 'this carrieth the colour white, and it is a very pure white, and therefore would be adorned with red Caraway Comfets,' wrote Gervase Markham, urging English housewives to pay particular attention to presentation and colour schemes. Markham suggests an alternative, ground-almond filling for a milk-white tart. His black tarts were filled with a rich prune purée, spiced with cinnamon, like the delicious *tartes aux pruneaux* still to be had in France. Any cook worth his salt (the phrase goes back presumably to an age before Lady Fettiplace's, when salt was too precious to be doled out to an inexperienced cook who might waste it) would have learned to produce black, white and yellow tarts with a whole repertoire of green and red ones as well. 'For green tarts, take green quodlings [codlin apples], green preserved apricocks, green preserved plums, green grapes and green gooseberries,' wrote Robert May in *The Accomplisht Cook*: 'For red tarts, quinces, pippins, cherries, raspberries, barberries, red gooseberries, damsins ...'

Red cherry and raspberry tart fillings may be found in Chapter Six, red quinces and barberries in this chapter, red pippins in the last one. Green gooseberry and green grape fillings are in Chapters Six and Eight respectively, and there is a green tart of spinach in Chapter One (May includes spinach, green peas and green sorrel in a second list of green tartstuffs). Here is a recipe for a particularly pretty green filling, which could be made with Granny Smiths, or any of the late-ripening apples that are picked at the end of this month or next to be stored through the winter:

TO MAKE TART STUF OF PIPPINS GREEN

Tart Stuff of Pippins Green

When you have scalded your pippins and made them greene, then take the greenest of them, & that which looks white put away, rub the greenest of them throwe a hayre sive, then way to every pound therof a pound of sugar, & a little rosewater, so boile it alltogether, still stirring it till it bee as thick as you will have it.

For a true green tart, turn to the directions for scalding and skinning green apples on pp. 167–8. But this is a good deal of trouble so, if you are prepared to settle for an equally handsome, pale amber colour, choose a good quality pippin or eating apple and simply peel it in the ordinary way. Don't try this method with a cooking apple like the Bramley, which may taste nice but will distintegrate into a nondescript mush (use Bramleys to make a deep red tartstuff in exactly the same way as the green, except that you simmer the apples very slowly in a covered pan for two to two and a half hours until they turn the shade you require, then turn up the heat and boil fast till setting point).

Red Tart Stuff

Either way, grate two pounds peeled or skinned apples on the coarsest mesh of the grater, discarding cores and pips. Weigh the fruit, measure out an equal weight of white sugar and make a syrup by dissolving the sugar in a little rosewater (triple strength, if you have it, gives a heavenly flavour). When all the sugar has dissolved, boil the syrup briefly then put in your apples and boil again briskly for ten to twenty minutes with no lid on until the tartstuff shows signs of setting. It should be a beautiful, glistening, pale greeny-gold mass of apple strips set in clear syrup; and it may either be put up like jam in sealed jars, or used right away to fill a pre-cooked pastry tart case.

These cases were often extremely elaborate, made in batches from paper patterns cut out, according to Markham, like garden topiary in the shapes of 'Beasts, Birds, Arms, Knots, Flowers and such like', with a thick rim or verge of pastry pinched up round the edges. Each pastry case was to be pricked all over to prevent air bubbles rising (it might be wise to fill it with haricot beans as well), baked blind—'thus you may do a whole Oven full at one time'—and left to cool, before being filled with a previously cooked yellow or white custard, a black prune purée, the green tartstuff given above or the red rosehip mixture in the next recipe. In *The English House-Wife*, Markham describes how to make a single tart of many colours in the shape of a beast with, say, black eyes, white teeth and scarlet talons, a bird with variegated tail feathers, a coat of arms or a knot of green and yellow ribbons. Set-pieces like these were much favoured at court—'As for the making of knots or figures with diverse coloured earths ...' wrote Francis Bacon scornfully in his essay 'On Gardens', 'they be but toys; you may see as good sights many times in tarts.'

English Tart Designs

Similar effects remained part of the English repertoire well within living memory, lingering on as an essential part of the traditional North country teas and beautiful, ornate farmhouse spreads described by writers like Arnold Bennett in fiction and Dorothy Hartley in fact. Her diagram (in *Food in England*) of 'Some English Jam Tart Designs' still current in the 1930s includes the Red Cross (redcurrant jelly on a white curd ground), the Star or Epiphany (popular at church socials: 'you could use twelve different sorts of jam if you wanted to show off'), the Well ('very effective with greengage round blackcurrant'), the ancient, crenellated Gable pattern for treacle tarts, the Cross, the Whorl and the Slits. Several of these designs clearly go back, like the skill and pride of the housewives who made them, to Lady Fettiplace's day when even a humble apple tart might come in three colours—red, amber, green—with its pastry case puffed, slashed, shaped, decorated with inset diamonds and spirals, or slit like the sleeve of a doublet to show a different coloured stuff underneath. This is the sort of showing-off that gave Petruchio an excuse, in *The Taming of the Shrew*, for a stand-up row over his unlucky wife's new dress:

> *What's this? a sleeve? 'tis like a demi-cannon.*
> *What! up and down, carv'd like an apple tart?*
> *Here's snip and nip, and cut and slish and slash*
> *Like to a censer in a barber's shop:*
> *Why what a' devil's name, tailor, call'st thou this?*

Red Tart Fillings

The three fruits that follow produce between them some of the most luscious of all red tart fillings. All three are unfamiliar, if not actually unobtainable nowadays, as outlandish in flavour though not in habitat as kiwi fruit or guavas. The first two—rosehip and barberry—are native to this country, while the beautiful golden quince, first introduced by the Greeks to the Romans, has been cultivated all over Europe for hundreds of years. All three were highly prized in Lady Fettiplace's day for both looks and flavour, and all would still be worth taking some trouble to find today. Rosehips, harvested for their precious vitamins all over the country in the second war, are still the easiest to come by: in spite of thorns, anyone with a pair of stout gloves can pick a pound or two of the brilliant scarlet, flask-shaped hips of the wild dog rose or eglantine that still festoons the hedgerows in autumn. Gardeners not addicted to dead-heading may use garden roses, as I suspect Lady Fettiplace must have done: some of the old roses produce exceedingly handsome hips as big as cherries or small plums, much easier to harvest and process than the wild ones. One curious thing is that where a rose petal conserve or jam tastes much as you would expect from the fragrance, a conserve of hips develops the same rich, fruity undertone—dark and mellow in so far as a flavour can be said to be either—as the dried rose petals in a pot-pourri. The bright orangey red of the uncooked fruit changes as well, turning an unexpectedly soft, deep, pinkish, velvety red.

TO PRESERVE HIPPS

Rose Hip Preserve

Take your hips & boile them in faire water, till they bee soft, but first pull out all the seeds before you boile them, then straine them, & weigh to every pound a pound of sugar, boile your sugar till it come to sugar againe, have the pulp of your hips over the fire, & to every pound theirof, put a good quantity of the iuice of barbaries, when they are both through hot, put it into the sugar, & let it boile up, & so keep it for tart stuf, you must pick your barbaries & put them in a posnet, & so let them boile, & stir them till they be all broken, then straine the iuice of them to your Hipps.

This is the second and more detailed of two virtually identical recipes, copied out at top and bottom of the same page, separated only by instructions To make Cakes of Greene Plums. The first thing to be said about it is that de-seeding hips is an interminably laborious process, especially with the tiny wild variety. It is important to get rid of the seeds, also of the 'blackhead' or calyx, and the tiny hairy filaments that would be extremely unpleasant in the finished tartstuff; but this can be more easily done, after the fruit has been stewed gently for anything up to an hour, by pushing it first through a colander, then twice through a hair sieve.

Now weigh out the sugar, pound for pound, dissolve it in a little water and boil till it candies according to the instructions for Plum or Gooseberry Preserve on p. 128. Heat the rosehip pulp carefully, stirring with a wooden spoon, and add a tablespoonful of barberry juice per pound of pulp (the juice of half a lemon will do instead, or you can substitute rosewater, as Lady Fettiplace herself suggests in a third recipe for preserved hips, in which case the preserve will probably need longer boiling to make it set). Amalgamate the two mixtures, and boil on if necessary until you have a smooth, thick purée which may either be dried out in little patterned moulds to make a set of garnet-coloured suckets, or put up in pots and kept to fill tarts.

Barberries

Barberries which, according to Grieve's *Herbal*, are so sour even birds draw the line at eating them, were often added to low-acid, drab-coloured fruits like pears or peeled quinces where a modern recipe would recommend lemon or redcurrant juice. Lady Fettiplace used them to colour and help set her quince cakes, and in the Marmalad of Peares given below. They are a pretty fruit, tiny, drop-shaped, coral-coloured, turning a clear ruby red when cooked; and they make what Ethelind Fearon (in *Jams, Jellies and Preserves*, 1953) described as 'to my mind, the most delicious jelly in the whole repertoire of a cook, partaking of the twin flavours of ripe redcurrants, and fresh lemon juice. For its sake, it is quite worth growing a whole row of *Berberis Wilsonae*, quite apart from their own intrinsic magnificence.' Lady Fettiplace's recipe for barberry conserve—identical to Miss Fearon's jelly—is given in the next chapter. Anyone meaning to try it may well have to grow his or her own fruit, since the wild barberry—*Berberis vulgaris*—has been almost entirely eradicated this century from English hedgerows in an attempt to wipe out the parasitic rust fungus, or wheat-mildew, to which it acts as host.

You would need at least a whole row of bushes to experiment with the barberry drops, sweetmeats and tartstuffs so popular in the seventeenth century. But a single established bush of garden berberis—a tough, ornamental, edging shrub often planted in municipal parks, shopping precincts or at the foot of blocks of flats—should yield enough for this pretty pink marmalade:

TO MAKE MARMALAD OF PEARES

Pear and Barberry Marmalade

Take poperine peares pare them and way to every pound a pound of Suger and halfe a pinte of water boyle them in the water untill they are very softe then breake them in peeces and pull out the kernells and put the Suger to them, and boyle yt untill yt will Cut, then strayne Barberries and take as much suger as you have Juce of barberries put yt together and stirr yt together till yt bee thicke, over the fier but let yt not boyle, then put yt to yor marmalad stir yt all together and so put yt in Boxes

Poperine pears were a popular variety originally imported from the Flemish town of Poperinghe: ordinary conference pears, not over-ripe, make a possible substitute. Adding barberry juice is a short cut to a red marmalade, very much quicker than the long slow simmering described in the last chapter. The fruit kernels or cores are to be included during the preliminary stewing so as to extract their pectin and encourage the marmalade to set: it is perhaps easier, and just as effective, to core the pears at the beginning so long as you cook them in a muslin bag with the chopped fruit. For how to boil the fruit pulp 'untill yt will Cut', and how to put it up in boxes, see the directions for Ruf Marmalad on p. 133. Have your barberry syrup ready to stir in at the end: you will need, to each pound of pears, four to six ounces of barberries, stripped from their spiny stems, softened in very little water in a small covered pan over a low heat, and strained. The juice should be mixed with an equal volume of white sugar, and it will mysteriously thicken as it heats without boiling, just as Lady Fettiplace says.

Quince Sweetmeats

And so to the magical quince, the golden apple of the Greeks, symbol of love and happiness, sacred to Venus who is often depicted holding one in her hand. Boxes of quince marmalade were a favourite mediaeval wedding present, and they remained a luxury gift for anyone from royalty downwards until well into the seventeenth century. Quinces grow easily in England, at any rate in the southern counties, and, if you have any garden at all, it is well worth planting your own: a basket of local quinces can sometimes be found for sale in markets, or at an old-fashioned greengrocers, but there is nothing to beat a sturdy, grey quince tree with its load of pink-and-white blossom in spring, and great, heavy golden fruit glimmering among dark green foliage in autumn. The fruit should if possible be picked when still a little unripe, and brought into the kitchen where it will turn a rich, warm, deep yellow and fill the room with its scent. When cooked, quinces turn cornelian pink. The famous quince sweetmeat called *cotignac*, produced for hundreds of years in the Orléans area of France, is this colour, and so are the quince pastes served all over the Spanish speaking countries as a dessert. In Argentina, quince paste cut in squares and served with cheese is practically a national dish. Lady Fettiplace's version (given below) is made in exactly the same way: its soft orangey-pink colour and rich mellow flavour go particularly well with a crumbly, white Wensleydale cheese, or for that matter with a good Cheddar.

Quince marmalades, sold in boxes or by the brick, were an established favourite in England long before the arrival of the orange variety that eventually got the upper hand on the breakfast table. Quince pastes identical to Lady Fettiplace's could still occasionally be found, stacked away along with other dried 'fruit leathers' in country farmhouses, when people like Florence White and Dorothy Hartley began collecting regional recipes in the first half of this century. Why the quince and its products should have fallen utterly out of favour in England, when they didn't elsewhere, is a mystery. No fruit was more highly prized in Tudor and Jacobean times: Lady Fettiplace gives fifteen different recipes, nearly twice as many as for any other single fruit, and the proportion generally holds good in later seventeenth-century cookery books. She stored them raw in barrels as well as making them up into preserves, pastes, red and white marmalades and little moulded or 'prented' cakes, dusted with sugar and stored in boxes. Here is her recipe for what the French call *pâte de coings* and the Spanish *pasta de Membrillo*:

TO MAKE PASTE OF QUINCES

Quince Paste

Take your quinces & rost them, then take the best of the meat of them, & way to every pound of it, a pound of sugar & beate it together in a morter, & boyle it till it be so thick that it come from the posnet, then mould it & print it, & dry it before the fire.

The quinces should be wiped with a cloth to remove the down, but not peeled. Roast or bake them in a low oven—this is easiest to do in a large, covered, earthenware cooking pot—for an hour or two until they are soft but not entirely collapsed. Leave them to cool, then cut them up and core them, discarding any hard or discoloured patches. Put the pulp through a coarse sieve, food mill or blender, weigh it and mix it with an equal amount of white sugar. A posnet is a three-footed metal cooking pot: any thick-bottomed pan will do instead. Bring it slowly to the boil, stirring well until the sugar has dissolved, and keep it gently cooking, with an occasional stir, for another hour or two until the mixture begins to candy and leave the sides of the pan, being 'so thick that it come from the posnet'. Ladle it out into patterned moulds, or in a half-inch-layer on a flat oiled tin; and dry it in a warm place till the paste is firm enough to turn out and wrap in greaseproof paper for storage.

This pink paste is what Lady Fettiplace meant by 'white' quinces: 'red' quinces come out almost black, darker even than a damson cheese. The rather startling contrast in colour is due entirely to the cooking technique explained in the recipe below, where the initial stage is similar, and the colour of the finished product depends on what you do next.

TO MAKE QUINCE MARMALAD RED OR WHITE

Quince Marmalades

Boyle your quinces till they bee very soft in water, then take them up, & when they are through cold, pare them & take the softest of them, & way to every pound of it a pound of sugar, boyle it till it come to candy, then put in the pap of your quinces, & stir it well togither, then put it in boxes, & so dry it; if you will have it red, put in a pint of water to a pound of sugar, boile it & scum it, then put in yor quinces, in pretie big pieces, cover it close & let it boile, till it bee red, then stir it togither, & boile it till it bee thick inough, then put it in boxes, & so keep it.

White Marmalades

Stew the whole quinces in just enough water to cover them for an hour or so until they are soft enough to pierce with the blunt end of a wooden skewer or spoon handle. Peel, core and slice them, and measure out an amount of sugar equal in weight to the sliced fruit. For white marmalade, proceed according to the method discussed more fully in the instructions for Plum or Gooseberry Preserve on p. 128.

Red Marmalade

For a red marmalade, water has to be added (use the water in which the fruit was stewed) to prevent the quinces burning or drying out during the long, slow cooking necessary to deepen and darken the colour. A white or pale-coloured preserve must always be boiled fast, uncovered, in as little extra liquid as possible. A red one must be left for hours simmering or seething very slowly in the oven, or over the lowest possible heat, in a pan with a lid on: 'uncover it not till it bee as red as you will have it,' writes Lady Fettiplace in another set of instructions 'To make Quince marmalade Red', 'which donne uncover it and stir it untill it bee boyled enough'. If you leave the quinces sufficiently long—probably between six and seven hours—they will turn a wonderful wine-dark red which looks black until it catches the light. This is the moment at which to remove the lid, raise the heat, and boil fast, stirring with a wooden spoon, until the liquid has almost entirely evaporated. This final stage will probably not take long. The sliced fruit remains whole, not squashy or disintegrated, so, if you want a smooth, glistening fruit paste for moulds or suckets, you will have to sieve or blend it at the end.

Quince Preserve

Quinces set with no trouble at all, and either white or red marmalade may be made into an excellent preserve, simply by stopping the cooking process as soon as the syrup shows signs of setting and putting it up in pots in the usual way. They make handsome presents, handsomer still if you pack up a pot each of the two colours together, when it is hard to believe till you taste the contents that they are made from the one fruit. The same is true of red and white marmalades, which may be cut into squares when dry and boxed up together in a checkerboard pattern. They will keep for years, and may be eaten by themselves, with cheese, or adapted to all sorts of modern dishes: try putting a square or two of quince marmalade into a beef stew cooked very slowly in red wine with rosemary and thyme; use them to complicate the flavour of a plain apple purée or apple meringue; slice them to decorate a blanchmane; melt them to make a fruit sauce, or to mix with whipped cream (include a few very small, solid cubes of marmalade) for a memorable quince ice. If you haven't time to make marmalade, or can only get hold of one quince, it might be worth trying the little uncooked sweets in this recipe, which is so quick and simple a child could do it:

Quince Ice Cream

TO MAKE SUGAR PLATE WITH QUINCES

Fresh Quince Sweetmeats

Take quinces and pare them, & slice them, & beat them in a morter with sugar searcht, take two spoonfulls of rosewater, & boyle it with gumdragon, & beat it with the sugar, & quinces till it come to dough, then roule it out, & put it into the moulds, & drie it at the fire. This way you maye make it of anie spice, or all of sugar.

Put the peeled, cored and roughly chopped raw quince or quinces into an electric food processor (this is another of those recipes which involve hard labour without a machine to do it for you) with an equal weight of sugar. Two small-to-middling quinces will yield round about half a pound of hard, grainy, peeled fruit reduced, when pulverised, to unexpectedly juicy fruit pulp (if the pulp produces a great deal of juice at this stage, it might be wise to strain off any surplus, following the advice given in the very similar recipe for Cakes of Orenges quoted in Chapter Two). Add the gum dragon or gum tragacanth (available from chemists), which should have been previously steeped and dissolved in rosewater: I reckon one heaped teaspoonful powdered gum tragacanth in two or three fluid ounces of rosewater per pound of sugar.

Work the mixture 'till it come to dough', when it may be rolled out and moulded (use little decorated tin moulds, fluted patty-pan trays or any convenient wooden moulds), or, if the paste is too runny, poured out onto an enamel plate or baking tin for cutting into squares later. Leave it for a few days in a warm airing cupboard, plate warmer, the bottom of a very low oven with the door open, or over a radiator, which is often the nearest modern equivalent to drying things out 'at the fire'. The colour will darken, turning from palest peach to a deeper apricot pink. Like the Cakes of Orenges on p. 70, these crunchy sweets have a freshness, fragrance and purity of flavour quite unlike modern fruit pastilles or boiled sweets.

Quinces were the last of the orchard crops, gathered 'about Michaelmas' (September 29, more like the middle of October in the modern calendar), according to William Lawson, and marking the end of a good six months' hard work in the stillroom processing successive flower, vegetable and fruit harvests. By the end of this month, any competent housewife would have built up sufficient stores, boxed, barrelled and potted, to withstand another five or six months' winter siege. Sixteen hundred and four, the year Lady Fettiplace's book was written, was the second of two exceptionally hot summers that had produced bumper yields throughout England: 'we had in our Gardens a second somer,' wrote Lawson's friend and Yorkshire neighbour, Lady Hoby, at Hackness on October 5, 1603, 'for Hartechokes bare twisse [artichokes cropped twice], whitt Roses, Read Rosses; and we having sett a musk Rose the winter before, it bare flowers now. I thinke the like hath seldom binne seene: it is a great frute year all over.'

11
NOVEMBER

At Hallowtide slaughter time entereth in
and then doth the husbandman's feasting begin;
From then unto Shrovetide, kill now and then some,
their offal for household the better will come.

This jingle comes from the earliest, and one of the most celebrated, of all popular gardening experts, Thomas Tusser, whose best-selling *A Hundreth Good Pountes of Husbandrie* went into thirteen editions between 1557 and 1600. All Hallows Day is November 1, Shrovetide marks the beginning of Lent round about four months later. November, when the grass failed, was a time of butchery and prodigious feasting, though scholars no longer believe, as they once did, that all stock not wanted for breeding was slaughtered and salted down this month. The sort of household that emerges from Tusser's manual, or the Ingatestone Hall accounts, or for that matter from Lady Fettiplace's book, had its own steady supply of fresh meat right through the winter.

Lady Fettiplace made her own sausages, black puddings and boiled haggis from the butchers' scraps that nowadays go straight to the sausage and pie factories. Nothing was wasted, not even 'the Ropes'—the sheep's pluck or stomach—which provided bags for boiled puddings, or the guts which turned into sausage skins. She gives two consecutive, almost identical recipes for boiling calves' and neats' feet (a neat was an ox, fattened for slaughter at this time of year if it could not be fed through the winter). There is probably small prospect for most people of experimenting with either today (or only, according to my London butcher, with calves' feet specially imported at prohibitive cost from Holland), but it would be a pity to overlook this traditional English recipe, still considered a dainty dish for a plain household right down to Victorian times.

TO BOYLE CALVES FEETE

Calves' Feet in Wine Sauce

Take a pinte of whight wine w^t^h halfe as much water put in the feete and w^t^h them a handfull of letisse or spinage, w^t^h a good many of currans, some hole mace pep salte & a little vergis, thicken yt w^t^h the yelke of an egge, and put therin a peece of sweete buter, so make sippetts and serve them

This recipe is for calves' feet previously prepared by being split, scalded and simmered slowly in water (it takes round about five pints to cover two feet) for four or five hours. The stock may then be strained off to produce a delicate, clear calves' foot jelly: Lady Fettiplace gives instructions elsewhere for making veal jelly from the stewing liquor, which was to be repeatedly strained ('then straine it into a verie deepe basin with a faire lynnen cloth, & doe not crush it, but let it run of it selfe'), de-greased, sweetened, spiced and clarified with egg whites in exactly the same way, and virtually the same proportions, specified by the Victorian chef, Francatelli, almost three centuries later. As soon as the calves' feet are cool enough to handle, the meat should be stripped from the bones, chopped into neat pieces and finished off in a sauce according to the instructions above. Quantities are unclear: Francatelli made aspic from eighteen calves' feet at a time; two would probably be more appropriate for an ordinary, small household (in which case it might be wise to cut down the white wine from a pint to, say, a wineglass each of wine and water or stock). Victorian cookery books follow Lady Fettiplace's recipe fairly closely, leaving out only the greens and currants, and thickening the sauce at the end with flour instead of an egg yolk.

Francatelli used boiled, minced cow's udder as a base for his elegant forcemeats. At the opposite end of the social scale, a 'muggety pie', made from the cow's umbilical cord, was regarded as a delicacy in Gloucestershire within living memory, according to an elderly farmhand who recommended it to Dorothy Hartley with considerable enthusiasm ('it was the jelly gravy was the best part—some did put in taters and a turnip, and sech, but 'twas best plain, and good cold'). Here is Lady Fettiplace's version, perhaps the original Gloucestershire ancestor of Miss Hartley's receipt:

TO MAKE A MUGGET PIE

Mugget Pie

First parboile them, then mynce them small, then take parselie, time, & marierome, & chop it small, & mingle it with the meat, & some suet, but no spice, put some mace beaten small, & put in some currence.

Parboil meant in those days to boil thoroughly. The mugget (defined by the Oxford Dictionary as a calf's or sheep's intestine, but Miss Hartley's field-work seems, in this context, more likely to be correct) should first be well washed and soaked in cold water. The twentieth-century recipe includes a little chopped onion, and also some of the gelatinous stock mixed with milk to fill up the pie. Gervase Markham's seventeenth-century version is thickened with beaten eggs and cream, then boiled in a bag rather than baked in a pie crust. The result should be white, suave, gelatinous and easily digestible, perhaps something like boiled tripe.

The absence of onion in Lady Fettiplace's meat and fish cookery (with the sole exception of her Stewed Oysters) points presumably to its mediaeval origins: onion is, by modern standards, the only significant ingredient missing from her Black Puddings, Sheepes Pudinges, and her instructions 'To make puddings of a Calfes haggas'. The haggis (or stomach bag) itself was to be boiled and minced, like the mugget, then mixed with breadcrumbs, flavoured with chopped sage and winter savory, cloves, mace and currants (spices and currants or raisins are still sometimes included in home-made Scottish Haggis, with part of the lights, liver and lungs as well). The mixture was bound with cream and four or five egg yolks, then stuffed into sausage casings—'& fill the guts with it'—with a lump of butter in the middle to counteract any dryness. Sheeps' and black puddings—the recipes are almost identical—were spiced, herby, meatless sausages, made from coarse oatmeal soaked in warm milk overnight till it swelled and thickened, mixed next morning with savoury herbs, nutmeg, suet, three beaten egg yolks '& no more bloud than will coller it red'. They were boiled, like dumplings, in the same pot as the meat with which they were to be eaten: a very similar oatmeal sausage or white pudding remained until quite recently a regional speciality in the West Country.

Boiled Haggis

Black Puddings

Eel pie, another ancient English dish, comes in Lady Fettiplace's book between Mugget Pie and the sweet, spicy fruit-and-marrow pie given on p. 59, with the mince pies given in the next chapter copied out at the foot of the page.

TO MAKE AN EELE PIE

Eel Pie

Take an eele and flay him, then take the bones out, & take some yelks of eggs hard rosted, & some corrans & some dates the stones pulled out, chop all these together, then season it with sugar cinamon, & gynger, & a little vineger, & some butter & so bake it.

Skinning an eel is easier said than done, but any fishmonger who is up to procuring one in the first place might perhaps be persuaded to skin and bone it as well. Chop it into two-inch pieces, and lay them in a pie dish on a bed of forcemeat made from pounded, hardboiled egg yolks, dates and currants. Season with a pinch each of sugar, cinnamon and ginger, sprinkle over a tablespoonful of white wine vinegar, and dot with shavings of butter. Cover with a puff pastry lid, and bake for one hour in a hot oven (Mark 7, 220°C, 425°F), turned down halfway to a more moderate heat.

These instructions come from Mrs Beeton's recipe for a very similar Eel Pie (she substituted parsley and chopped shallots for the ancient flavouring of dried fruit), which was to be baked dry, like Lady Fettiplace's, then finished off, as it came from the oven, by pouring in a quarter of a pint of very thick béchamel sauce. I think something of the sort—perhaps 'a good deal of sweet cream' as in the recipe for Creamapple Pie given on p. 58—should also be understood in Lady Fettiplace's recipe. This outlandish pie clearly goes back directly to Tudor times, perhaps even before. Traces of mediaeval origins regularly survive in much later versions of the same dish: quartered, hardboiled eggs are an ingredient in the celebrated Thames watermen's Richmond recipe—'a pie worthy of Eel-pie Island'—given in *Food in England*, dating from the 1860s or 70s, by which time nutmeg and pepper had replaced cinnamon and ginger as spices, and the vinegar had been upgraded to sherry.

Fruit Flavourings for Meat

The dried fruit had disappeared altogether, relegated strictly to the sweet course in conventional British cookery except in a very few cases, like the handful of currants allowed on account of oriental connections in a kedgeree. Even so, the old liking for fruit to flavour and sweeten a meat dish still surfaces occasionally in the orange juice and peel added to a game sauce, the custom of serving apple sauce with pork, goose and duck, currant jelly with venison, cranberries with a roast turkey at Christmas. This last American habit, only fairly recently re-introduced to this country, originated presumably in attempts by the first English settlers to find a substitute for their native barberry, highly prized all over Britain in the seventeenth century as a garnish when fresh fruit and vegetables were hard to come by in winter. The brightly coloured berries, pickled, jellied or crystallised in bunches, remained a traditional standby: Mrs Beeton used them with curled sprigs of parsley to decorate an 'exceedingly pretty' dinner-party dish of creamed chicken, and Miss Hartley produced the same effect with an autumnal bowl of white puffballs cooked in milk ('In a round brown dish, the smooth white puffs in their own creamy sauce, white against the translucent scarlet berries and the vivid green parsley, look good and taste delicious').

Lady Fettiplace made a liquor from equal parts of white wine and white wine vinegar, boiled together with sugar, in which 'To keepe Barberries all the yeare'. She also gives directions for Paste of Barberries, a preserve and two conserves or jellies, both excellent with chicken, turkey or mutton. For connoisseurs, Miss Hartley recommends barberry jelly with mutton bred in Leicestershire, Norfolk and the flat eastern counties, redcurrant jelly for the valley breeds of Gloucestershire and Oxfordshire, rowanberry for the sweeter, Welsh mountain mutton. Barberries, if you can find any (see p. 199), should be gathered in October or November, the later the better, provided they are not frost-nipped.

TO MAKE CONSERVE OF BARBERRIES

Barberry Conserve or Jelly

Take Barberries & pick them from the stalks, then put them into a chafar, with as much rose water as will wet them but none to bee seene in the bottome, then set them on the fire, & as they warme still prick them, till they are all broken, then straine them, & put to the iuice of them, as much sugar as you think good, then set it on the fire, & keep it warme till the sugar bee melted, then let it boyle verie fast, till it bee inough.

A chafar is a chafing-dish or pan heated by charcoal, which provides a more easily adjustable heat than an open fire for tricky operations like jam-making. Softening the fruit over a low heat, and pricking or mashing it till the juices run, should be done very gently: failing a charcoal stove, the traditional alternative is to put the fruit in a covered stone jar and leave it in a slow oven, or a saucepan of barely simmering water, until it is thoroughly soft and broken. Rosewater gives a heavenly fragrance to the cooking but, if you haven't any, simply use the water that clings to the berries after washing, without any surplus to collect on the floor of the pan—'as much . . . as will wet them but none to bee seene in the bottome'. Strain through a jelly bag, previously wetted and wrung out. Instructions as to quantity, given in Lady Fettiplace's second recipe, are to weigh the juice (put it on the scales in a deep plastic box or jug, then subtract the weight of the box), and weigh out an equal amount of sugar. Mix the two together, and stir until the sugar is all dissolved. I have never managed to pick enough barberries for this recipe, but I have made it with imported cranberries, and the jelly set almost as soon as it came to the boil.

Lady Fettiplace poured her hot, liquid jelly into what were evidently watertight metal boxes: 'then put yt in Marmalad Boxes and when the howshold bread is drawen and that the oven hath stood for a while after, set in yo[r] Boxes and let them stand untill yt bee stiffe to Cut set upp yo[r] oven lidd when you have put in yo[r] boxes, this way you may make good Conserve of Raspice [raspberries]'. This sort of firm fruit jelly stiff enough to cut was still being turned out and sliced in strips in Mrs Beeton's day for decorating white creams, or as a garnish for meat. Any stiff marmalade or paste made from the sharper fruit can be used in the same way—barberries, gooseberries, perhaps even the little green apple cakes on p. 167 which would go well with a dish of cold pork. They begin to lose their looks after a year or so, but they seem to mature in flavour: I have had some success with a re-cycled, dark-red quince fish—left over from a party two winters before, beginning to crack a little and dim its glossy sheen—cut in cubes and served like chutney with cold ham. Try dropping a square or two of the highly concentrated, Seville orange sweetmeat on p. 71 into the roasting pan juices when making gravy for a pheasant or pigeon, or use strips of Lady Fettiplace's thick marmalades melted down in a little hot water, with a glass of port wine or sherry, as the basis for one of the excellent fruit sauces for game evolved in the nineteenth century.

Fruit Sauces for Game

A hot fruit sauce made from jam or marmalade became the traditional accompaniment to an unsweetened batter pudding, prepared according to a formula that remained unchanged from Tudor and Jacobean times until it made its way into manuals like Bee Nilson's famous *Penguin Cookery Book* and the no less comprehensive *Constance Spry Cookery Book* in the 1950s.

FOR A PUDDING

Boiled Batter Pudding

Take flower & twoe eggs, & a little nutmeg and suet, and as much creame, as will make it somewhat thicker, than butter, so put it into the bag and boile it.

Proportions are 6 oz. flour, 1 tablespoon suet, and between ⅓ and ½ pint of thin cream to 2 eggs. Make it up into a thick batter, beating hard (it takes a minute at most in an electric blender). Add nutmeg and a pinch of salt but no sugar, and steam it for 1½ to 2 hours in a greased china pudding basin with a foil lid.

If you want to turn this pudding out, it is safer to put a round of well-buttered paper in the bottom of the bowl before you pour in the batter. But it rises so nicely—like a little, firm, springy, perfectly spherical ball—that it might look best served as it is in its bowl on a plate. Bright red barberry jelly goes well with this pale, cream-coloured pudding, and so does a sauce made from one of the concentrated orange marmalades, well diluted with water and perhaps a spoonful of gin. Here is a slightly more elaborate, baked, bread-and-butter pudding which makes a substantial and comforting dish for a chill autumn evening:

TO MAKE A PUDDING

Baked Bread and Butter Pudding

Take the top of the morning milke, & a good deal of grated manchet and some flower, but not so much flower as bread, then put in three eggs yolks & whites, some cloves & mace, & a little salt, some great Reasins, *a good piece of butter melted, so temper all this well together, let it bee somewhat thicker than batter, so bake it, & serve it.*

Manchet is fine white bread which should be two or three days' old, if it is to make good breadcrumbs. Take 2 pints thick, creamy milk, or milk mixed with cream, and set it to heat gently with 4 oz. breadcrumbs. Mix 2 heaped tablespoons of flour to a paste with a little of the milk, and amalgamate it with the rest. Beat 3 eggs till they are thick and frothy, and stir them into the warm mixture. Add 2 or 3 cloves, a blade of mace (these first two items should either be ground, or tied in a scrap of muslin for removal later) or a grating of nutmeg, 1 generous level teaspoon salt, 2 oz. melted butter and 4 tablespoons raisins, preferably the big, soft, sticky kind that will need to be stoned and chopped first.

Leave the mixture to stand for twenty minutes or so in a warm place, until the crumbs have swelled to the correct consistency, 'somewhat thicker than batter'. Now bake it in a well-buttered dish for 45 to 50 minutes in a moderate oven (Mark 4, 180°C, 350°F). This pudding may be served with cream or a wine sauce, but, so long as it includes raisins as sweetening, I don't think it really needs more than a thick strewing of brown sugar and more flakes of butter dotted over the top as it comes from the oven. Leave it in a warm place for the topping to melt and soak in a little while you serve the first course.

The Marow Pudinge which follows is very similar both to the nameless pudding above (from which it is separated in the manuscript by more than forty pages), and to the second of the two fools given in Chapter Eight. I include it to suggest something of the multiplicity, antiquity and high standing of the British bread pudding that flourished from Tudor times until relatively recently. Mrs Beeton collected a dozen or more, ranging from Cabinet or Chancellor's Pudding to a Very Plain Bread Pudding (two pints stale crusts soaked in boiling water and flavoured with salt, nutmeg, sugar and a few currants), which may go far towards explaining why the whole family fell out of favour. But, unless you overdo the starch, there is no reason for these puddings to be stodgy. A properly made bread pudding will be finely flavoured, 'tenderly firm' in texture, and, from the cook's point of view, uncommonly good-tempered: quantities, proportions, oven temperatures and times may all be adjusted to taste in these recipes. Some frugal cooks recommend as much as three quarters of a pound of bread to a single pint of milk; richer batters call for more eggs and only an ounce or two of breadcrumbs or flour. Lady Fettiplace's puddings are very little trouble to prepare and equally good to eat hot or cold. A large one makes simple, nourishing and, in my experience, popular convenience food for the sort of household where fluctuating numbers of people are apt to drop in, especially children and teenagers, who may want feeding at odd times in a hurry without warning and often with friends.

TO MAKE A MAROW PUDINGE

Marrow Pudding

Take good milcke and Crummes of bred and a little fflower the yelkes of 4 egges and the whights of 2, a little Cloves and mace and some suger with a feaw Reasons of the sunne, stir all these well together and boyle it in a possnet untill it bee somewhat thicker then batter, then when it is boyled put to it 2 Or 3 spoonefulls of Rosewater, and then buter the sides of a dish and sett it in the oven (put in your marrow when you set et in the oven)

The last sentence was an afterthought, added in Elinor Fettiplace's own handwriting. The addition of beef marrow and rosewater (the marrow from a single marrowbone will be enough, with 4 to 6 tablespoons rosewater to 2 pints creamy milk) gives a particularly delicate flavour, but the pudding will taste more familiar, and perhaps just as good, if you substitute butter for marrow. Otherwise follow quantities and method given for the previous pudding, bearing in mind that 'boyle it' means the sort of slow, gentle heating—more seething than simmering—used to swell and flavour the crumbs for a bread sauce.

The two puddings above are comparatively homely, if not exactly poor relations of the next one, named for the Earl of Devonshire, who was said by his secretary, Fynes Morison, to be extremely particular about both his clothes and his food. He was Charles Blount, Lord Mountjoy, whose career reached its height in 1604, the year Lady Fettiplace's book was written. Triumphantly vindicated after his implication in the Earl of Essex's plot, covered with glory from his recent military campaign in Ireland (where he was served both by Elinor's kinsman, Sir Edmund Fettiplace, and by her old family friend, Sir Henry Danvers) and newly ennobled, he stood high in favour with the new King James. He was the lover of Penelope Rich—Sir Philip Sidney's beautiful Stella, sister to the dead Essex—and their sad and scandalous story, which ended with his death in 1606, is said to have provided the seed of John Ford's tragedy, *The Broken Heart*. But fortune still smiled on him at the time this recipe was copied out, and his pudding is a suitably lordly affair, rich and fruity, light as a soufflé, the most sumptuous of all these baked batter puddings.

THE LORD OF DEVONSHIRE HIS PUDDING

The Lord of Devonshire His Pudding

Take manchet and slice it thin, then take dates the stones cut out, & cut in pieces, & reasins of the Sun the stones puld out, & a few currance, & marrow cut in pieces, then lay your sippets of bread in the bottome of your dish, then lay a laying of your fruit & mary on the top, then another laying of sippets of bread, so doo till your dish be full, then take creame & three eggs yolks & whites, & some Cynamon & nutmeg grated, & some sugar, beat it all well together, & pour in so much of it into the dish as it will drinke up, then set it into the oven & bake it.

The point to remember with this pudding is that the bread should be sliced exceedingly thin: use a stale loaf, and be lavish with the layers of dried fruit in between. Quantities for 6 or more people are 6 to 8 slices of crustless bread; a generous handful of dates, and another of raisins; 1 tablespoonful of currants; the marrow from a beef marrow bone (butter the bread instead, if you can't get marrow); 1 pint single cream; 3 eggs; 1 pinch each of cinnamon and nutmeg; and 1 or 2 tablespoons of sugar. Dredge the top with more sugar, strew on spices, and bake the pudding for ¾ to 1 hour in a slow oven (Mark 3, 160°C, 325°F). Serve it at once—it will rear up out of its dish, and should be rushed quickly to table before it collapses—with a jug of thin cream.

But it tastes perhaps even better eaten cold next day, when the flavours have had time to develop. I don't know if the Lord of Devonshire reckoned his pudding suitable eating for an expeditionary force in the field, but I have eaten one, baked, sliced and transported in a loaf tin, as part of a late autumn picnic on one of those rare, clear, sunny November days when it made an admirable end to the meal, part sweet, part moist, squashy fruit cake. This was the sort of last course, apparently unknown in France, that delighted the Frenchman, Henri Misson, whose otherwise dismal account of English cooking at the very end of the seventeenth century breaks off for a rhapsody on puddings: 'Flower, Milk, Eggs, Butter, Sugar, Suet, Marrow, Raisins, etc., are the most common ingredients of a *Pudding*. They bake them in an Oven, they boil them with Meat, they make them fifty several Ways: BLESSED BE HE THAT INVENTED PUDDING, for it is a Manna that hits the palates of all sorts of people . . . Ah, what an excellent thing is an *English Pudding*! *To come in Pudding-Time*, is as much as to say, to come in the most lucky Moment in the world . . .'

October and November are the months for gathering the glistening, richly-flavoured, purple-black elderberries that grow in such abundance all over motorway verges and municipal waste ground as well as in country hedgerows. They are fully ripe, and ready to pick, when the tassel of fruit turns over, drooping downwards under the weight of the berries instead of bearing them up on its cluster of stalks. Lady Fettiplace used them for colouring and flavouring home-made vinegar (she recommends substituting elderflowers in spring, and red rose petals in summer). Towards the end of her book, among the miscellaneous contributions before the index, are two sets of almost identical instructions for Elder Wine, copied out on consecutive pages in two quite different hands, belonging presumably to a couple of her Horner or Fettiplace relations. The first—To make Elder wine—is in a large, flowery, unformed writing that appears nowhere else in the manuscript; the second—which, being the fuller and more detailed, is the one reproduced below—is in a crabby, black hand, much closer to Elinor Fettiplace's own, perhaps the same hand that had already copied out a little cluster of fruit wine recipes (see Chapter Six) only two pages before in the manuscript.

BETTER, TO MAKE ELDER WINE

Elderberry Wine

to 20 pound of malago: raisons clean rubbed picked & small shred you must put 5 gallons of water, w^{ch} *hath boiled one hower, & is coled to y*^{e} *temper of new milke, soe let them infuse 8: or 10. daies stirring them once in a day or two then pass it through a hair sive, al w*^{ch} *time you must have readie 6 pints of y*^{e} *juice of elder berryes, so prepared in a jugg in a kettel of water over ye fier, as for ye sirup, it must be cold when tis put to ye other liquor mix it very well, & soe tun it upp in a vesseel letting it stand 8 or 10 weekes, before you bottel it, It is not fitt to drinke under 6 monthes old, but a yeare or two yeare old is better,*

Smaller and more manageable quantities, given in the first of these two recipes, are 4 lb. raisins to 1 gallon of water and 1 pint elderberry juice. Raisins from Malaga in Spain were the big, fat ones needing to be picked over and chopped, still sometimes sold loose by old-fashioned grocers or the more serious sort of health-food shop. Their sweetness serves in place of sugar to feed the wild yeast present on unsprayed and untreated fruit skins: modern recipes for home-made wines generally insist on the inclusion of commercial wine yeast, but I have found that the instructions above work very well, without yeast, even with four pounds of ordinary, pre-packed, supermarket raisins. Chop them, or give them a brief whirl in an electric blender, before adding a gallon of water, previously boiled and cooled to blood heat. Leave them for eight to ten days in a covered jar or plastic bucket, and don't forget to stir them every so often. Now strain off the liquor, crushing and pounding the raisins as hard as you can in a large hair or nylon—not metal—sieve: the first recipe advises squeezing the fruit with your hands, which is messy but effective (the remaining, slightly fizzy, fermenting raisin debris makes delicious fruit cakes or moist, fruity gingerbread).

Pick your elderberries as soon as the time is up: you will probably need three and a half to four pounds of berries to produce a single pint of thick, black juice. Stand the fruit in a stone jug or jar in a pan of barely simmering water, and pour off the juices every half hour or so as they collect in the bottom of the jug. Lady Fettiplace's own detailed instructions for making all sorts of fruit syrups are given at the end of Chapter Seven: I take it that 'ye juice of elder berryes, so prepared . . . as for ye sirup', means that the juice should be mixed, as that recipe directs, with sugar in the proportion of two pounds per pint. Heat the mixture gently, without boiling, until the sugar is dissolved, and leave it to grow cold. This sweet syrup, added to the original gallon of water and raisin juice, will start the liquor fermenting strongly again. Leave it in a glass jar with an airlock for two months or so, then siphon it off, bottle and cork it. It is so good after six months—rich, dark and fruity, not over-sweet, nice with soda water in long summer drinks—that it is not easy to keep from drinking it for another two years.

Imported Red and White Wines

Elderberries make one of the best-known of all full-bodied country wines, and this must be among the earliest elder recipes, since home-made fruit wines seem to have been virtually unknown in the sixteenth century. Apart from raspberry wine, wines made from grapes were the only ones acknowledged by the Tudor physician and wine buff, Andrew Boorde, whose tips (in *The Fyrste Book of the Introduction of Knowledge*, 1540) remain as useful today as they were then: 'Chose your wyne after this sorte: it must be fyne, fayre and clere to the eye; it must be fragraunt and redolent, having a good odour and flavour in the nose; it must spryncle [sparkle] in the cup when it is drawne ... it must be cold and plesaunt in the mouth; and yt must be strong and subtyll of substaunce.'

Home-brewed ale, beer, cider and mead remained the English staples although there was already, by the end of the sixteenth century, a brisk trade in imported wines. Lady Fettiplace used them for cooking as freely, and in much the same ways, as we still do to flavour sauces, soups and meat dishes. White wine and sack or sherry enriched her creams, fools and sweet puddings. Red wine was a tonic regularly prescribed for the sick, infirm or enfeebled at either end of the age scale:

Give a neaw borne Child on spoonefull of Clarret wine the first thinge yt taketh and yt shall never bee troubled wth the fallinge Sickness

By Docto^r^ Padway.

Claret also went into toothwashes ('Myrrhe, sodden in claret wine, & the teeth washt therewith, fasteneth the teeth and maketh them cleane'). It was flavoured with musk and ambergris, mixed with herbs or flowers of lily-of-the-valley (this was a cure 'For the Pashion of the Harte', supplied by Mistress Gresham Thynne of Longleat), then distilled into stiff little nips, pegs and cordials to help people get through the day, or face the night, to calm the nerves, brace the spirits and relieve depression.

A WATER FOR MELANCHOLIE

A Water for Melancholy

Take claret wine one pottle, & an handfull of borrage flowers, and as many buglos, and three ounces of cynamon, & still it all together in a still, & then drink it with your wyne at your meate.

Debility of both mind and body had to be catered for, perhaps especially at this low ebb of the year. The start of the banqueting season meant laying in stocks of digestives—orange marmalades to settle the stomach, strong, spicy boiled sweets or Cakes for the Wind in the Stomach, senna pills to lighten it, wormwood plasters to warm it, violet syrups to cool it. A herbal bread poultice in a linen bag worked like a hot-water bottle ('lay it to your stomack as hot as you can, & you shall find great ease thereof'). Another poultice, made from roasted red onions stuffed with frankincense and applied to the navel, cured the colick or stomach cramps. Then there was the Surfet Water, a highly spiced pick-me-up much in demand at this festive season, made from two gallons of malmsey distilled and laced with bitter aloes. 'A water for the dulness of the stomach and to put away any heaviness of the heart' was what would now be called a pre-dinner drink, distilled with herbs from 'good rennish wine and sack ... and when the fire is out of the water, drink of it fasting and an hower before supper: it is best in the winter.'

Whereas people needed toning up in spring with sharp, astringent, anti-scorbutic drinks to cleanse the system, in winter they needed sustaining with rich, fragrant, reviving stimulants, great bowls of spiced ale and bragget sweetened with honey, sack possets and hot caudles to drive out the cold. It is hard to draw a line, with some of these drinks, between general-purpose and strictly medicinal restoratives.

A DRINKE TO STRENGTHEN

Milk Caudle or Punch

Take a pinte of Cowe whot milk, the yolks of ten egges, beat it very well together, put therto halfe a pinte of good rose water, & a pinte of sack, & as much sugar as will sweeten it, & between two cups brew it as you doo butterd Beere, & in the morning fasting drink a good draught of it.

This method of brewing 'between two cups' sounds like the traditional winter stirrup cup, made by pouring a pan of steaming hot, spiced, buttered beer or ale into a bowl of beaten eggs, then shifting it back and forth between pan and bowl to whip up a froth and cool the cup enough to drink. The parting guest, setting out on horseback or in a draughty, unheated coach on a cold day, must often have stood in need of this kind of fortification. Quantities, for a couple of comforting doses, are half a tumbler of hot milk beaten up with two or three egg yolks, a spoonful of sugar, half a wineglass of rosewater and a full one of sherry.

Thomas Baskerville gives a cheerful glimpse of Berkshire hospitality on his way from Faringdon to Bristol, the journey on which he stopped off to visit Edmund Fettiplace, Elinor's last descendant in the direct male line. Baskerville was an inquisitive traveller, pausing often to inspect the gentry's homes and gardens, report on new building projects, admire the view and jot down a series of jingles listing produce in local markets, homegrown or imported specialities, and the kind of refreshments available to anyone travelling through Fettiplace country on the road to Bristol in the seventeenth century:

A Flanders mare
A Lancashire lass
And Hampshire honey is current goods for every man's money.

Stroud water reeds
Burford saddles
Banbury cakes and Dutch cradles
Indian pea cakes
French spaniels
Barbary horses *Arabian camels.*

Canary sack and Bristow sherry
Will make a sad man's heart to be merry.

12
DECEMBER

Christmas is the time when modern eating habits cling closest to a dietary pattern laid down well before the seventeenth century in England. 'Every Family against *Christmass* makes a famous Pye, which they call *Christmass* Pye,' wrote M. Misson, with a note of respect in marked contrast to his generally dim view of English cooking: 'It is a great Nostrum the Composition of this Pastry; it is a most learned Mixture of Neats-Tongues, Chicken, Eggs, Sugar, Raisins, Lemon and Orange Peel, various kinds of Spicery, etc . . .' Recipes for Christmas mince pies in Victorian and Edwardian cookery books still normally included a proportion of meat (chicken and tongue, rumpsteak or mutton). This, together with all the other ingredients—suet, dried fruit, citrus peel, sugar, spices and alcohol—goes directly back to the Middle Ages. Mince or 'shred' pies were on Thomas Tusser's list of standard Christmas fare which, apart perhaps from pig's brawn and souse, has not changed a great deal between 1557 and the present day:

Christmas Pie

Good husband and huswife, now chiefly be glad
Things handsome to have, as they ought to be had . . .
Good bread and good drink, a good fire in the hall,
Brawn, pudding, and souse, good mustard withal.
Beef, mutton and pork, shred pies of the best,
Pig, veal, goose and capon, and turkeys well drest.
Cheese, apples, and nuts, joly carols to hear,
As then in the country, is counted good cheer.

The ingredients listed in Lady Fettiplace's instructions To Make Pies (given below) sound so familiar from any modern recipe for home-made mincemeat that, the first time I made them and handed them round, in place of the usual variety made from a jar of commercial mincemeat, they came as a considerable shock to the palate. They turned out to be in fact little savoury pies, rich and fruity but not at all sweet, and quite unsuited to tea time. My mistake lay in failing to realise that, though the ingredients remain the same, proportions have changed drastically. Lady Fettiplace's quantities are unusually precise for the period—'put as much currance as meat, & twice so much sugar as salt'—and clearly mean that you need, to a teaspoon of salt, no more than two teaspoons of sugar. In other words, sugar in this recipe is only a seasoning, like salt (Gervase Markham's mince pies contain none at all), which gradually increased out of all proportion as the meat was first reduced, then—quite recently—dropped altogether. A little minced tongue, beef or mutton—say, one part to double the quantity of suet and four or six times as much fruit—greatly improves the texture of a modern, sweet mince pie, without adding any identifiable meaty flavour.

But Lady Fettiplace's recipe remains much closer to mediaeval meat pies, baked without any extra liquid in their stout, freestanding pie crusts, liberally spiced, and moistened only by fruit and butter or suet, much easier to eat in the fingers than a pie filled with gravy. The effect, strongly recalling the Arab origins of European cooking, will be familiar to people who like samosas and other dry, mildly spiced meat pasties of the Middle East. Something very like it is still popular in Argentina where they serve small, spiced, fruity meat pies, called *empanadas*, with no sugar inside but icing sugar sprinkled on top, hot as a first course or appetiser. A tray of Lady Fettiplace's hot pies makes a nice change from sausage rolls at a party. They are particularly good to eat out of doors on a winter picnic, or for a Boxing Day lunch with claret, a sharp green salad and a bowl of plain redcurrant, barberry or cranberry jelly.

TO MAKE PIES

Mince Pies

Parboile your mutton, then take as much suet as meat, & mince it both small, then put mace & nutmegs & cinamon, & sugar & oringes peels, & currance & great reasins, & a little rose water, put all these to the meat, beat yor spice & oringe peels very small, & mingle yor fruit & spice & all togither, with the meat, & so bake it, put as much currance as meat & twice so much sugar as salt, put some ginger into it, let the suet bee beef suet, for it is better than mutton suet.

Quantities for four dozen tiny pies, or one large, flat one that will feed ten or twelve people, are: 8 oz. lean, leftover cooked, minced mutton ('parboile' means to boil thoroughly, but it is hardly worth boiling meat specially in such small quantities: Sir Kenelm Digby, who reckoned a pound each of meat, suet, currants and raisins 'enough for once in a large family', assumed that any reader would be catering for a household of anything from twenty to forty people); 8 oz. shredded beef suet, 8 oz. currants, 8 oz. raisins. Mix all these together with a big pinch each of powdered ginger and ground mace, ½ level teaspoon grated nutmeg and 1 level teaspoon cinnamon, 1 well-rounded teaspoon of salt and 2 of sugar. Add the finely grated rind of an ordinary orange, or rather less of a Seville orange if you can get one. Allow round about 6 tablespoons of rosewater to moisten the mixture (Digby suggests including a little sack or sherry as well).

Puff Paste

You will need 1½ lb. pastry, rolled very thin, for small pies, half this amount for a single, double-crust pie baked on a pie plate or shallow tin. Use ordinary shortcrust, or bought puff pastry, or make your own richer puff paste according to Digby's instructions, which he got from my Lady Lasson: 'Her finest crust is made by sprinkling the flower (as much as it needeth) with cold water, and then working the past with little pieces of raw Butter in good quantity ... And this makes the crust short and light.' Standard modern specifications are equal parts of butter and flour, mixed with iced water, alternately rolled and folded, then rested in the refrigerator, six times in all.

Whichever you use, roll the pastry out as thinly as possible, cut it in rounds to fit either a pie plate or patty-pan tins, and mound up the filling in the middle (between one and two heaped teaspoons for a small pie), squeezing it together a little as it will shrink in the cooking. Cut out slightly smaller rounds for the lids, or what Digby calls Liddles, moisten the edges with cold water, and crimp them together. Little pies need only to be pricked with a fork but a big one might be worth decorating with knots, flowers, coats of arms, seasonal slogans, or simply initials and the original date, to show that this is no ordinary mince pie. Glaze the pastry with top of the milk or a beaten egg yolk, and bake in a hot oven (Mark 7, 220°C, 425°F), 20 to 30 minutes for small pies ('Half an hour baking will be enough': Digby), 10 minutes longer with the heat turned down for a big one.

The next recipe is for a single large mutton pie in which the dried fruit and orange peel have been replaced by savoury herbs and chopped hardboiled egg: already Lady Fettiplace has arrived at much the same formula we still use today for a pork or veal-ham-and-egg pie.

TO MAKE A PIE

Mutton Pie *Take mutton, mince it with beef suet, & take a good handfull of parseley, as much tyme, & as much marierom, & the yelks of fowre eggs, & the whites of two, & so chop all this togither very small, then take cloves, mace, cynamon & ginger, & a little sugar, & season the minced meat withall, & some salt, & so bake it, in fine crust, let it bake the space of two howers, & then serve it.*

I have tried this recipe with and without liquid, and on the whole prefer the compromise suggested below which produces something spicier than a modern meat pie, moister and not quite as fat as a mediaeval one would probably have been. It is very good though surprisingly unlike the traditional, gravy-filled, mutton pies, cooked with onion and perhaps a few mushrooms, still made in Scotland and some parts of this country. Lady Fettiplace's version is well-flavoured, juicy and succulent, more like a home-baked pork pie (which is also greatly improved by the addition of a few spices). Quantities given here will feed six to eight people.

For the filling, take 1½ to 2 lb. lean lamb or mutton (best end of neck or boned fillet), mince or chop it into small pieces, and mix it with 4 level tablespoons beef suet. Add a handful or scant tablespoonful each of chopped fresh parsley, thyme and marjoram (1 teaspoon each if dried), 2 chopped hardboiled eggs, and 2 extra yolks (3 whole eggs is generally simpler), a scant level teaspoon each of ground mace or nutmeg, cinnamon and ginger, and 3 or 4 crumbled cloves. Add 1 rounded teaspoon of salt, and 2 of sugar.

This might have been baked in a raised pastry crust (see the instructions for Rabbit Pie on p. 57), as mutton pies still are in northern parts of Great Britain. But a 'fine crust' sounds more like the rich puff paste Digby recommended for mince pies, in which case you will probably need round about one pound of pastry. Line a pie dish with just over half of it, put in the filling with an inverted egg cup or pie funnel to support the crust, pour in half a pint of cold water or stock (made by simmering the meat bones and trimmings with herbs and a few vegetables), and cover with a pastry lid. Two hours baking in a Jacobean bread oven would have meant two hours in an oven slowly cooling throughout that time: a smallish pie like the one given above should be baked for 20 minutes in a hot oven (Mark 7–8, 220°C, 425°F), to raise and colour the pastry, then left for another 45 minutes to 1 hour for the meat to cook at a much lower heat (Mark 2–3, 160°C, 325°F).

These two pie recipes belong recognisably to the same ancient tradition, which seems to have been in the process of splitting off to produce, on the one hand, the savoury meat pie and, on the other, the sweet fruity article we still eat at Christmas. But it is not only mince pies that go back beyond Lady Fettiplace's day to the middle ages. Admittedly, no modern meal bears any exact resemblance to the sort of spread laid on by Tudor and Stuart cooks for a company still accustomed to eat with the fingers. But it is not perhaps going too far to detect traces of the mediaeval origins of English cookery in all the standard ingredients (except for the roast potato) of a conventional Christmas dinner consisting of turkey, bread sauce and cranberry (or barberry) jelly, plain buttered vegetables and gravy enriched with red wine, followed by boiled plum pudding and sherry- or brandy-butter, not forgetting the little dishes of sweets, nuts, candied peel and crystallised fruit that are the nearest most people at home ever come nowadays to a final banqueting course. Rich, fat, fruity forcemeats were traditionally used to moisten a large, dry bird (my favourite turkey stuffing, from Bee Nilson's *Penguin Cookery Book* of 1952, is based on the venerable combination of dried prunes, herbs and spices, with a thickening of breadcrumbs and an essential sharpening of wine vinegar). The layer of almond paste or marzipan on a Christmas cake is another ancient invention. All these were firmly established by Tudor times as part of the festive season that reached its climax with the twelve days of Christmas, and Lady Fettiplace gives instructions for most of them (Christmas pudding and hard sauce are discussed in Chapter One, bread sauce under sippets on p. 93, barberry or cranberry jelly is given in the last chapter, sweetmeats in too many places to list, and marzipans or marchpanes come next in this chapter).

Christmas Feasts

People long before Lady Fettiplace's time hung up Christmas decorations of mistletoe, holly and yew. Even modern Christmas crackers recall the mock guns, with real gunpowder trails, blazing and banging away at the sort of Jacobean dinner party described by Robert May, which ended with people pelting one another with water-bombs, wine spilt, candles extinguished and ladies shrieking as they cut open a pie full of live birds or frogs. Guests at the banquets recorded by Henri Misson and John Nott, at the turn of the seventeenth century, were commonly given little going-home presents—knots of coloured ribbon or gilded baskets filled with sweetmeats and fancy biscuits—to take away just like the participants in a children's party today. Indeed, the paraphernalia of a modern children's party remains a shrunken and juvenile reminder of the great court feasts of Lady Fettiplace's day with their fools and trifles, their coloured tarts, striped sweets and gilded sugar-paste baubles, their edible saucers and bowls, marzipan birds, beasts and fish, spectacular table decorations in the shape of pasteboard castles and battleships, not to mention the shrieking, giggling and rowdy games with the lights out. Here is Lady Fettiplace's recipe for the sort of fancy biscuit that was essential party-food, or 'Banqueting stuff':

TO MAKE FRENCH BISKET BREAD

French Biscuit Bread or Macaroons

Take one pound of almonds blanched in cold water, beat them verie smale, put in some rose water to them, in the beating, wherein some musk hath lien, then take one pound of sugar beaten and searced and beat with your almonds, then take the whites of fowre eggs beaten and put to the sugar & almonds, then beat it well altogether, then heat the oven as hot as you doe for other bisket bread, then take a paper, & strawe some sugar upon it, & lay two spoonfulls of the stuf in a place, then lay the paper upon a boord full of holes, & put them into the oven as fast as you can, & so bake them, when they begin to looke somewhat browne they are baked inough.

Other seventeenth-century recipes for French bisket are generally for the kind of light Savoy biscuit, or ladies' fingers, given in Chapter Five. But this one is, in fact, a classic recipe for almond macaroons, which are still made in exactly the same way today (except for the flavouring of musk, a secretion of the musk deer's sex gland, highly prized in perfumery but currently forbidden, at any rate by US law, in food). They are extremely easy to make, and infinitely nicer than the bought variety: try them with a plain, white Almond Leach, a bowl of Buttered Gooseberries, or simply by themselves with coffee.

Almonds are expensive, but quarter quantities will make a generous plateful of biscuits. You will need 4 oz. ground almonds, 4 oz. icing sugar, 1 beaten egg white, and a little rosewater for mixing. Work all these together, beating hard, to make a pliable dough: this is one of those laborious processes which become simplicity itself in an electric blender or food processor. A metal baking sheet placed on an oven shelf will do very well instead of the pierced wooden board, which was raised on feet off the stone floor of the Jacobean oven, so that the underside of the biscuit cooked as fast as the top.

The instruction to 'lay two spoonfulls of the stuf in a place' means, I think, that two large spoonfuls of dough (probably the equivalent of four modern tablespoonfuls) make a single, large, round biscuit or flat cake, which should (according to Digby's recipe for my Lord of Denbigh's Almond Marchpane) be 'about the bigness of your hand, or a little larger, and about a finger thick'. Thickness is important, as the biscuits should be crisp outside but still soft and chewy in the middle. They will be firm, well risen and lightly browned, or 'baked inough', after probably 35 to 45 minutes in a low to moderate oven (Mark 4, 180°C, 350°F, turned down a little after the first quarter of an hour).

This firm, fine biscuit dough can very easily be rolled out and stamped with cutters, or 'printed' in tin or carved wooden moulds (old butter moulds, previously soaked in cold water, do very well), to make the fanciful shapes and patterns that appealed so greatly to Tudor and Stuart cooks. French Bisket Bread is sweeter, and slightly more solid in texture, than the next recipe for Maccaroonds, which produces another rich, light, little almond pastry to serve with a fruit fool or white cream.

TO MAKE MACCAROONDS

Almond Macaroons

Take a pound of Jordaine Almonds, blanch them and beate them in a morter, when they are somethinge smale, put in now and then a spoone full of suger finely beatne, and if you see it begin to oyle put into it a little rosewater to keepe it from oylleinge, when you have beatne it reasonable fine ad unto it the whight of an egge and halfe the yelke of an egge beinge beatne with halfe a dozen spoonefulls of Rosewater, *after you have put it into yor beatne almonds stir it well together w^{t}h a spoone and it will make yor almonds looke like butter, then put it into a hoate oven a little, and when it is through warme, take it out againe and stir it well together w^{t}h a spoone, then power it in little lumpes uppon wafers, and bake it, when it is halfe baked you may wash it w^{t}h* Rosewater *and the yelke of an egge beatne together, or if please you when it is through baked you may Ice it over.* * * *

A rounded Jacobean spoonful of fine, powdered sugar would probably be the equivalent of a couple of ounces in weight: even so, a spoonful added 'now and then' can hardly have come to much more than half a pound of sugar to a pound of ground almonds. If you grind your own almonds in an electric mixer, leave a few recognisable fragments of nut to give crunch and bite to the macaroons or, if you use bought, ready-ground almonds, add a few whole ones, blanched, skinned and finely chopped. A second recipe for 'Makeromes' says that the almonds should be ground 'not too small'. It also advises adding 'to everie two spoonfuls of sugar, one of flower' (which would presumably help prevent oiling, and make the mixture less rich: I haven't tried it as the tendency to add flour seems, on the whole, better resisted in English cookery).

A whole pound of almonds would make round about four dozen little biscuits. For a smaller but still ample batch, grind 8 oz. blanched and skinned almonds in an electric mixer, gradually adding 4 oz. icing sugar. Now add half of the white of an egg (the easiest way to halve an egg white is to beat it lightly first: alternatively, you could just use the whole white), with a teaspoonful of the yolk, keeping the rest to make icing, and 6 tablespoons of rosewater (go carefully with the liquid: half this amount may be enough). A dough so soft that it looks 'like butter' should be runnier still by the time it has been warmed briefly in a hot oven as Lady Fettiplace directs: beat it again, and drop or 'power' (pour) it in spoonfuls onto a baking sheet lined with Bakewell paper (edible rice paper would be perhaps the nearest equivalent to seventeenth-century wafers, made in a waffle iron).

A smoother biscuit, suitable for icing over, can be made with a forcing nozzle or, easier still, by rolling the dough (don't let it get too runny during the preliminary warming) between your fingers, a teaspoonful at a time, to make a ball, then flattening it out. The macaroons will be 'halfe baked' after 10 or 15 minutes in a moderate oven (Mark 4, 180°C, 350°F). Have ready a glaze made from the egg yolk, beaten with a little rosewater, and apply it with a pastry brush or, following authentic Jacobean practice, a quill feather. Return the tray of biscuits to a slightly lower oven for another 20 minutes or so, until they are thoroughly dried out and the glaze has set.

Sir K. Digby's Icing

Alternatively, for a more decorative macaroon, leave the trayful to get quite cold and cover them with an icing made, according to Digby's instructions, from fine powdered sugar mixed to 'a thick pap' with lemon juice, rose- or orange-flower-water, and a little egg white: 'Lay this smooth upon the Cake with a Knife, and smoothen it with a feather.' As soon as the icing has dried and hardened, Digby advises applying a second coat:

> *if there be any unevenness, or cracks or discolouring, lay on a little more of that Mortar, and dry it as before. Repeat this, till it be as clear, and smooth, and white, as you will have it. Then turn the other sides, and do the like to them . . . they must be pure, white and smooth like Silver between*

polished and matte, or like a looking Glass. This Coat preserves the substance of the Cakes within, the longer moist.

Digby's sugar coating is, of course, what we should call royal icing, laid on in successive, thin layers according to the technique still followed by professional caterers to produce the hard, glossy, white surface on a Christmas, wedding or christening cake. The layer of almond paste that goes under this royal icing is also still made in exactly the same way as the macaroons given above, or the marchpane below (recipes for a modern, sweet tooth's almond paste usually call for equal parts of sugar and almonds, as in Lady Fettiplace's marchpane, which follows; but many people today prefer the less sugary formula she used for macaroons).

Marchpane, Marzipan or Almond Paste

Marchpane is the original, English form of the German marzipan, or almond paste, which appears nowadays in most households only as part of the ritual at Christmas (none of Lady Fettiplace's almond pastes, incidentally, bear any resemblance whatsoever to oily, ready-mixed, commercial marzipan which is as pliant as plasticine, and can taste almost as nasty). The Maccaroonds given above were little individual versions of the grander Marchpane, which seems generally to have been baked in a single cake or flat tart, sometimes with a raised rim round the edge, weighing perhaps three to four pounds or more, exceedingly rich and sumptuously decorated: a centrepiece of much the same size, and occupying the same commanding position on the table, as the twentieth-century Christmas cake (apparently a fairly late German import, like so much else on the modern Christmas scene). In the order of importance drawn up by Gervase Markham for a banqueting table, the Marchpane always takes precedence: 'Marchpanes have the first place, the middle place and last place; your preserved fruits shall be disht up first, your pasts next, then your Marmalades, and Cotiniates [quince confections], then your Comfets of all kinds; Next your Pears, Apples, Wardens, bakt, raw, or rosted, and your Oranges and Lemons sliced; and lastly your Wafercakes.'

A marchpane was evidently dazzling to look at, whether it was iced snow-white and shining like a looking glass, or gilded as in the recipe below:

A RECEIT TO MAKE A MARCHPANE

A Marchpane

Take a pound & a half of almonds, blanch them & bruise them in a morter by themselves, then take a pound & a half of sugar & pound it smal, search out as much of it as you think will serve to ice your marchpane, & to mould it up in, Take the rest of your sugar & mingle it with your almonds, & beat them in a morter till they come to paste, not putting too much at once in your morter for feare of oyling, you must have gum dragon steep it in rose water all night, & in your pownding put some of your gumdragon upon your pestills end, when you have pounded it all mould it upon on a bottome made with marchpane bread, make your conceits as you think fit, set your marchpane in the oven not being too hot, & when it is reasonable well hardned take it out & ice it, & set on your conceits, then put it in the oven againe, untill yor iceing bee hardned, then take it out, & stick on your comfits, & when it is cold gild it, your iceing is made with nothing but rosewater & sugar beaten togither, it must bee somewhat thick, I think some 3 greate spoonfulls of sugar will serve for the iceing of it.

The '3 greate spoonfulls' of icing sugar to be reserved for icing and rolling out the paste would have weighed round about 3 oz., leaving 1 lb. 5 oz. sugar with 1½ lb. ground almonds for the marchpane itself. One gently rounded teaspoon of gum dragon, or powdered gum tragacanth from a chemist, should be enough for this quantity (although the Victorian Francatelli used a whole half ounce of gum dragon to stiffen his exceedingly sweet marzipan, made from half a pound of almonds mixed with three times as much sugar). Leave it to soak for a few hours in a coffee cupful of rosewater, then work all three ingredients together into a paste with a wooden spoon in a large bowl (if you start off in an electric blender, be prepared to decant the mixture into a bowl if it grows too stiff). Reserve some of the paste to make your conceits—fancy figures or cut-outs—and bake the marchpane in a moderate oven in a single thick layer in a cake tin.

Gilding and Decorating the Marchpane

The thick glaze of rosewater and sugar, to be applied halfway through, gives a slightly shiny, transparent glaze, ready for gilding at the end with gold leaf, which was readily available, if exceedingly expensive, in 1604, and may still be obtained at exorbitant cost from specialist art shops (gold spray paint, unlike gold leaf, is inedible and emphatically not a viable substitute). You might produce a similar effect today with gold lace, gold paper cut-outs, and the gold-wrapped chocolate coins, animals and angels sold for Christmas decorations. Fancy gold and silver or gaily coloured Christmas tree baubles are precisely the sort of thing Lady

Fettiplace's contemporaries meant by 'conceits'. Hers were made at home in special 'standing moulds', then baked and coloured, iced or gilded; but, according to Sir Hugh Plat, always a great one for commercial short-cuts, they could also be bought ready-made: 'and of this paste our comfit-makers at this day make their letters, knots, Armes, escocheons [escutcheons, or painted armorial shields], beasts, birds and other fancies.'

The eye was only one of the senses to be pleased in the party season. Christmas, or a few weeks before it, was the time for mixing aromatic compounds of dried herbs, flowers and spices, making up new 'sweet powders', and renewing old ones with dried rose petals stored from the summer before in great, corked, lead-lined earthen pots. Plat strewed his windowsills and washbasins 'al winter long' with individually dried, bright-coloured, sweet-scented pansies, rose petals and gilliflowers. Sir Francis Bacon, according to Aubrey, 'had his Table strewed with Sweet Herbes and Flowers' at every meal. Lady Fettiplace describes how to pound damask rose petals with precious gums, barks and balsams 'in a whot morter, which must bee kept hott all the while you bee a working of it', to make pomanders, half a dozen perfumed toilet waters, and three sorts of pot-pourri powder.

TO MAKE DAMASK POWDER

Damask Rose Powder

Take Negeloromano, Calamus, Ciprus, origanum, arris roots, storax, Beniamyn, Cloves, lignu rhodium, orenge pilles, damask roses, sweet marioram, beat all the woods & gums and roots by themselves into small powder, and dry your roses and marioram verie drie, & beat them into powder, then mingle them all together, to such a quantitie, as the smell may best like you.

Negeloromano is *Nigella romana*, or fennel flower (no relation to ordinary fennel), which produces the spicy seeds known in France as *quatre epices*; *Calamus aromaticus* is the fragrant root of the sweet flag, which gave scented rushes for strewing floors; Ciprus is another aromatic root, belonging to the sweet cyperus (not to be confused with the cypress tree); origanum was perhaps wild marjoram, *Origanum vulgare*, as distinct from the sweet garden herb; orris roots belong to the flower de luce; storax and Beniamyn, or gum bezoin, are balsamic resins imported from the East; *Lignum rhodium* is sweet-scented candlewood.

These strong powders, said to last sometimes as long as half a century, were never kept in the lidless china bowls often used nowadays for pot-pourri. They were stoppered and enclosed, stuffed into 'sweet baggs', strewn between layers of clothes in a chest or linen press, kept tightly sealed to imprison the scent which rushed out, filling a whole small room or withdrawing chamber, when the lid was removed from a jar previously warmed on the hearth.

Table Laying

People who set such store by the strong scents, gay colours and bravura display of a summer garden took particular satisfaction in reproducing them all on the winter banqueting board. A table laid with marchpanes at top, middle and bottom, flanked on all side by knots and borders of dishes, reproduced the strict symmetry of pattern and riotous profusion of colour in a Jacobean garden. Great importance was attached to presentation: 'for what availes it our good Housewife to be never so skilled in the parts of Cookery, if she want skill to marshall the dishes, and set every one in his due place . . .' wrote Gervase Markham, giving detailed instructions on table-laying. 'It is like to a Fencer leading a band of men in a rout, who knows the use of the weapon, but not how to put men in order.' Markham allowed a minimum of thirty-two dishes ('which is as much as can conveniently stand on one Table') to each of the three courses at dinner. The housewife was to marshall the last course round her marchpanes, the first round an equally splendid centrepiece called the Grand Salad, 'setting the Sallets extravagantly about the Table . . . the Fricases [fricassées, or fried dishes] about them, then the boyld meats amongst the Fricases, rost meats amongst the boyld, baked meats amongst the rost, and Carbonadoes amongst the bak'd . . .'

Winter Banquets

The effect must have been something like a buffet table laid out for a modern wedding breakfast or a formal evening reception, at which guests help themselves to whatever they fancy. I have tried following Markham's plan for the final or banqueting course of a Christmas dinner, using sixteen dishes (which is as much as my table can conveniently hold) of Lady Fettiplace's fruit sweetmeats: red, green and clear amber apple suckets, coral-coloured and dark inky-purple quince pastes (what Lady Fettiplace calls 'white' and 'red' quinces), orange marmalades, soft, pinky-red rosehip- and much deeper red plum-cakes, stamped out in squares and circles, or moulded into fluted flowers, diamonds, shell-shapes and ornate, stylised fish. It made a pretty but, by seventeenth-century standards, pitifully meagre display. Even a humble feast for ordinary people—as opposed to 'the extraordinary great Feasts of Princes'—should have included double the number of dishes, eked out by gilded marchpanes, coloured tarts, almond creams, white fools, sweet cream-cheeses and custards, little bowls of iced macaroons, sponge biscuits, wheels of red-white-and-green or cowslip-and-violet-coloured sugar plate.

For all its magnificence, this sort of display was not nearly so much trouble to produce as it sounds for an Elizabethan housewife relying on the contemporary equivalent of convenience foods. By far the greater part of it came out of marmalade boxes, biscuit boxes, the gallipots and glass jars filled earlier in the year with tartstuffs, conserves and jellies. A traditional banquet, or 'dessert' as it was called by the eighteenth century, might require considerable designer's skill but (apart from a few perishable items) very little actual cooking. 'I have endeavoured to set out a Dessert of sweetmeats,' wrote Elizabeth Raffald in 1769, explaining the labour-saving system which still obtained for winter parties, 'which the industrious Housekeeper may lay up in Summer, at a small Expense, and when added to what little Fruit is then in Season, will make a pretty Appearance after the Cloth is drawn and be entertaining to the Company ...'

The delicate lemon and orange creams, tea creams, stone creams and solid syllabubs so popular in the eighteenth century could be run up by the cook in the morning or overnight with relatively little effort. Two of them have been copied out at the end of Lady Fettiplace's book in the same flowing hand that contributed recipes for Lemmon-Mead, Rattafia, Morella Brandy and brandy-based Orange and Cinnamon Waters. Both are quick to make, and the result in each case hard to beat for elegance and simplicity.

TO MAKE BARLEY CREAM

Barley Cream

Take 2 Ounces of Pearle Barley, boyle it in 2 or 3 waters till 'tis tender, then strain it from ye water & boyle it in a Quart of cream, then put in ye yelks of 6 Eggs & sweeten it to your Taste, & keep it stirring till tis pretty coole, & then put it in Glasses. you may boyle in ye cream a little Cinnamon or Mace.

For half quantities, which will be enough for four to six people, you will need 1 oz. pearl barley, 1 pint single cream and 3 egg yolks. Put the barley in a small pan of cold water, bring it to the boil and cook for five or ten minutes, then replace the reddish-brown liquid with fresh cold water, repeating the process twice more. Add the cooked and drained barley to the warm cream, and amalgamate this mixture, little by little, with the well beaten egg yolks in a bowl. Tip the custard back into the saucepan and warm it on a gentle heat, preferably over hot water, stirring all the time until it will coat the back of your wooden spoon. Add about a tablespoonful of sugar, and a generous pinch of powdered cinnamon. When the cream is pretty cool (stirring it from time to time, as it cools, will prevent the custard continuing to cook unevenly in the hot pan), pour it into individual round wine glasses or bowls, and leave to stand for several hours in a cold place.

This suave and subtle Barley Cream, added to the manuscript towards the end of the seventeenth century or perhaps even later, was one of the first recipes I tried out of Lady Fettiplace's book, and it remains one of my favourites. But the pale foamy cream copied out next to it (handily placed for using up leftover egg whites) runs it fairly close.

TO MAKE CHOCOLATE CREAM

Chocolate Cream

Take a Quart of cream, 3 Ounces of Chocolate grated, boyle it well together & let it stand till tis cold, & y[n] put in y[e] whites of 6 Eggs beaten to a Froth & sweeten it to your Taste, & then mill it up.

Chocolate from the New World began to be sold in England in the 1650s: the first London chocolate house was opened in 1657, White's Club in St James' started life as another shortly afterwards, by which time chocolate was well on the way to becoming an exceedingly fashionable drink. This mixture makes one of those semi-solid confections like syllabub, part dessert, part thick, frothy drink. For 6 generous glassfuls, scald a pint of single cream by bringing it to the boil, then coarsely grate in 2 or 3 oz. of the best quality black chocolate (this is double the amount specified above, but the cocoa butter in natural cocoa beans made seventeenth-century chocolate richer than ours), and simmer the mixture gently for a few minutes. When it is quite cold, beat up 3 egg whites until they stand in peaks, with a heaped tablespoonful of sugar (more if you like a sweeter taste), and fold in the chocolate cream. Beat it well: 'mill it up' meant whipping the mixture with a specially designed, notched wooden chocolate-beater, or mill. Pour the cream into glasses, leave it to set in the fridge, and serve with more grated chocolate scattered on top. It should develop the stiff foam, or head, so much liked in the seventeenth and eighteenth centuries, with a runnier chocolate underneath, less cloying than chocolate mousse, frothier and more ethereal than a cold soufflé set with gelatine.

Both this and the previous cream are particularly good with Lady Fettiplace's plain Maccaroonds, served alone at the end of a meal, or as part of one of the grand, coloured spreads that rounded off any festive occasion right down to Victorian and Edwardian times. The traditional ending to a Christmas dinner has only comparatively recently narrowed itself down to a single plum pudding, accompanied by hard sauce and either preceded or followed, at an uncomfortably short interval, by mince pies at tea time with an equally rich plum cake, encased in successive layers of even richer almond paste and royal icing. It seems ironic that the diet-conscious twentieth century should have restricted itself to what would have seemed even—perhaps especially—to Tudor or Jacobean eyes a small and thoroughly unbalanced selection of their richest, heaviest and most indigestible sweets, while at the same time jettisoning the grace notes supplied at the lighter end of the scale by fruit jellies, plain biscuits and white creams.

It might be worth reviving the custom of serving, if not a full-scale banquet, perhaps a carved apple tart, a white leach or the simple, refreshing fresh cream on p. 100 as an alternative to Christmas pudding. A single cook catering at home without regular help for four, six, eight, probably at most twelve persons, including extras at Christmas, can hardly be expected to provide the choice and variety supplied for a seventeenth-century family that included everyone—parents and children, workmen and waiters, cooks and their assistants, household and hind (or farm) servants—who slept under one roof, together with visiting friends and relations. A household of twenty members or more might easily be doubled at Christmas, and further swelled by a fair proportion of the local work force, who had produced the various crops and now came in for the distribution.

Christmas hospitality in Lady Fettiplace's day was taken to astonishing lengths, even by twentieth-century Western standards of unbridled consumption. For all its extravagance, ostentation, outright frivolity, a properly laid banqueting table represented the triumph of summer over winter, art over nature, plenty over the want that was never far from anyone's door in seventeenth-century England; and in a sense the same might still be said to be true today. 'This Collection full of pleasing variety, and of such usefulness in the Generality of it, to the Publique, coming to my hands, I should, had I forborn the Publication thereof, have trespassed in a very considerable concern upon my Countrey-men ...' wrote Sir Kenelm Digby's publisher, recommending his cookery book to the reader in 1668: 'There needs no Rhetoricating Floscules to set it off ... Fall to therefore, and much good may it do thee.'

Select Bibliography

I. COOKERY, KITCHEN GARDEN AND HOUSEHOLD MANAGEMENT

Beeton, Isabella. *Beeton's Book of Household Management*, 1861; facsimile edition, Cape, 1968.

Brears, P. C. D. *The Gentlewoman's Kitchen. Great Food in Yorkshire 1650–1750*, Wakefield Historical Publications, 1984.

David, Elizabeth. *A Book of Mediterranean Food*, John Lehmann, 1950.
French Country Cooking, J. Lehmann, 1951.
Italian Food, Macdonald, 1954.
Summer Cooking, Museum Press, 1955.
French Provincial Cooking, Michael Joseph, 1960.
Spices, Salt and Aromatics in the English Kitchen, Penguin, 1970.
English Bread and Yeast Cookery, Allen Lane, 1977.
An Omelette and a Glass of Wine, Jill Norman, 1984.

Davidson, Caroline. *A Woman's Work is Never Done. A History of Housework in the British Isles, 1650–1981*, Chatto & Windus, 1982.

Digby, Kenelm. *The Closet of Sir Kenelm Digby, Knight, Opened, 1668*; ed. Anne Macdonnell, London, 1910.

Drummond, J. C. and Anne Wilbraham. *The Englishman's Food. A History of Five Centuries of English Diet*, 2nd edition, Cape, 1957.

Estienne, Charles (Charles Stevens) and Jean Liebault. *Maison Rustique or the Countrey Farme*, tr. Richard Surflet, revised by Gervase Markham, London 1616 (Lady Fettiplace had a copy of a pre-Markham, 1600, edition, given her by Sir Henry Danvers in 1624).

Grieve, M. *A Modern Herbal*, ed. C. F. Leyel, 2 vols., Cape, 1931.

Hartley, Dorothy. *Food in England*, Macdonald and Jane's, 1954.

Hess, Karen. *Martha Washington's Booke of Cookery*, a seventeenth-century family MS., transcribed and edited by K. Hess, Columbia University Press, 1981.

Lawson, William. See Markham.

Markham, Gervase. *A Way to Get Wealth*, 13th edition, London, 1676 (incorporating Markham's *The English House-Wife*, 1615, and *A New Orchard and Garden* with *The Country Housewifes Garden* by William Lawson, 1617).

May, Robert. *The Accomplisht Cook or The Art and Mystery of Cooking*, 1660; 5th edition, 1685.

Nott, John. *Cooks and Confectioners Dictionary*, London, 1726; facsimile ed. with an introduction and notes by Elizabeth David, Lawrence Rivington, 1980.

O'Hara-May, Jane. *Elizabethan Dietary of Health*, Coronado Press, U.S.A., 1977.

Oxford, A. W. *English Cookery Books 1500–1850*, 1913, 2nd impression, Holland Press, 1977.

Plat, Hugh. *Delightes for Ladies*, 1602; ed. G. E. and K. R. Fussell, Crosby Lockwood, 1948.

Raffald, Elizabeth. *The Experienced English House-Keeper*, Manchester, 1769.

Tusser, Thomas. *A Hundreth Good Pountes of Husbandrie*, 1557; *Five Hundred Points of Good Husbandry*, ed. W. Mavor, London, 1812.

Wheaton, Barbara Ketcham. *Savouring the Past. The French Kitchen and Table from 1300 to 1789*, Chatto & Windus, 1983.

White, Florence. *Good Things in England*, Cape, 1932.

Flowers as Food, Cape, 1934.

Wilson, C. Anne. *Food and Drink in Britain, From the Stone Age to Recent Times*, Constable, 1973; Penguin, 1976.

The Book of Marmalade, Constable, 1985.

2. GENERAL

Atkyns, Robert. *Ancient and Present State of Gloucestershire*, London, 1712; 2nd edition, 1768.

Aubrey, John. *Brief Lives*, ed. A. Powell, London, 1949.

The Natural History of Wiltshire, ed. J. Britton, London, 1847.

Baskerville, Thomas. 'Thomas Baskerville's Journeys in England', *MSS of the Duke of Portland at Welbeck Abbey*, vol. ii., 1893.

Bindoff, S. T. (ed.) *The House of Commons 1509–1558*, 3 vols., Secker & Warburg, 1982.

Bradley, Katherine and Richard. 'William Bush—The Flying Boatman', *Berkshire Arch. Journal*, vol. 71, 1981–2.

Byrne, Muriel St. Clair. *The Lisle Letters*, abridged by B. Boland, Secker & Warburg, 1983.

Carleton, Dudley. *Dudley Carleton to John Chamberlain 1603–24*, ed. with an introduction by Maurice Lee, Jr., Rutgers University Press, 1972.

Chamberlain, John. *Letters of John Chamberlain*, ed. N. E. McClure, American Philosophical Society, Philadelphia, 1939.

Clifford, Anne. *The Diary of the Lady Anne Clifford*, introduction by V. Sackville-West, Heinemann, 1923.

Dent, Emma. *Annals of Winchcombe and Sudely*, John Murray, 1877.

Dunlop, J. Renton. 'The Fettiplace Family', *Transactions of the Newbury District Field Club*, vol. v, 1895–1911.

Pedigrees of the Fettiplace Family, nos. I (N. Denchworth), III (E. Shefford and Besselsleigh), IV (Swinbrook and Childrey) and VII (Fernham), *Miscellanea Genealogica et Heraldica*, vol. ii, 5th series, 1916–17.

Pedigree of the Pooles of Sapperton and Coates, *Ibid.*, vol. iii, 5th series, 1918–19.

Emmison, F. G. *Tudor Secretary. Sir William Petre at Court and Home*, Phillimore, 1970.

Fraser, Antonia. *The Weaker Vessel. Woman's Lot in Seventeenth-Century England*, Weidenfeld & Nicolson, 1984.

Fuller, Thomas. *The History of the Worthies of England, 1662*, ed. P. Nuttall, 1840.

Girouard, Mark. *Life in the English Country House. A Social and Architectural History*, Yale University Press, 1978.

Hasler, P. W. (ed.). *The House of Commons 1558–1603*, 3 vols, H.M.S.O. for the History of Parliament Trust, 1981.

Hoby, Margaret. *The Diary of Lady Margaret Hoby, 1599–1605*, ed. Dorothy M. Meads, Routledge, 1930.

Joseph, Harriet. *Shakespeare's Son-in-law: John Hall, Man and Physician*, Arden Books, Connecticut, 1964.

Mildmay, H. A. St. John. *A Brief Memoir of the Mildmay Family*, privately printed, 1913.

Misson, Henri. *Memoirs and Observations in his Travels over England*, tr. M. Ozell, London, 1719.

Nichols, J. G. *The Progresses of Queen Elizabeth*, vol. iii, London, 1823.

The Progresses of James I, vol. i., London, 1828.

The Unton Inventories with a Memoir of the Family of Unton, Berks. Ashmolean Society, 1841.

Stone, Lawrence. *The Crisis of the Aristocracy 1558–1641*, Oxford University Press, 1965.

Family and Fortune. Studies in Aristocratic Finance in the Sixteenth and Seventeenth Centuries, Oxford University Press, 1973.

Strong, Roy. 'Sir Henry Unton and His Portrait: An Elizabethan Memorial Picture and its History', *Archaeologica*, 1965.

Thorpe, J. D. 'History of the Manor of Coates', *Transactions of the Bristol and Gloucester Archaeological Society*, vol. 50, 1928.

Thynne, J. and M. *Two Elizabethan Women: Correspondence of Joan and Maria Thynne 1575–1611*, ed. Alison D. Wall, Wiltshire Record Society, 1983.

Verney, Frances Parthenope and Margaret M. *Memoirs of the Verney Family*, 2nd edition, 1904.

Winchester, Barbara. *Tudor Family Portrait*, Cape, 1955.

Notes

Dates, here and elsewhere, follow the modern style introduced in 1752 when January 1 replaced March 25 as New Year's Day (before that, dates between January 1 and March 24 were commonly given by the English in dual form e.g. Jan. 1604/5). Books cited here in short form appear in full in the Bibliography. Abbreviations are the usual ones, e.g. *D.N.B.* = *Dictionary of National Biography*, *O.E.D.* = *Oxford English Dictionary*, P.R.O. = Public Record Office, *S.P.* (*Dom.*) and (*For.*) = *State Papers* (*Domestic*) and (*Foreign*), *V.C.H.* = *Victoria County History*.

INTRODUCTION: A FAMILY AND ITS FORTUNES

1. Burke, *Extinct and Dormant Baronetcies*, 1844; J. R. Dunlop, Fettiplace pedigrees.
2. *Visitations of Berkshire*, vol. ii, Harleian Society, vol. 57, 1908, pp. 21, 127; see also *Elinor Fettiplace's Receipt Book*, p. 36 (the Colonel Fettiplace commanding the parliamentary garrison against Prince Rupert at Cirencester in 1642 was John Fettiplace of Colne St. Aldwyns in Gloucestershire, first cousin to Elinor Fettiplace's father-in-law, Bessells Fettiplace).
3. Will of Sir Henry Poole, prob. 1616, P.R.O.
4. *Ibid.*, and J. D. Thorpe, 'History of the Manor of Coates'.
5. S. T. Bindoff, *House of Commons*, vol. iii, pl 129; Thorpe, *op. cit.*; information from W. J. Tighe, whose thesis on Gentlemen Pensioners under Queen Elizabeth is deposited with the Cambridge University Library.
6. July 1, 1573, *MSS of the Marquess of Bath at Longleat*, vol. v, *Talbot, Dudley and Devereux Papers 1533–1659*, ed. G. Dynfallt Owen, H.M.S.O., 1980, p. 240; for a present from Sir Giles Poole to the Earl of Leicester in 1559, *ibid.*, see *Elinor Fettiplace's Receipt Book*, p. 56.
7. Bindoff, *op. cit.*
8. *Brief Lives*, pp. 321–2.
9. Thorpe, *op. cit.*; will of Sir Henry Poole.
10. Muster roll, December 16, 1591, *S.P.* (*For.*), *1591–2*, ed. R. B. Wernham, H.M.S.O., 1980.
11. Dunlop, 'The Fettiplace Family'; *V.C.H., Berks*, vol. iv, p. 338.
12. For Fettiplace sales, see Dunlop, Pedigree III; *V.C.H. Berks*, vol. iii, p. 104, vol. iv, pp. 236, 525; J. G. Nichols, *Unton Inventories*, pp. lxxx, lxxxii.
13. Dunlop, Pedigree III.
14. Margaret Hoby, *Diary*, p. 21.

15. *MSS of the Marquess of Salisbury at Hatfield House*, ed. M.S. Giuseppi, Part XVII, 1938, p. 388.
16. J. Chamberlain, *Letters*, pp. 101–2.
17. *S.P.* (*Dom.*), *1598–1601*, ed. M.A.E. Green, 1869, pp. 444, 648; see also *Salisbury MSS*, Part X, 1904, pp. 178, 199, 208; and Nichols, J. G. *Progresses of Queen Elizabeth*, vol. iii, p. 499.
18. See Nichols, *Unton Inventories*; R. Strong, 'Sir Henry Unton and His Portrait'.
19. *S.P.* (*Dom.*), *1598–1601, op. cit.*, p. 35.
20. Chamberlain, *Letters*, p. 57.
21. Nichols, *Unton Inventories*, p. 34.
22. *S.P.* (*Dom.*), *1598–1601, op. cit.*, p. 478.
23. J. and M. Thynne, *Two Elizabethan Women*, p. 37.
24. *Ibid.*, p. xxvii.
25. Will of Sir Richard Fettiplace, prob. June 18, 1617, P.R.O.
26. Chamberlain, *Letters*, p. 130.
27. J. G. Nichols, *Progresses of James I*, vol. i, pp. 220, 415.
28. *Ibid.*, p. 257.
29. Nichols, *Unton Inventories*.
30. R. May, 'Triumphs and Trophies in Cookery', preface to *The Accomplisht Cook*.
31. *S.P.* (*Dom.*), *1601–3*, ed. M. A. E. Green, 1870, p. 294.
32. *Natural History of Wiltshire*, p. 78; see also *Aubrey's Brief Lives*, ed. O. L. Dick, 1949, p. 78.
33. *V.C.H. Berks*, vol. iv, p. 335; *Berkshire Archeological Journal*, vol. liv, 1954–5, p. 18; N. Pevsner, *Berkshire*, Penguin, 1966.
34. *V.C.H. Berks*, vol. ii, p. 281, vol. iv, p. 340.
35. *D.N.B.*
36. K. Hess, *Martha Washington's Booke of Cookery*, pp. 449–55.
37. Thorpe, *Unton Inventories*, p. 34; *S.P.* (*Dom.*), *1598–1601, op. cit.*, p. 34, for the letter quoted on pp. 73 and 78 in *Elinor Fettiplace's Receipt Book*.
38. For a history of English household MSS, see Hess, *Martha Washington's Booke of Cookery*, pp. 449–55.
39. *Natural History of Wiltshire*, p. 79.
40. *MSS of Lord de L'Isle and Dudley at Penshurst Place*, vol. iii, ed. W. A. Shaw, 1936, p. 132.
41. *Salisbury MSS*, Part XVI, 1933, pp. 304, 318.
42. *S.P.* (*Dom.*), *1603–10*, ed. M. A. E. Green, 1857, p. 424.
43. L. Stone, *Family and Fortune*, p. 63
44. *Natural History of Wiltshire*, pp. 92, 102.
45. Stone, *op. cit.*, Chapter VIII.
46. Sir Egerton Brydges, *Memoirs of the Peers of England during the Reign of James I*, 1802.
47. May, *Accomplisht Cook*, biographical foreword by 'W.W.'.
48. G. Markham, *English House-Wife*, p. 99.
49. *Ibid.*, p. 98.
50. *Ibid.*, p. 100.
51. Mathena Blomefield, *Nuts in the Rookery*, Faber, 1946, p. 15; see also her *The Bulleymung Pit*, Faber, 1946.
52. F. G. Emmison, *Tudor Secretary*, p. 155.
53. Thorpe, *Unton Inventories*, p. 1.

54. K. Digby, *The Closet Opened*, pp. 142, 155–6.
55. E. David, *An Omelette and a Glass of Wine*, Jill Norman, 1984, pp. 59–60.
56. Sir Henry Poole's will, *op. cit.*
57. Will of Edward Rogers, prob. September 1, 1623, P.R.O.
58. Dunlop, Pedigree III.
59. Will of Sir George Horner, 1676, P.R.O.
60. Dunlop, Pedigree III; *Cal. of the Committee for Compounding*, ed. M. Green, Part II, 1890, p. 1050; *Committee for the Advance of Money*, p. 430.
61. Thorpe, 'History of the Manor of Coates', p. 245.
62. See Morris R. Brownell, *Alexander Pope and the Arts of Georgian England*, Oxford University Press, 1978.

Index